From Agadir to Armageddon

From Agadir to Armageddon

Anatomy of a Crisis

Geoffrey Barraclough

HM

HOLMES AND MEIER PUBLISHERS
New York

First published in the United States of America 1982 by
Holmes & Meier Publishers, Inc.
30 Irving Place, New York, N.Y. 10003

Library of Congress Cataloging in Publication Data

Barraclough, Geoffrey, 1908–
    From Agadir to Armageddon.

    Includes index.
    Bibliography: p.
    1. World politics—1900–1918.   2. Europe—Foreign
relations.   3. Agadir incident. 1911.   I. Title.
D455.B328   1982   327'.09'041   82-15476
ISBN 0-8419-0824-9

Printed in Great Britain

Contents

Preface

Back in 1979, when the throne of the Shah of Iran was toppling and the United States' Seventh Fleet was on its way halfway around the globe from the Philippines to the Arabian Sea and the Persian Gulf, I had a visit from a charming, intelligent German journalist. 'Is this July 1914 again?' he asked. 'No, no,' I replied, '1911.' And when he looked surprised and a little disconcerted, I added by way of explanation: 'Agadir, Kiderlen-Wächter, the *Panthersprung* – don't you remember?' Evidently he did not remember. 'Kiderlen-Wächter,' he said, 'who was Kiderlen-Wächter?'

This book is an attempt to answer his question. Its subject, narrowly defined, is what soon became known as the 'Agadir crisis', the last of the confrontations between the great powers before the July crisis of 1914 and the outbreak of the First World War. But it does not follow the conventional pattern of diplomatic history. The crisis in 1911 was the crisis of a whole society, and it is that crisis, not merely its international ramifications, that I have tried to depict. I shall say something about Kiderlen-Wächter and his opposite numbers in Paris, Rome and London – 'the new Machiavellians' in the seats of power, as I have called them – but my concern is not with individuals but with the social and economic tensions with which they failed to cope. They seem to me to have many similarities, most of them disconcerting, with the tensions and turmoil confronting the world today.

It is in that spirit, and with no particular claim to originality, that I have written this book. It was completed in 1981, on the seventieth anniversary of Agadir, and though I have subsequently revised the text, I have not changed it in any substantive way. Events in 1982 – the Anglo-Argentinian war in the Falkland Islands, the Israeli invasion of Lebanon, continuing instability in the Persian Gulf, and a sharp deterioration in the world economy – only confirm the picture of growing international disorder, so reminiscent of the growing international disorder between 1911 and 1914. That is why it seemed to me that the story of the little gunboat, the *Panther*, and its sequel was worth re-telling. I am aware that no historical parallel fits neatly and tidily. As Lenin once said, we must take account of 'the fundamental differences between socio-economic formations'. But that does not mean we can learn nothing from history, even at this late date.

G.B.
Boston,
15 July 1982

I

'Serious News From Agadir'

'The Emperor has sanctioned my Morocco programme, including ships for Agadir.'
The German Secretary of State for Foreign Affairs, 11 May 1911

At eight o'clock on the evening of 1 July 1911, a German gunboat, the *Panther*, dropped anchor in the harbour of Agadir, a small and impoverished port on the Atlantic coast of Morocco, and set the world in turmoil.

It was an unexpected move, hatched in secrecy, and it echoed round Europe like a pistol-shot. Not one in a thousand of those who read the story in their newspapers in the following days had even heard of Agadir before. Now the *Panthersprung*, or 'the leap of the *Panther*', as it soon came to be called, hit the headlines even in far-away Mexico, which had problems enough of its own to think about. If the German government intended to create a sensation, which undoubtedly it did, it certainly succeeded. What were the Germans doing in this remote, sandy bay? What hidden calculations lay behind their action? No one knew the answer, not even (it later transpired) the Germans themselves, and the very fact that no one knew the answer heightened the sense of crisis.

Nevertheless, the opening scene reads less like a melodrama than a comedy of errors, with all the bungling, confusion and lack of co-ordination we have learned to associate with such actions in our own day. The naval demonstration itself got off to a bad start, the result of a failure of liaison between the Foreign Office and the naval authorities. The original plan, drafted on 12 June, was to send four cruisers to Agadir and the nearby port of Mogador, and the Chancellor and Foreign Minister finally secured the Kaiser's reluctant and unenthusiastic consent on 26 June. But when the moment for action came it turned out that no cruisers were available, and so it was necessary to fall back on the *Panther* – despite its ferocious name, a distinctly unimpressive vessel, with a crew of 125, and (as the Kaiser put it) 'two or three little pop guns on board', unlikely to strike fear in the hearts even of the few Moroccans who might sight it lying idly off-shore. The *Panther*, it is true, was subsequently relieved by the light cruiser *Berlin*, and also by its sister ship, the gunboat *Eber*; but one cannot but wonder about the feelings of the officers and crews, mute hostages to fortune, as vulnerable as the American hostages in Teheran in 1979 and 1980, who must have been well aware that they could be blown out of the water at a moment's notice by the British navy, if the Admiralty in London gave the order.

Equally ludicrous were the pretexts put forward for German intervention. According to the official announcement drawn up on 30 June the *Panther* was despatched to Agadir because 'German firms established in the south of Morocco' had asked for 'protection of life and property'. This, perhaps, was technically true. In response to an urgent Foreign Office directive issued on 19 June, a number of German firms, including the Mannesmann brothers ('those rogues', the Kaiser called them), had conveniently discovered that they had major interests in alleged (but non-existent) iron ore deposits in southern Morocco, and two days later a petition for protection was submitted to the government. No one believed it. (When Bethmann-Hollweg, the German Chancellor, later trotted out the story before the Reichstag, the Assembly greeted it with roars of laughter.) There was, to begin with, no evidence that German interests were in danger or German citizens being molested, but, worse still, there were (as the German ambassador in London later admitted) no Germans at all at Agadir or in the neighbourhood. To remedy the deficiency, the story goes, a mining prospector in the service of the Hamburg firm of Warburg was hurriedly despatched to Agadir, where he was last seen on the beach, signalling desperately to the ship's officer on the *Panther* to pick him up.

The fact, of course, was that the German action had been hastily put together without troubling to plan its execution in detail, and from the start it moved from expedient to expedient. This was typical of Alfred von Kiderlen-Wächter, the new German Foreign Minister, who had assumed office the preceding year. Kiderlen believed in action for its own sake; anything was better, in his view, than the stagnation which had characterized German foreign policy under his predecessors. Hence Agadir – chosen, according to his own statement, because it was so far from Gibraltar that intervention there would not alarm the British. Certainly, it was not chosen because Kiderlen believed that Germany had serious economic interests in southern

Morocco. Impetuous and rash he may have been, but he was not naïve enough to believe stories of that sort.

When Kiderlen first hatched his Agadir plan is uncertain. Probably it began to brew in his mind in early March when news arrived of growing unrest in Morocco and of French preparations to put it down. Precisely what he had in mind is more uncertain still. He later claimed that he never intended to remain at Agadir permanently; his 'only object' was 'to make the French negotiate'. But as early as April he had told his friend, the Prime Minister of Württemberg, that he was thinking of occupying the place. In fact he never did so; the German ships were ordered to anchor off-shore, a mile from the harbour, to avoid incidents. Probably his idea (he himself indicated as much) was to wait and see what happened and what he could pick up – hence the lack of detailed planning. There were plenty of attractive alternatives, 'compensations' (the weasel word of 1911), a slice of Moroccan territory, perhaps just to drive a wedge between France and Britain and so create new possibilities for Germany: why be too precise?

But this policy, or lack of policy, had another side which Kiderlen does not appear to have appreciated. The very vagueness and ambiguity of his plans made them seem sinister; the very speciousness of the pretexts for sending the *Panther* to Agadir was itself a ground for suspicion. Kiderlen may or may not have intended simply to put pressure on France; but the crisis that followed was real – far more serious, almost certainly, than he had bargained for. The three months beginning on 1 July were punctuated by rumours of war, even by preparations for war. Inflammatory speeches were delivered; fleets were alerted; troops were moved, and manoeuvres cancelled lest armies should be caught off-guard; and the newspapers blew hot on the embers, as is their wont. We know in retrospect that the danger of war was not great; but that is not how it seemed to contemporaries, or at least to the experts in the European chancelleries who spent their days and nights following the course of events move by move and despatch by despatch.

Ironically, it was Germany itself that was worst affected. 'Black Monday', 4 September, saw a panic on the German Stock Exchange, with industrial securities falling 10, 20, 30 per cent in one day. Worse still, there was a run on the banks as anxious depositors hurried to withdraw their savings and convert them into gold. According to the best available estimates, withdrawals in September totalled no less than 35 million marks, and it has even been suggested (not very plausibly) that it was the panic at home that caused the German government to back down from confrontation with France and Britain, and bring the Agadir crisis to an end.

That is the story in a nutshell. Was it a storm in a teacup? Or was it the first gust of a gale that would blow down the imposing structure of a European-dominated world which had been built up during the nineteenth century? Whatever the reason, tension subsided almost as quickly as it had arisen. Actually, the Kaiser had made it clear at an early stage that he would not consent to measures he considered likely to lead to war; and though this was not known to the British or French, William II's attitude meant that Kiderlen's hands were tied. He intimidated, bluffed and threatened; and for 151 days, beginning on 1 July, there was always a German warship stationed at Agadir, a symbol of Germany's supposed readiness to fight. But the bluster was more apparent than real, and on 28 November, the *Eber* (which meanwhile had relieved the *Panther*) was withdrawn, and the crisis was over. When the British ambassador in Berlin visited the German Chancellor on 17 December, they parted, Sir Edward Goschen reported, 'with the mutual hope that 1912 would prove a better year all round than 1911'. Neither, probably, believed the other, and with good reason. Peace was still intact; but no one can unscramble eggs, and (as we shall see) quite a lot of eggs had been scrambled during the last six months of 1911.

2

1911 : 'The Critical Year'

'We parted with the mutual hope that 1912 would prove a better year all round than 1911.'
The British ambassador in Berlin, 17 December 1911

Not surprisingly, 1911 has gone down in our history books as the year of Agadir. Historians, particularly diplomatic historians and all those concerned with the origins of the First World War, have singled out the 'leap of the *Panther*' and the crisis which ensued as the outstanding event of that year, a key link in the chain of events that led, stage by stage and move by move, to August 1914.

This is, no doubt, legitimate and in some respects illuminating. Certainly, anyone today who sees a similar chain of events leading apparently in a similar way to the Third World War will find much to ponder, most of it disquieting, in the diplomatic history of Agadir. Nevertheless, it is only one side of the story. Diplomatic events are the visible tip of the iceberg; our subject in this book is the iceberg itself, the whole complex, swirling mass of forces, many of them hidden below the surface, which led to the disaster. Before we come to the crisis itself, it is therefore important to form a picture of the world in which it occurred. More than one historian has described 1911 as 'the critical year'; and the fact that the crisis was temporarily overcome, or postponed, does not make it less critical. It could be the same in the 1980s.

The diplomatic story is adequate enough if all we want to know about are the political consequences of the Agadir crisis. It is less useful if we want to know the causes and the circumstances – to know, in other words, how and why the crisis occurred and, perhaps, to get by analogy an insight into the pressures and circumstances which may lead to a similar crisis, and even to war, at some other time in some other place. Even in chess, as anyone knows who followed the Spassky–Fischer or the Korchnoi–Karpov matches, we cannot ignore either the psychology of the players, or the atmosphere in which they are playing. The same was true of statesmen, diplomats and politicians in 1911. They too were not playing a diplomatic game in a vacuum, were not impervious, and could not be impervious, to the world around them. That is why, if we wish to know why Kiderlen-Wächter took the plunge and embarked on the Agadir adventure, the diplomatic record will tell us only half the story. For the other half we must turn elsewhere, to the frustration and discontent that permeated every section of German society in 1911, perhaps still further to a worldwide sense of malaise and disillusion. Kiderlen was, indeed, reacting to a specific constellation of diplomatic events; but his reactions were conditioned by other factors in the situation. In this, we may think, he was in no way exceptional and we may suspect that statesmen and politicians are more likely than not to react in a similar way today. That is why the Agadir crisis is still worth thinking about.

It was Theobald von Bethmann-Hollweg, the German Chancellor, a typically sensitive, cultivated, upper-class German who liked to play a couple of Beethoven sonatas every night to soothe his nerves before going to bed, who put his finger on the essential characteristic of 1911. 'My dear friend,' he remarked to the British ambassador as the year drew to its close, 'how can I play my beloved old music with the air full of modern discords?' Bethmann was thinking about the conflicting interests of Germany, France and Britain; but the discords cut much deeper. 1911 was not simply a year of crisis in international relations, it was also a year of revolutionary ferment. 'No responsible statesman,' a great French historian has written, 'would have said ... that he felt safe against the perils of some kind of revolutionary outburst.' A wave of unrest and disaffection was running through the world, and we cannot measure the mood and temper of 1911 without taking it into account. It would be surprising – though they would probably have been the last to admit it – if it had not affected the minds and attitudes of those charged with the conduct of foreign affairs.

*   *   *

If we try, at a distance of seventy years, to put ourselves back in the position of people in 1911 – not only senior officials in ministries and Foreign Offices, but also the man on the Clapham omnibus, commuting to Bishopsgate or Throgmorton Street – the first thing to note is that Agadir was only one event, or incident, in a disturbed and eventful year. It certainly did not loom so large for them as it does for us. Anyone who reads the debates on foreign policy in the British

House of Commons, for example, will find, perhaps to his or her surprise, that people there were as much concerned about the affairs of Persia as they were about the affairs of Morocco. But they will also find that Persia and Morocco together received far less attention than more urgent and alarming happenings at home. If Agadir was a first tremor of the earthquake which erupted in August 1914, it was not high enough on the Richter scale to worry contemporaries unduly.

There were good reasons for this. By 1911, to begin with, people had got used to crises and war scares. They had learnt (mistakenly) to live with them, just as we have learnt (mistakenly) to live with the atom bomb. Morocco had been a source of trouble and international friction ever since 1905. There had been a war scare after the Austrian seizure of Bosnia and Herzegovina in 1908, followed by an Anglo-German naval crisis in 1909. All had been settled without war, much as the Cuban missile crisis of 1962 was settled without war. Why should it be different in 1911?

Furthermore, the public was not fully apprised of the risk of war until the danger had passed. Agadir was the concern of cabinets and chancelleries, and for the most part they played their cards close to their chests, and the ordinary man – even the ordinary Member of Parliament, or his French or German opposite number – had little idea of what was going on. What they sensed, correctly enough as it turned out, was that no government, however loudly it talked, was likely to gamble its country's future, or to pit German soldiers against French soldiers, or English sailors against German sailors, for the sake of a place of which few people had ever heard, and about which fewer still cared. That was not, of course, the real issue, and statesmen in London, Berlin and Paris were fully aware of that fact. But they had no intention of confiding the arcane secrets of international diplomacy to the public, not least of all Sir Edward Grey, the British Foreign Minister in Asquith's Liberal administration, who knew that the Liberal majority was far from sharing his sceptical view of German intentions. The fact that the Liberals, on the whole, were pro-German, just at the time when Grey and the Foreign Office were becoming increasingly suspicious of German aims and ambitions, was one – but only one – of the cross-currents which muddied the diplomatic channels in 1911.

No less important was the fact that Morocco was only one of many flash-points around the world which might detonate an explosion. Possibly it was knowledge of this possibility – or at least a subconscious awareness of the risks involved – that finally convinced the French,

7

German and British governments that a compromise solution of the Agadir crisis was in their interests. Explosions abroad, and still more, explosions at home, were too high a price to pay. No one who lit the long fuse could be sure what it might, and what it might not, blow up. Ironically, it was just when the drama was ending that the Italians, bystanders rather than actors during most of the play, ignored the risk and lit the fuse. The Italian invasion of Tripoli on 29 September was an unintended by-product of Agadir, but it touched off a conflagration which spread far and wide until it exploded in the First World War.

There was, indeed, plenty of combustible material in the world in 1911 quite apart from Morocco, and contemporaries were well aware of the situation. Ancient empires – the Ottoman Empire, the Manchu Empire in China, perhaps even the Habsburg Empire in Europe – were visibly falling apart, and people were already worrying about the impending scramble for the spoils. In Persia and Turkey the reverberations of the revolutions of 1906 and 1908 were still being felt, destabilizing influences in an unstable and hotly contested region, and there was nervous talk of the possibility of a great Moslem resurgence and of holy war sweeping through North Africa until finally it reached 'the Shiah Mohammedans in India'. In the British House of Commons, a Member warned the government that, if it condoned the Italian action in Tripoli, it might have a widespread Moslem revolt on its hands which could endanger the stability of the Empire.

If the unrest among the Moslem peoples of North Africa was the direct result of French and Italian provocation, unrest in Persia was no less clearly the result of British and Russian interference. Anglo-Russian rivalry in Persia dated back many years, but was supposed to have been settled in 1907 by a division of spheres of interest, Russia in the north, in the area adjacent to the Caucasus, Great Britain in the south-east adjacent to India, with a neutral zone in between. By 1911 it was obvious that this arrangement was not working, and that is why (as we have noted) Persia was as big a bone of contention in 1911 as Morocco. But now there was a new factor in the situation: oil. This had played no part in the 1907 agreement, and it was only after 1913, when the British decided to switch their new battleships, the super-Dreadnoughts, to oil, rather than coal, that oil became a major issue. But 1911 was the first year (it was also, as it happened, the first year in which a commercial shipment of oil left the British West Indian island of Trinidad) in which oil impinged directly on international relations.

British interest in Persian oil dated back to 1903, when a certain

William d'Arcy, a gold millionaire from Australia, obtained an oil-prospecting concession from the Persian government which, combined shortly afterwards with the interests of a Canadian oil tycoon, Lord Strathcona, was the germ of the Anglo-Persian (later Anglo-Iranian) Oil Company, in which the British government took a controlling interest in 1914. D'Arcy's company operated, to begin with, in southern Persia, but in 1911 it turned its attention to northern Persia, that is, to the Russian sphere of interest. It was helped in this by a certain Mr Morgan Shuster, an American who had been brought in officially as financial adviser to the Persian government, but who was also an agent for the New York banking firm of Kuhn, Loeb & Co, which was closely involved with the British and European financial interests (Cassel, Samuel, Deterding) which were backing d'Arcy's ventures. Not surprisingly, Shuster's interference in the north provoked a strong Russian reaction, which in turn provoked a serious anti-Russian uprising, not unlike that in Afghanistan in 1980.

There is no need to follow the rest of this story, which culminated in the recall of Shuster. The important points, from a longer-term point of view, are two: first, the hostility among Persians provoked by western interference and exploitation, foreshadowing a similar reaction in 1978 and 1979; and, secondly, the emergence of oil as an international bone of contention. No one, probably, foresaw in 1911 the role that oil was going to play in international relations – not even the oil tycoons themselves – but here was an issue which was destined to dominate the future. Once again, 1911 turned out, almost accidentally, to mark a turning-point in history.

On another level, 1911 also marked a decisive shift in the relations between Russia and the United States. The estrangement of the two powers, which had been drawn together by hostility to Great Britain during most of the nineteenth century, is conventionally traced to the Bolshevik Revolution of 1917. In reality it goes back to 1911, when President Taft, bowing in an election year to Jewish pressure groups in Congress, unilaterally abrogated the seventy-nine year old commercial treaty between the United States and Russia which James Buchanan had negotiated in 1832. This gratuitous action, like that initiated in 1972 by Senator Henry Jackson, did more harm than good to the Russian Jews whom it was supposed to help, but it put a spoke in Russo-American relations which remained henceforward (in the words of a Russian newspaper) in a state of 'cold indifference'. Like the Soviet government today, the Czarist government in 1911 had no intention (the Russian Foreign Minister declared) of allowing 'any infringements from abroad of the inalienable right of Russia, as a sovereign state, to regulate its internal legislation'. The United States, on the other hand, had embarked on the humanitarian crusade which has coloured – and sometimes thwarted – its foreign policy ever since.

Here again, though contemporaries may not have perceived it, 1911 was a critical year, with consequences reaching far into the future. The other two events which stand out in any longer view of history were the Mexican revolution at the beginning of the year, and the Chinese revolution at its end. So much so that, from the perspective of the present, we shall not be far wrong in concluding that these, rather than Agadir, were the most significant events of 1911.

*   *   *

The Mexican and Chinese revolutions are outstanding because they mark the opening of a new era in history, a decisive stage in the unfolding of the revolt against the West, and against western exploitation of the wretched of the earth, which has become a central theme of contemporary history. In 1911 the coloured world of Asia, Africa and Latin America was on the move, and the Chinese and Mexican revolutions symbolized the change. Because almost everywhere the native dynasties and governing élites had been suborned and corrupted by the West, liberation took the form of revolt against the government in power; but the ultimate aim was to throw off the western yoke. In China, it was the activities of western rail interests, scrambling for concessions, that touched off the revolt. In Mexico the enemy was not so much Porfirio Diaz as the United States ambassador, Lane Wilson – described by an American historian (somewhat unfairly, since he has subsequently had many rivals for this distinction) as 'the worst envoy in the history of his country' – who quickly called in the American marines and almost as quickly disclaimed any intention of interfering in Mexico's internal affairs. This was not true, but it illustrates the ambiguities of United States' policy in Mexico and Latin America, and the moral perplexities of the West in its relations with the Third World.

In 1911 the western preponderance, going back to Christopher Columbus and Hernando Cortés, was beginning to crumble. A few people on the spot were aware how precarious the position was; for most people, imbued with the Eurocentric view of the world which was characteristic of the age, what happened in China and Mexico was peripheral. In the short term, this is easily comprehensible. The

10

displacement of Porfirio Diaz by Madero was not, on the face of it, a world shaking event; it signified little more than a shift in the ruling Mexican junta. The revolt against the Ch'ing, who had ruled China ever since 1644, was an event of a different magnitude; but the fall of the Ch'ing dynasty had long been discounted, and the general view was that Yuan Shih-kai, the strong man recalled from retirement to cope with the unrest, would stabilize the situation without too much difficulty, and that through Yuan western interests, particularly western investments in the Chinese railways, would be preserved.

These calculations were reasonable enough. The important fact is that they were wrong, like similar calculations about Iran in 1978 and Egypt in 1980. What contemporaries failed to see was that peasants and workers would take a hand, both in Mexico and in China, and transform the whole situation. Already before the end of 1911 Emiliano Zapata, the legendary leader of the oppressed peasantry, had come forward with a new and stirring message, repudiated Madero, and proclaimed in the famous Plan of Ayala a programme that fired the Mexican revolutionaries and shook the seats of power. This was the beginning of a revolutionary movement that would drag on to 1934, or even to 1940, just as the Chinese revolution dragged on unresolved until 1949, inflicting terrible injuries in both cases on the peoples involved in the struggle. But the result was a fundamental and lasting change in the balance of world power, an ongoing challenge to the preponderance of the white world which everyone in 1911 took for granted.

China and Mexico were not the only places in 1911 where western exploitation was challenged and resisted. The unrest in Morocco, which led step by step to German intervention and the *Panthersprung*, was a direct response to the subordination of the weak Moroccan ruler, Mulay Hafid, to western interests and his reliance on French support. A wave of anti-western resentment was agitating the Moslem world, and spreading from there to Hindu India, where a series of assassinations kept alive the protest against British rule, and even to darkest Africa. Perhaps the most percipient comment on the atmosphere in the colonial world in 1911 came from the British Governor of Northern Nigeria. 'It must never be forgotten', he wrote, 'that we are "protecting" a people in spite of themselves, and that almost every improvement and development initiated by us is absolutely opposed to all their instincts and traditions.... The emotional nature of the negro and the fanaticism of the Moslem may flare up at any moment.'

Unfortunately, few people in 1911 were disposed to listen to Sir Hesketh Bell's warning. The belief in the superiority of the white race – or at least in the persuasiveness of the Maxim gun – was still unshaken. In spite of the seeds of doubt sown by the Boer War, 1911 was still a heyday of imperialism. But the rumblings of discontent were there, not always far below the surface, and they contributed to the sense of malaise, the realization that things were not working out according to plan, which made 1911 a disturbed and critical year. With China and Mexico in upheaval, with disaffection spreading from Morocco through Tripoli to Persia, where would the rot stop? These were not the uppermost questions in people's minds, but they were still another complication, compounding and intensifying the existing atmosphere of uncertainty and insecurity.

*   *   *

But China and Mexico – and even Morocco – were peripheral in 1911, and few Europeans needed to look beyond their own frontiers to see that trouble was brewing. If 1911 was a critical year, it was because the consensus upon which the whole existing system rested – or was supposed to rest – had broken down. There was unrest among the working classes; there were divisive constitutional issues; and for Britain at least there was the Irish question, the legacy of an earlier phase of predatory imperialism, which looked as though it was now on the point of taking its revenge.

In Britain 1911 was the year of the great constitutional crisis over the right of the House of Lords to reject legislation approved by the House of Commons. In fact the controversy over the Parliament Bill excited politicians and constitutional lawyers far more than it did the man in the street, and contemporary chroniclers noted with pained surprise 'the apathy of the public'. The question of Home Rule for Ireland cut deeper. The Irish question only came to a head in 1913 and 1914, but 1911 was the year when the lines of battle were drawn – the year when Carson and Bonar Law (the latter shortly to replace Balfour as leader of the Unionist Party in Westminster) raised the standard of Ulster revolt and uttered scarcely veiled threats of civil war. For most English people, to say nothing of the Irish, the future of Ireland was a far more important issue than anything that occurred overseas in Africa or Asia, or even on the continent of Europe.

But even Ireland was overshadowed, in 1911, by the great wave of industrial unrest which came to a head in August. Unrest among the workers was, significantly, practically the first subject touched upon by King George V in his conversation with the German ambassador in London, Count Metternich, when the latter visited the new sovereign at Balmoral in September. It was, His Majesty observed, 'increasing disturbingly in all civilized countries' – but (though this he did not add) nowhere more disturbingly than in the United Kingdom. Already in the previous month the German Foreign Ministry was speculating 'how much strikes and disturbances in England are likely to hamper her action in foreign affairs'. It had similar thoughts about France, and in Russia the assassination of Prime Minister Stolypin, on 14 September, was evidence, if any were needed, that the unrest of 1905 was still continuing: in fact, it came to a head again in the famous Lena Goldfield strike of 1912.

We shall return to the industrial unrest, which was one of the most significant aspects of the 1911 scene. The other aspect which deserves at least mention, so far as England is concerned, is the mounting feminist agitation which had begun earlier and went on with increasing violence until July 1914, but which also contributed to the atmosphere of unrest. The coronation ceremonies, which took place in June, were marked (or, as some old-fashioned people thought, were marred) by a great procession, four miles long, of 40,000 suffragettes; and though this was a peaceful demonstration, as befitted the occasion, later in the year the mood changed, windows were smashed, and Lloyd George, sitting back in his motor-car, was hit on the head by a despatch box hurled through the open window by a male sympathizer. Here again the future – a future very different from the male-dominated society of 1911 – was knocking on the door.

*　　*　　*

It would, of course, be misleading to suggest that alarms and excursions at home and abroad were the only, or even the main, preoccupation of 1911. It has already been suggested that Agadir looms larger for historians today, who know the sequel, than it did for contemporaries, who did not. Time marches on, and threats of war did not prevent people from going to Goodwood for the races – those, at least, who could afford it – or to cricket at Lords (where, in 1911, Oxford beat Cambridge, and Eton beat Harrow), any more than events in the Persian Gulf or the crisis in Poland, and doom-laden messages from the President, prevent people from going to watch the Celtics or the Los Angeles Dodgers today. I myself paraded happily in carriage-and-four in Manningham Park with my grandparents, looking down smugly on the crowd of mill-girls and shop-assistants who stood around enjoying the warmth and brightness of one of the sunniest years on record. No doubt it was the same in Munich, Hamburg and Elberfeld. That, also, is part of the reality of 1911.

For many Englishmen and Englishwomen the highlight of the year, without much doubt, was the coronation of King George V on 22 June, a ceremony attended by the Crown Prince of Germany and his brother, who were received with special enthusiasm by the crowds. This – a happy interlude, a contemporary observed, when 'for three or four days party strife was suspended' – weighed more for contemporaries than the diplomatic clouds over Morocco. The other memorable feature of the year (some people even went so far as to hold it responsible for the bad temper of striking workmen and the obduracy of diplomats) was the heatwave, which registered an almost unbelievable 100° F at Greenwich on 9 August. Even diplomacy was affected in an age still innocent of air-conditioning. A temperature of 90° F or more, the British ambassador in Berlin told his opposite number in the Foreign Office in London on 27 July, 'is not suitable for carrying on worrying and delicate negotiations'. No doubt he was right; but those who were not carrying on worrying and delicate negotiations profited where they could from the run of good weather. Once again, for the second time on record, the Channel was successfully swum (it was, no doubt, the coolest place to be); and the Cowes Regatta, held on schedule despite the political situation, was won predictably by the German Kaiser.

*   *   *

This urbane and optimistic view of 1911 is, nevertheless, deceptive. Later, people looked back nostalgically to the years before the Great War (or the First World War, as survivors of the Second World War now choose to call it) as *la belle époque*. For some, no doubt, including myself, walking happily in the park with my German Fräulein, who wept bitter tears when she was shipped back to the Fatherland at the end of 1914, it may have been true. But on any closer look the times were not so beautiful. Even the more affluent middle classes, the beneficiaries of the system, were beset by anxiety. We were certainly unaware, as we walked through Manningham Park with my younger brother in his pram, of the seething discontent of the workers, which had erupted twenty years earlier in the great Manningham strike of

1891. We still had servants in plenty to tidy up for us, and to light the fire before we came down to breakfast in the morning. But there was an uneasy feeling that the good times were coming to an end, that we stood at the end of an epoch. The smell of grime and sweat was kept at a distance, but it could not be entirely banished. Strikes, revolutions, assassinations and armed clashes were a reminder of the existence of another world, different from ours and fundamentally hostile to ours.

That is why historians have called 1911 'the critical year'. All the countries of Europe stood on the edge of civil strife, and outside Europe resistance to European rule and European pretensions was gathering force. The crisis was not only a crisis of war and peace, it was the crisis of a whole society. And if war was the only way out – or at least the easiest way out – people were bracing themselves to take it: not today but tomorrow, if necessary, or the day after. Looking back on 1911, it is this change of mood – the growing sense of anxiety and the fatalism that accompanied it – that is the final impression. In the following chapters we shall examine its causes, beginning with the economic strains and tensions which, more than anything else, sapped people's confidence about the future. In 1911 the great boom, which had begun in 1896, was running out of steam, just as the boom of the 1950s and 1960s ground to a halt around 1974, and the result in both cases was to leave people shaken and bewildered, and ready for desperate remedies.

3

'The Sense of an Impending Crash'

'Some people talk about Morocco, everyone talks about the rise in the
cost of living.'
Welt am Montag, 4 September 1911

If people in 1911 were oppressed by a sense of impending crisis, it was
not simply – not even mainly – the crisis in international relations that
worried them. What they saw, or felt, or instinctively anticipated, was
another of those frightening downturns in the economic cycle which
had made the 1880s and most of the 1890s nightmare years for businessmen. (This was the time when my paternal grandfather moved
out of his comfortable, ugly, middle-class mansion into an uglier,
uncomfortable terrace house, where he remained until his business
was almost miraculously rescued by war, and an almost insatiable
demand for blankets for Serbian, Greek, Romanian and other distant
armies, thus enabling him to pay off the bank and return to an even
larger mansion, high on the moorside above the River Aire, with a
magnificent view across the valley to the Brontë country on the other
side.) What businessmen like my grandfather were beginning to feel
in 1911, and not only in England, was that they were about to repeat
this frightening experience, and that the repeat performance might be
even more frightening.

There is at first sight something paradoxical about these anxieties.
1911, and the immediately preceding and succeeding years, are traditionally seen as a time of lavish spending, luxury, ostentation and high
living. Walther Rathenau, the millionaire Jewish industrialist and
head of the great German electrical corporation, AEG, walking
through the streets of Berlin in 1911, was appalled by 'the insolence of
our wealth gone crazy', and in England the coronation was accompanied by wild parties, lavish fancy-dress balls, and what *The Times*
ponderously denounced as 'general light-heartedness'. But we must
not make the mistake of confusing the very rich and the much publi-
cized antics of lordlings, with the wealthy and not so wealthy but

established and reasonably affluent middling classes. Their anxieties were real.

Here again, no doubt, we must be careful not to exaggerate. The gloom about the future of capitalist society, which settled on the business community in the 1930s, and is again obtruding in the 1980s, was only dimly foreshadowed in 1911. It needed another sharp jog in the economic cycle before anyone spoke in the dramatic terms of Dean Acheson when he proclaimed, in 1944, that 'we cannot go through another ten years like the ten years at the end of the twenties and the beginning of the thirties, without having the most farreaching consequences upon our economic and social system.' But by 1911 the writing was on the wall, the impending downturn too visible to be denied; and, as in 1981, no one knew what to do about it.

*   *   *

It was a critical year for the economy in practically every country about which we have adequate information, and certainly in the world's leading industrial nations. 1911, one of the most percipient of contemporary observers wrote, was dominated by a feeling of 'uncertainty' and 'misgiving', of 'nervousness' and 'disquiet', on the part of the commercial and industrial classes, and this was not simply a consequence of the Morocco crisis. It preceded and ante-dated it.

At first glance the judgement of the financial editor of the *Frankfurter Zeitung* may seem wide of the mark. In 1911 the world economy was on the last leg of the remarkable economic upswing which had followed the ending of the great depression in 1896. The temporary setback of 1907-08 had been surmounted, as in our own day the temporary setback of 1974-5. There was, indeed, one serious exception, the United States; and Europeans (particularly, it would seem, Germans) who speculated in American securities in 1911 got their fingers badly burnt. But elsewhere, by all the conventional indices, the picture was good, indeed more than good. There were some soft spots (building, for example); but output of basic raw materials (coal, iron) was up on 1910, which had also been a highly satisfactory year, shipbuilding was flourishing (the intake of new orders was healthy, particularly in the United Kingdom), the export trade was expanding rapidly, unemployment was down, and nothing could hold back the new branches of industry, electricity and chemicals, which had even withstood the recession of 1907 and 1908. 1909 and 1910 had seen recovery from the recession; 1911 looked even better.

But we know today from our own experience of the Johnson years, and from memories of the Coolidge years, that the last leg of a period of boom has its own peculiar problems. These were as evident in 1911 as they were in the early 1970s and the late 1920s, and had the same familiar characteristics. They explain the 'misgiving' and 'disquiet' which afflicted the business world.

First of all, though the recovery from the 1907–08 recession was quite marked, it was not proving easy to get back to – still less to surpass – the prosperity of the pre-recession years. Wholesale prices in Germany, for example, in July 1911 were still well below the level of July 1907 – in the case of the sensitive and politically powerful metallurgical industry, by almost 10 per cent. By comparison with the early years, the boom was running out of steam, or (as one commentator put it) was 'short of breath'. It was also decidedly uneven, and even in Germany major branches of industry, notably textiles and construction, were depressed. In cement, for example, even the larger, more competitive firms were only working at 50 per cent capacity, the smaller ones at 30 per cent or less. This, as Sir Francis Oppenheimer, the able British representative in Frankfurt, pointed out, was far from 'the uniform activity characteristic of a boom'.

The fact was that, by comparison with the early years of the boom, the growth of productivity was definitely slackening. Business was going ahead, but at a slower pace; the return on capital was declining, and profits were harder to earn. In England, it would seem, total productivity increased by no more than 0.5 per cent a year during the first ten years of the century; and although England is often treated as a special case, there is no doubt that a similar process was at work in Germany, and probably also in the United States. It is significant that the dividends paid out by eighteen leading German businesses in 1911 were over 20 per cent lower than they had been in 1906; in fact, only three of the eighteen actually increased their payments.

The slowing of growth – the inevitable progress towards stagnation, or even 'stagflation' – in the later stages of an economic cycle is a phenomenon as familiar to businessmen as it is to economists, and it has predictable results, all of which were as visible in 1911 as they are today. Three, in particular, deserve mention, since they characterize the whole economic climate: (i) a wave of takeovers and mergers (not, indeed, as high as that of the 1970s, but high enough), as business tried to counter declining profitability by economies of scale; (ii) an aggressive attack on export markets to make up for stagnant demand at home; and (iii), perhaps most ominous and most characteristic of all, a speculative fever which reached its peak in 1912, and put share prices far ahead of their intrinsic value.

In all these respects, no doubt, reactions were modest by comparison with later times. Certainly, speculation was far more hectic in 1929, and again in 1973, when the common stock of McDonald's, the hamburger king, was trading at seventy-six times earnings (implying, on the unlikely assumption that McDonald's would double its earnings every six years, that the 1973 investor was buying earnings of the year 2005). But for contemporaries the implications were clear enough. As Sir Francis Oppenheimer soberly observed, prices had reached levels 'which no confidence in the future, however sanguine, could justify'. Before the market finally broke, in October 1912, the shares of the Vogtländische Machine Works had risen 354 per cent above the level of 31 December 1911. Nice pickings for some lucky punter, but scarcely a healthy portent for the economy as a whole! The onset of the depression, already beginning in 1913, but fended off by the outbreak of war in 1914, was clearly visible.

* * *

The most striking and most commented upon feature of the 1910–13 boom was the vast, unparalleled expansion of exports. Virtually the whole of the increase in British manufactures in this period went to the export market. In Germany, where exports had fallen in 1908 by more than 6 per cent below the 1907 level, by 1911 they had reached the record high of 8106 million marks, over 18 per cent above the 1907 figure. For us today, nurtured on the mythology of 'export-led growth', this seems a major achievement. In reality it was a reflection of the growing difficulties. Exports were sought not for their own sake but because of the saturation of the home market and the pressure of overproduction, and in many cases they were dumped at unremunerative prices.' It only needed a crisis abroad – a crisis which in fact arrived in 1913 – for markets to shrink and the whole overheated prosperity to collapse. By mid-summer of 1913 newspapers were writing of 'signs on the economic horizon' of 'approaching catastrophe'.

Along with a boom in export markets, 1911 also saw a boom in foreign investment, a sure sign of over-capacity and the drying-up of investment opportunities at home. Rather than put money back into their businesses, people found it safer and more profitable to invest in the international capital and money markets. In Britain only 2.2 per cent of the national income had been invested abroad during the first quinquennium of the new century, as compared with 8.2 per cent at home; between 1910 and 1913 the figure was 9.3 per cent, and domestic investment had sunk to little more than 4 per cent. During the two years 1911 and 1912 something like 30 per cent more capital was exported from the United Kingdom than during the whole decade betweeen 1890 and 1901, and in each of the two years vastly more than in any peak year of capital export during the 1880s or the 1870s. As the great English economic historian, Sir John Clapham, later pointed out, the effects at home were far from good: 'a relatively small diversion of resources from foreign to home investment', he says, 'would soon have wiped out the few per cent of extra unemployment in the building trades'. But investors knew better – or thought they did. Foreign investment seemed more remunerative; perhaps 'the gambling element' in it attracted them.

There is, in fact, no doubt that what motivated the more or less monied middle classes, the *rentiers* in England and Germany and elsewhere, was the desire to maintain their standard of living in an inflationary climate. By 1911, 'the hope of an increased income' had become, in the words of Sir Francis Oppenheimer, 'an irresistible temptation'. The result was that investors moved out of fixed interest stocks into industrial equities, and then – when (as we have seen) industrial equities failed to produce the expected increments – into speculative counters – gold mining shares (at that stage, like the Australian mining market and the oil exploration market today, full of dubious and sometimes fraudulent flotations), rubber shares, American rails (long after railway building had passed its peak), and even such gambling issues as cinematographs and skating-rinks. British consols (standing, as I write, at $19\frac{5}{8}$) fell in September 1911 to $76\frac{3}{8}$, at that date an all-time low. The collapse, one contemporary wrote, 'was due to the insistence by ordinary investors on higher yields than a few years ago, consequent on the increased cost of living'. But even this was not literally true. Industrial equities and more speculative shares were bought, not for their higher yields, but in the hope and expectation of quick capital gains – which, in those halcyon days, were not subject to taxation.

*   *   *

'Speculation,' Sir Francis Oppenheimer rather ponderously reported, 'increased with the force of an avalanche' in 1911. This was, in his opinion, the distinctive feature of the 'last commercial recovery'.

Perhaps, with the benefit of hindsight, we can go further and say that the boom – like the last leg of subsequent booms – was a speculative boom, without real substance, that the economy was riding for a fall, and that anyone who was capable of looking beyond the end of his nose was aware of it.

If one hasty, short-term way out was to push up exports at any cost, another was to put pressure on the government to keep up orders, particularly in armaments and military hardware, which were the best supports of heavy industry. This, unfortunately, is something about which we do not, for obvious reasons, know as much as we might wish, but we know something. There is no doubt that German heavy industry, Krupps and the other 'steel kings' of the Ruhr, was deeply involved in the activities of the *Flottenverein*, or Navy League, and in the propaganda campaign for naval building. The same was true of their opposite numbers – Vickers, Armstrong, Whitworth – in Great Britain and elsewhere. Dreadnoughts were for them a matter of life and death, of profitability or recession. Count Zedlitz-Trützschler, the Comptroller of the German Kaiser's household, had no illusions in this respect. 'It would be very interesting,' he noted in his diary in 1909, 'to learn something about the connections that exist between the fleet fanatics and the manufacturers engaged in building the fleet. The power of the steel kings weighs heavily and their worries about their business, their desire to keep the share index high, has often been put before us as a national concern.'

There was, of course, a third way out of the impending crisis, and that was to wring more out of the workforce, to get greater productivity without higher wages. This policy was pursued both in Britain – particularly after the foundation of the Engineering Employers' Federation in 1896 – and in Germany, and was accompanied by an attack, not unlike that in Britain in 1979 and 1980 and in the United States in 1980 and 1981, on social security and social welfare. The Central Federation of German Industrialists called for a 'rallying of all employers' against the 'insurance epidemic'; industry could not afford the burden, it was undermining its competitiveness on world markets. At the same time it demanded new legislation to deal with strikes, asking the imperial government, on the very day that the *Panther* steamed into Agadir, to take action to prevent picketing. What we need, a shipbuilding magnate announced a few months later – anticipating by seventy years the thought processes of Prime Minister Thatcher – is 'a law for the protection of non-strikers'.

From all this there emerged a confrontation which rapidly assumed revolutionary dimensions. 'We are in the midst of a revolution today,' wrote Albert Ballin, William II's wealthy friend and head of the Hamburg-Amerika line, in July 1910. 'It is a revolution,' a Hull shipowner told E. R. Askwith, the able arbitrator of the British Board of Trade, eleven months later; 'and so', Askwith commented, 'it was.' 'War has begun,' declared the Secretary of the British Railwaymen's Union on 18 August 1911; but what he was talking about was not war between Britain and Germany, but class war.

Fear of revolution was widespread among the beneficiaries of the *status quo* in Germany, France and the British Isles in 1911 – more widespread, probably, than the realities justified – and we shall not understand the Agadir crisis nor its dénouement unless we take this fact into account. As early as 1907 the German General Staff had carried through a study of counter-insurgency, designed to combat revolutionary outbreaks in the industrial centres. In 1910 the military commander in the Ruhr drew up plans to arrest all socialist leaders in the event of war. And even in 1914, when it might have been expected to have been concentrating all its thought and efforts on the offensive against France, the army took elaborate precautions to forestall the possibility that the Social Democrats would attempt to obstruct mobilization by proclaiming a general strike. It was, it realized, fighting a war on two fronts; and there is no doubt that the revolutionary front at home, though obviously not the first priority, was taken very seriously.

Even in Germany, it is only fair to add, the military represented an extreme and unrepresentative fringe, and in the end the civil administration was able to curb, though not control, what Bethmann-Hollweg called 'the follies of the "Red-baiters" in uniform'. Nevertheless, revolution was in the air from 1911 onwards, and the possibility of revolutionary outbreaks can never have been far from the minds of statesmen and politicians during the disturbed pre-war years. And, apart from revolution, they faced, perhaps in some ways no less disturbing, a growing discontent and disillusionment on the part of the middle-class electorate, on which both Bethmann-Hollweg in Germany and the Asquith administration in Britain depended for support. Together, these facts go far to explain why 1911 was 'a critical year'.

4

'Workers of the World, Unite'

'Let those now strike who have never struck before, and those who have always struck strike all the more.'
W. Marsland, Manchester Cotton Spinners' delegate, Trade Union Conference, Newcastle, 8 September 1911

The revolutionary unrest which was, all in all, the outstanding feature of 1911, was a direct consequence of the economic situation sketched in the preceding chapter. Some writers have sought its origins in the spread, from its home in France, of the philosophy of syndicalism, a derivation of the ideas of Bergson, Gustave Hervé and Georges Sorel, whose influential *Reflections on Violence* had appeared in 1906. But this view certainly exaggerates the intellectual component. As Mr George Dangerfield has stated, syndicalism had not 'the slightest appeal to British workmen'; their 'political barometer was wages and nothing more' – unless, perhaps, it was the closely related question of the cost of living. And the same questions exercised workers in the other industrialized countries of the world. What is significant is that action soon carried them further; but prices, wages and the cost of living were the starting point.

That workers were restive and dissatisfied is not surprising. The opening years of the twentieth century were everywhere a time of inflation – not, no doubt, so steep as the inflation rate of 10 per cent a year, if we are lucky, or 75–100 per cent, if you happen to live in Brazil, Israel, Turkey or Argentina, we are accustoming ourselves to living with today, but disturbing and alarming enough. And there is no doubt, either, that the rate of inflation was increasing, rather than diminishing, as 1910 passed over into 1911. The bourgeois *rentiers*, the German *Mittelstand*, the English investors who lined up on 'dividend day' at the Bank to collect their unearned increment, were not suffering an illusion in believing that their standard of living was being slowly but surely eroded. But what they were experiencing was nothing by comparison with the deterioration in the position of the workers. Did 'the better-off classes whose comfort is assured' realize what poverty really meant, Lloyd George asked in a famous speech at Swansea in 1908.

By poverty, I mean *real* poverty – not the cutting down of your establishment, not the limitation of your luxuries. I mean the poverty of the man who does not know how long he can keep a roof over his head, and where he will turn to find a meal for the pinched and hungry little children who look to him for sustenance and protection.

Lloyd George was a great orator who spoke with the wizardry of a Welsh bard. But however rhetorical his language, the grim reality bore him out. At a time of apparently increasing prosperity and ostentatious living on the part of the very rich, the relative position of the working classes, not only in England and Wales, was getting worse not better, the gap between rich and poor, which is so familiar to us today – though today we think of it in terms of rich nations and poor nations, rather than of rich classes and poor classes – was widening, not closing. Leo Chiozza Money, in a book which first appeared in 1905 and which quickly ran through three printings, and came out in a revised and updated edition in 1911, estimated that, in 1908, 12 per cent of the population of Great Britain enjoyed half the national income, and that of this 12 per cent the wealthiest class (the 125,000 he classified as 'the rich') were in possession of a little over one-third. Money's estimates, inevitably, have been challenged by later 'experts', but there is no doubt that his picture is true in all essentials; and it is as certain as certain can be that the situation in Great Britain was more favourable – favourable, that is to say, from the point of view of the dispossessed and disinherited masses – then we should get from a similar picture, if we had one, of the maladjustment of wealth in Germany or the United States, or probably in France.

It is notoriously difficult even today, with all our sophisticated statistical techniques, to estimate either the cost of living or the real value of wages, but one thing about which all writers, contemporary and modern, agree is that workers in 1911 were worse off than workers ten years earlier. Estimates vary, as one would expect, and there are variations from country to country (Italy, in particular, appearing to go against the trend). But even the most conservative (and least convincing) economic historian I have been able to consult concedes that the level of real wages was no better in 1914 than it had been in 1896.

If true, this was a situation that was scarcely likely to fill the working classes with enthusiasm; and that is perhaps why, as another historian has written, by 1911 discontent had come to focus 'not on specific evils and localized enemies, but on the performance of the entire system'. If you substitute for the word 'performance' the word 'malperformance' or 'malfunctioning', and for 'entire system' the words 'capitalist system', that is not a bad description of the situation when the Agadir crisis broke in July 1911.

*   *   *

Not much is gained by arguing, as economic historians delight to do, about the exact figures. One historian calculated that prices in Britain rose by 7.6 per cent between 1906 and 1911, and that, as nominal wages failed to keep pace, real wages decreased by 6 per cent over the same period. Another wrote (in terms only too familiar today) that the purchasing power of the pound sterling had shrunk by 1910 to 16s 11d. The new Conservative, or Unionist, leader in the House of Commons, Bonar Law, alleged in November 1911 that there had been a rise of nearly 10 per cent in the cost of living with no corresponding rise in wages under the Liberal government, but he may have been exaggerating for political purposes.

In this welter of opinion, the safest course is probably to follow Sir John Clapham, my father's neighbour and friend in Cambridge after my father retired from the fray, after many buffetings by the economic cycle, just when Chamberlain took over from Baldwin in 1937. Clapham, the historian of the Bank of England, was certainly no radical, still less a revolutionary, but he calculated that by 1912 food prices were 14 per cent above the 1900 level, and that 'a rise of 1s in 7s on food bills ... is not a thing to be ignored', particularly when wages were more likely to have gone down than up, and when average weekly pay would rarely (and then only if you were lucky) be likely to top 35s.

In fact, far from increasing to meet the rising cost of living, wages (or some wages at least) were under attack. Employers were not slow in exploiting the 1907–08 recession to cut down their wages bill. In 1908, in Great Britain alone, over 140,000 workers struck, not very successfully, against wage cuts. Some leading sectors, the aristocrats (it might almost be said) of labour, were substantially worse off. In Germany, for example, miners at the seam face, who had earned over 6 marks a shift in 1907, were only earning around $5\frac{1}{2}$ marks in 1911, although meanwhile the cost of everything had risen. Their position in Britain was as bad, if not worse. In 1911 miners' wages were still 11 per cent below the 1900 level. With food and clothing costs up around 10 per cent, this was a very noticeable difference – noticeable, at any rate, to those whose budgets had to bear the costs.

It would be easy to add to these statistical figures – to take into account, for example, the fact that unemployment, though undeniably less severe than during the recession years of 1907–08, never again until 1913 matched the low level of 1900. This is simply in line with the observation we have already made that the recovery after 1909, the last leg of the secular boom beginning in 1896, was in many ways a 'phoney' upsurge, dependent less upon a real recovery of the economy as a whole than upon an unstable speculative boost, which had no real substance and could not last.

More significant was the reaction of the workers, who were, in effect, paying for the phoney boom, and who had reached – or seemed to have reached – the limit of their patience. I say seemed to have reached because when, in 1914, the appeal to national solidarity came they fell into line, and the revolutionary situation, which seemed to be on the point of boiling over, collapsed like a pricked balloon. But that does not mean that the situation in 1911, and during the three succeeding years, did not scare the bourgeoisie, or that the sense of impending revolution, however much the threat may have been exaggerated, did not impinge on international politics. How do you circumvent and defeat internal discontent? President Galtieri and Prime Minister Thatcher were not the first – and no doubt will not be the last – political leaders to play the national card, rallying support against the enemy outside to fend off discontent and criticism at home. The tactic was as well understood in 1911 as in 1982. The Italian Prime Minister, Giolitti, for example, writes openly about 'encouraging diplomatic incidents abroad in order to extinguish domestic political conflicts', while denying that this had ever been his policy. But it was in Germany that the connection between internal and external affairs was most clear. For imperial Germany, or for those upholding the existing system of government in Germany, it was by now a matter of life and death to find a way out of its social and political dilemmas, no matter how desperate the means; and the fact that Bethmann-Hollweg failed to do so – that Agadir raised more problems than it solved – was a decisive factor in the situation. By the end of 1911 the road to 1914 was pretty clearly – though not irremediably – marked out.

*   *   *

But these reflections carry us away from 1911, and from the revolutionary situation that was building up in 1911. It is true, if we judge only by the extant documentation, that no government anywhere (except perhaps in Spain) appears to have been terribly worried by the challenge. Perhaps they were confident that they could control it, if necessary, by a whiff of grape-shot, a cavalry charge, a few rounds from the fusiliers. Perhaps the documentation conveys less than the truth. If we look more closely, it is impossible to escape the conclusion that, as 1911 progressed, ministers were beginning – incredulously at first – to realize that they were in the grip of something new, unprecedented and unpredictable. They were right.

Without doubt a new spirit was abroad. Consider, for example, the railway workers' strike manifesto in August 1911: 'Today', it proclaimed, 'the railwaymen are worse than slaves.' This was something altogether different from the reasoned exposition of concrete grievances and complaints which any reasonable government, especially a Liberal government, would listen to, even if it did nothing about them – particularly when it was accompanied (and here was something unheard of) by a twenty-four hour ultimatum. So also was the threat from a South Wales miners' agent to the local mineowners' management: 'there is going to be murder – by God, I mean it!' The English middle classes – unlike their German brethren, for whom even the most innocuous railway porter or train driver was a red revolutionary in disguise – liked to comfort themselves with the belief that they could count on what they called 'the good sense of the working classes'. But the reality in 1911 was better expressed by the Prime Minister fulminating in frustration: 'Your blood be upon your own head', and by the Home Secretary, Winston Churchill, despatching troops in all directions without even waiting, as the letter of the law demanded, for the local authorities to ask for them.

In fact, the English working classes had plenty of good sense, but their definition of good sense and the middle-class definition of good sense were fundamentally different. They smarted, with every justification, under a sense of injustice. They were well aware that, in a time of rising prices, they were being left behind; and they knew that Parliament, left to itself, would do nothing to right the balance. In Britain, the Liberals prided themselves on their social legislation, particularly Lloyd George's National Insurance Act, introduced and passed in 1911. It did nothing to appease the workers. What they were interested in was wages, not health insurance, and so far as they were concerned, the immediate effect of the Act was to subtract 4d a week from an already meagre wage packet. True, it had tacked onto it a tenuous unemployment scheme, but Lloyd George himself went out of his way to point out that it applied only to 'the precarious trades' (or about one-sixth of industrial workers) and excluded unemployment due to strikes or lock-outs. With one single exception, and this a very timid measure dealing only with the most notorious 'sweated industries', the great Liberal programme of social reform, which figures so large in our history books, had not raised anyone's pay by as much as one penny.

Not surprisingly, by 1911 working men and working women had begun to realize that, if they were ever to get anything, they would have to get it by themselves. In 1906, with over fifty Labour representatives in Parliament, they were ready to give political action a chance. Five years later it was obvious that political action was getting nowhere. The alternative was direct action, and direct action meant the strike. The day of the barricades was past, as Marx and Engels had perceived after the defeat of the Paris Commune in 1871; terrorism and assassination, the weapons of the 1890s, were futile, though they still occurred from time to time in India and Russia. The strike was the workers' only effective weapon, and workers everywhere resorted to it on a grand scale. Labour unrest, spreading and intensifying, was the hallmark of 1911, and it was far more deeply imprinted at the year's end than at its beginning.

There was, of course, nothing new about strikes, and nothing particularly alarming about their intensification. All this had happened before, and would doubtless happen again. What was new and alarming was the realization, with gathering force as the year passed, that their character had changed. Nothing could be more misleading than to classify the strike wave of 1911 under the old heading of 'industrial disputes'. No doubt, they still were industrial disputes, but they were also a great deal more. H. G. Wells was one of the first to put his finger on the difference. 'The old-fashioned strike', he wrote, 'was a method of bargaining, clumsy and violent perhaps, but bargaining still.' But now the worker was 'beginning to strike for unprecedented ends' – or even to strike for no visible ends at all, to strike not for this or that concession but 'against the fundamental conditions of labour'.

This was the first big difference, perhaps the fundamental difference. The issue was no longer boss versus worker, employer versus employee, something the mediatory organs of the state – Mr Askwith, for example – could fairly easily iron out. Now the issue was the state itself, the state as the embodiment of bourgeois society (which included, alas, most Labour Members of Parliament, and a large majority of trade union officials). Trade disruptions were one thing, but this was a rebellion of the underdog which threatened the whole existing dispensation, the distribution of the spoils, and the giddy, extravagant, irresponsible life style of what, very untruthfully, was called *la belle époque*.

There were also other, more specific differences, which gradually impressed themselves on contemporary observers, not least of all upon middle-class observers who did not like what they saw. The first was a spirit of militancy and violence, which struck terror in middle-class hearts. Someone who claimed to have been in Paris in 1871 during the Commune told Askwith in Hull that 'he had never seen anything like this' – 'women with hair streaming and half-nude, reeling through the streets, smashing and destroying'. It was, needless to say, no different in the forbidding valleys of South Wales. Here also, when Churchill's troops appeared, women and children threw themselves into the fray, hurling stones, flints, bricks, anything they could lay hands on. In Tonypandy and Pontypridd, in Penycraig and Llwynypia, the poor and dispossessed had at last reached the end of their tether. It was not an industrial dispute in any ordinary sense, but a desperate struggle for survival. The reaction of the German Ruhr miners was little different.

Another fact which impressed contemporaries was the participation – perhaps, indeed, the leading, activist role – of the unskilled and unorganized, of the horde of casual labourers, of men who had no union affiliations. The great strikes of 1911 almost invariably began among non-union workers; they were forced upon the reluctant and conservative unions from below. But their effect was to transform the unions, to drive them into combined action by federation and amalgamation, the final result of which was the famous 'Triple Alliance' of miners, railwaymen and transport workers, forged in 1913. The outcome was a new spirit of solidarity, so that the half which had no direct interest at stake came to the help of the other half which had. Earlier strikes had been local and sporadic; now they were national. The national strike declared by the railwaymen on 15 August – 'our first', as their historian wrote, with militant pride – was a landmark.

Furthermore – and perhaps more ominously still, for the upholders of the *status quo* – the strike movement of 1911 was international. The signal for an international strike of seamen was given on 14 June. It is usually said that it was obeyed in England, but went unheeded elsewhere. But that is less than the truth. The response was, indeed, lukewarm in France and Germany. But there were strikes in Belgium on 16 June and in Amsterdam and Rotterdam later in the month, strikes in which strikers were fired on, soldiers were stoned, and twenty-one of the thirty-five liners in the port of Amsterdam were immobilized. In Bilbao and Lisbon, also, the dockers came out, and tried, not without success, to draw other groups – carters, porters, lightermen – into the movement.

The threat of a general international outbreak was certainly real enough. The Germans, perhaps, hoped that the troubles in England would prevent the government there from taking a strong line over Morocco, and to that extent the strikes were not entirely unwelcome to the authorities in Berlin. But they were also aware that the ferment might spill over at any moment into the Second Reich, with consequences no one could foretell. When we take into account, in addition, nationalist unrest, in Austria-Hungary for example, and the linkage, very clear in the case of the Czechs, between national disaffection and labour disaffection, we can only conclude that those – a growing number – who believed that Europe stood on the edge of civil war were not far wrong.

*   *   *

In 1911, almost paradoxically, Great Britain was the country most affected. The story of the great strike movement – 'the workers' rebellion', one historian has called it – has often been told, and this is not the place to recount it once again. It is a stirring, dramatic, sometimes deeply moving story, the story of a spontaneous uprising in which the real heroes were the workers themselves, and the two remarkable leaders, Tom Mann and Ben Tillett, who inspired and directed them, often in defiance of the tepid, legalistic trade union bureaucracy.

It was a movement which had its martyrs when the troops, called out to occupy strategic points and provide guards and convoys, fired on the crowds in Liverpool and Llanelly, and killed and wounded a number of demonstrators. The intervention of the military heightened resentment and unrest. In Parliament, Keir Hardie, one of the few genuine socialists in the Labour ranks, denounced the Home Secretary, Winston Churchill, and, in words familiar enough today but strange and revolutionary then, shocked the House by proclaiming that the men shot at Llanelly had been murdered in the interest of the capitalist system.

The strike movement had begun, in Britain and elsewhere, in 1910 – this, Halévy correctly observes, was the moment when the wealthy classes first became seriously alarmed – but 1911 was the year of the great campaigns. In 1910 there were 531 strikes involving 385,000 workers. In 1911 the number rose to 903 – more than twice the level of 1909 – and 831,000 workers came out on strike or were locked out. In 1912 the number of strikers was half as large again, and it has been calculated that over 40 million working days were lost. By the standard of the time – by almost any standard – it was a staggering figure.

But what was happening in Great Britain was by no means exceptional. Throughout the world the failure of wages to keep up with the inflationary spiral was provoking a wave of revolutionary agitation, and everywhere the number of strikes and the number of strikers increased dramatically. Europe was most directly affected; but the movement was not confined to Europe and serious strikes broke out in Brazil, Uruguay and Argentina, where half the population was said to be in 'hopeless financial embarrassment' as a result of the soaring cost of living. And everywhere the strikes had the same disconcerting characteristics: the leading role played by workers in the basic industries (railways, docks and mines) whose concerted action could paralyse bourgeois society; the prevalence of 'strikes in sympathy' by workers not directly involved; the call (not necessarily successful, but symptomatic) for a general strike; and finally an increasing recourse to violence. In Germany, the strike of Ruhr miners at the beginning of 1912 was every bit as bloody as the strike of Welsh miners in the Rhondda valley at the end of 1910, and both were only beaten down by military force and starvation. In France, as well as in Wales, women threw themselves into the fray ('viragos' and 'carrion crows', *The Times* called them), particularly when troops were sent in to quell revolt. In Vienna, a demonstration organized by the Social Democrats to protest against the high cost of living turned into a riot, and a number of demonstrators were killed when the cavalry charged the mob.

Even the bare statistics are a striking testimony – perhaps the most striking testimony – to the rampant discontent among industrial workers. We have seen the sharp rise in the number of strikes and strikers in industrial England. In practically every country of Europe for which we have evidence the picture is the same. In Germany, there were 2,914 strikes in 1911 involving some 325,000 workers; ten years earlier the corresponding numbers had been 727, and fewer than 50,000. In France the comparable figures were 541 strikes in 1901 and 1,489 strikes in 1911. In Belgium the number of strikes during the same period increased from 117 to 310. In Denmark the number of strikes remained virtually unchanged, but the number of strikers rose sevenfold, and the number of working days lost increased from a mere 57,000 in 1901 to 648,000 in 1911, or more than eleven times. Quite clearly, a new spirit was abroad among the industrial workers of Europe.

But these figures, confined to industrial disputes, are only part of the story because in many countries with a large agricultural population agrarian unrest was as serious and widespread as industrial unrest. This was true in Portugal, where agitation among the agricultural workers of the Elvas region was widespread early in the year, and in Spain, where armed bands of peasants roamed the countryside, occupied the town hall at Cullera and shot the magistrate, and actually proclaimed the republic at Caroagente, the centre of the orange growing industry. With the dockers out at Bilbao and the miners on strike in the province of Asturias, with the whole Basque region brought to a standstill, and discontent spreading to Barcelona, Valencia, Saragossa and Malaga, Spain, by the end of 1911, was virtually in a state of civil war.

The situation in France was not very different. Here also agrarian unrest, particularly among the wine growers of the Marne and Aube, underpinned industrial discontent. For contemporaries the movement among the wine growers was the gravest threat to French stability in 1911. It amounted, according to contemporary reports, to 'a positive insurrection' – a rebellion in many ways as bellicose and disruptive as the simultaneous uprising of the Mexican peasantry under Zapata – and the result was that, for a considerable period, 'the rich district of Epernay and Reims was delivered over to revolution'.

Ironically, it was Aristide Briand, once the apostle of the general strike, who took in hand the work of repression with the peculiar ferocity of the poacher turned gamekeeper; but the unrest continued long after the fall of the Briand ministry in the spring of 1911, and in August the agrarian revolt, driven underground but not assuaged, was matched by violent popular uprisings in the industrial *départements* of the Nord, Pas de Calais and Aisne. This, by a curious coincidence, was the moment when the Agadir crisis reached its peak, when rumours of war were loudest, and preparations for war most advanced.

*　　*　　*

Not surprisingly, the 'Labour unrest' – to employ the anodyne phrase contemporaries used to hide from themselves the spectre of revolution

– was accompanied by a sharp swing to the left in politics. For us today, aware of the unrevolutionary (if not positively anti-revolutionary) attitude of the working-class political leadership, particularly of the Social Democrat representation in the German Reichstag, there is nothing startling or especially significant about the growth of the left-wing parties. They were not likely to rock the boat. But contemporaries did not see it that way. Socialism, for them, had still all the frightening connotations of 1848 and 1849, and of the Paris Commune of 1871, and – except, perhaps, in England, where people were trained to keep their cool (and where, later, Willie Gallagher, the single Communist Member of Parliament, was one of the most popular and beloved members of 'the Club') – they reacted accordingly.

The swing to the left politically was bad enough. It was made worse by a steep rise in trade union membership. In England, for example, it increased by some 600,000 in 1911. But it was not only a question of numbers, but also of the entry of a new, militant class which stiffened the unions and also stiffened the socialist parties. The change of mood over the five years between 1906 and 1911 left the leadership little choice except to respond to the rank and file. It did so often unwillingly, but it did so nevertheless. In Britain, the comfortable 'Lib-Lab' coalition of 1906 began to fall apart after 1911, and Labour candidates came forward who secured the defeat of Liberals, either to their own advantage or (more often) to that of the Conservatives.

The swing to the left was general. In Austria, the Social Democrats emerged from the 1911 elections as the predominant party in Vienna. They increased their strength considerably in Switzerland and made substantial gains at the expense of the right in Sweden. In France, where the socialists had made progress in 1906, they did even better in 1910. Their successes should not, of course, be exaggerated. Nowhere was the left within measurable reach of securing a majority (though it might have been in Germany if the representative system had not been heavily and systematically rigged). But the left-wing parties were in a position in a number of countries to hold a balance, particularly where, under the stress of the growing crisis, the main bourgeois blocs were falling apart. Already in 1906 a coalition of the Social Democrats and Centre Party in the Reichstag had defeated the German government and forced an election. In Britain after the elections of 1910 the Liberal government was dependent on the Irish and Labour vote and compelled to trim its policies accordingly. In France the Radical bloc, which had dominated since 1902, was dissolving into dissident factions, and when the Radicals failed to win an absolute majority in the elections of 1910, the short-lived ministries that followed were driven willy-nilly into an uneasy alliance with the socialists under Jaurès.

Clearly, the unspoken assumption that politics was the preserve and prerogative of the monied classes, of landed wealth and of industrial wealth, the assumption which had governed the political scene for the last fifty or sixty years, was crumbling. And now, to the crumbling from within was added, in 1910 and 1911, the assault from without, the direct, unparliamentary, or even anti-parliamentary, action of the under-represented or unrepresented masses. In Britain in 1911 there were still 4 million adult males without the vote, and neither there nor in France nor in Germany did women have the vote at all, though under the pressure of rising prices, simply in order to make ends meet, they were taking jobs in rapidly increasing numbers and were already a very substantial part of the industrial workforce. These were the people demanding the right, in 1911, to make their voices heard, through working-class parties if possible, but if not by the only means left open to them – agitation, strikes, demonstrations. The Bermondsey women's strike in August 1911 got less attention at the time than the great battles of the London transport workers; but as a spontaneous movement of revolt by the most downtrodden and worst paid sector of the working class (the average weekly wage was 7s–9s for women, and 3s for girls), it was a landmark both in women's history and in labour history.

*   *   *

All countries were affected by the new militancy and the swing to the left, but Germany, where parliamentary elections were due in 1912 and were looked forward to with growing apprehension, was affected most seriously of all. Ever since 1907, when the socialist vote had increased by a quarter of a million, by-elections to the Reichstag had shown a steady drift to the Social Democrats. Could the socialist flood be halted before it swept down the dams against democracy which Bismarck had so carefully constructed? What is certain is that, by 1911, the upholders of the existing order were not far from despair. Even Bethmann-Hollweg, who had succeeded Bülow as Chancellor in 1909, did not believe that the peculiar, anachronistic political and social system foisted on Germany by Bismarck could survive much longer, but he did not know the way out. Others, more radical, were toying with the idea of a *coup d'état*, suspension of the constitution, and rule by bayonets. But would a conscript army obey?

The problem in Germany was not merely the advance of socialism, but the cleavage in the ranks of those who benefitted from and had every reason to support the Bismarckian constitution. If Conservatives, Liberals and the Catholic Centre co-operated, all might still be well. But the policy of co-operation, or *Sammlung*, was easier to preach than to implement. The issue, as usual, turned on taxation. Liberals were enthusiastic advocates of a great German navy; Conservatives were equally determined to have a great German army. But who was to pay for either, and still more for both? Over this central issue, which touched everyone's pocket, the hope of a common front of the possessing classes broke down. The detail we can pass over. The result was that by 1911 the German domestic scene was in total disarray. Dissatisfaction with the existing order had reached dangerous proportions, even among those who were its beneficiaries, and the prospect was that the Reichstag elections of 1912 would return a clear centre-left majority, which would proceed to demolish the autocratic empire. By comparison, the constitutional crisis in Britain, which caused so much uproar in political circles there in 1911, was not much more than a storm in a teacup.

The situation in Germany was not without irony. Everyone was aware in 1911 that the Ottoman Empire, the Habsburg Empire and the Manchu Empire in China were falling apart, but paradoxically none of these ancient empires was in a more crippling impasse than the youngest and most recent recruit to the imperial ranks, the forty-year-old Hohenzollern Empire. On the surface, it is true, the Second Reich seemed immensely vigorous, prosperous, self-assertive and successful. But its vigour and self-confidence were more apparent than real; a psychologist might have described them as a posture sub-consciously adopted to conceal the weaknesses and uncertainties lurking below. Certainly, as the elections of 1912 drew near, as the economic recovery began to look precarious, as the prospect loomed up of another recession in 1913 or 1914, the uncertainties became more oppressive. Perhaps, as Max Weber had dimly foreseen in 1895, the imperial dream had been an aberration, 'a youthful indiscretion which the nation would have done better to omit'. But how, at this late stage, to draw back? And how to move forward?

The German problem in 1911 was that, failing a total reconstruction of the antiquated Prussian social and political system, which was probably impossible in view of the entrenched position of the conservative classes, it could only fend off discontent at home by a series of *coups* abroad. But how could you expect to bring off a series of *coups* abroad without alarming and antagonizing the other powers and conjuring up the spectre of war? This was the situation in which Bethmann-Hollweg found himself in 1911. Six weeks before the Agadir crisis, the German Foreign Secretary reported that Bethmann was 'anxious for success and becoming impatient'. The implication is that he hoped that a diplomatic victory in Morocco might serve as a catalyst for bringing together the nationalist parties and securing a much needed strengthening of the imperial government. It might even take the wind out of the Social Democrats' sails. But suppose there were no victory – or only a minor victory – which neither satisfied the Right nor appeased the Left? These questions, and the dilemma they posed, were to weigh heavily on Bethmann-Hollweg during the hot summer of 1911; but the very fact that he embarked on the Agadir adventure at all shows how desperate he was to find a way out.

* * *

If this was the situation, we shall not be far wrong in seeing in the exigencies of domestic policy – that is to say, in the social tensions and economic strains which all countries of Europe were experiencing – the underlying explanation of the diplomatic crisis of 1911. In any broader view, the crisis at home and the crisis abroad were two sides of the same coin, manifestations of the breakdown of the existing order. In such a situation, it was clearly tempting to stave off criticism and disaffection at home by a spectacular success abroad, or at least by a patriotic appeal to the national cause. In 1907, in the so-called 'Hottentot elections', when the issue was the savage suppression of the great Herrero revolt in Africa, Bülow had defeated the Social Democrats in this way, cutting their representation in the Reichstag from 79 to 43, the first and only reverse they suffered in the whole history of the Second Reich. Why should not Bethmann achieve an equal success in the elections of 1912 by a bold stroke of foreign policy?

It is hard to think that such calculations were ever far from the minds of statesmen and politicians in 1911, but, except in the case of Germany, concrete evidence is difficult to come by. We do not know, for example, why the weak Monis government in France decided, in spite of the misgivings of Delcassé and Clemenceau, to embark on a forward policy in Morocco. Was it intended, in an unexpressed and perhaps never clearly thought out way, to offset the rampant discontent in France and make the government more popular? The only thing we can be certain about is that the ostensible reasons put forward for the Moroccan adventure were not the real reasons; and yet it was this action by the French that started the train of events that led to the Agadir crisis.

In the case of Germany the position is altogether different. The Social Democrats had, from the start, no doubt whatsoever about the purpose of the despatch of the *Panther* to Agadir. It was, they said, a manoeuvre 'to divert attention from internal conditions' and 'to create a favourable atmosphere for the Reichstag elections'. It may be objected that this is a partisan statement which should not be taken at face value. But there is plenty of evidence that the connection between foreign policy and domestic policy was well understood in German official circles as well. The crown witness is the Foreign Secretary himself, who set it out in all clarity in the elaborate memorandum he drew up to persuade the Kaiser to sanction the Agadir *coup*. If Germany succeeded in obtaining 'tangible advantages' from the 'liquidation of the Moroccan question', Kiderlen wrote, this would be important 'for the future development of political conditions at home'. In particular, it would 'change the views of many dissatisfied voters' and might thus have 'a significant effect upon the outcome of the pending Reichstag elections'.

Although, in the event, the outcome of Agadir was to unleash (as we shall see) an outburst of frustrated nationalism, the initial reactions showed that Kiderlen's calculations were not far wrong. It was not merely that the whole of the right, Conservatives and Liberals alike, rejoiced in the demonstration of German power (as if, one newspaper put it, 'the German dreamer awakes after sleeping for twenty years'). They also welcomed an active foreign policy, even (perhaps particularly) if it carried with it the threat of war, as 'the only cure for our people'. 'The domestic situation', the *Deutsches Armeeblatt* pronounced, 'would benefit from a bold passage of arms, even if it means tears and anguish for individual families.' Or, as the conservative *Post* observed on 26 August 1911, it would ensure the 'restoration to health of many political and social institutions'.

Kiderlen-Wächter was also not altogether wrong in thinking that an active foreign policy was the best way of meeting and defeating the Social Democrat challenge. Superficially, the great socialist success in the elections of January 1912 seemed to give him the lie. But the success was purchased at no little cost – namely, by a sacrifice of principles, which led to internal dissensions within the party and, six years later, to the secession of the left wing. In that sense 1911 marked a fateful watershed in the history of German Social Democracy. The

37

despatch of the *Panther* to Agadir placed the party leadership in a nasty predicament. Should it follow the lead of the left and denounce it as a naked act of imperialist aggression? But in that case would it not lose the support of all patriotic Germans, and so make it possible for Bethmann to dish socialist chances in 1912 as Bülow had dished them in 1907? In the anxious, unedifying debates and manoeuvres that followed, the temporizing policy and tepid reformism of the right wing won out, but the price was the alienation of the rank and file and of all who called for action. Paradoxically, the great Social Democrat victory at the polls was accompanied by stagnation, if not actual decline, in party membership and disillusion among the workers. For a few short years, between 1906 and 1910, when the call for mass strikes was at its height, it looked as though German Social Democracy had real revolutionary potential, enough at least to frighten the middle classes. After 1911 it was a spent force.

This was something not as obvious at the time as it became later, and the fears of the middle and upper classes and their desire for war as a way out of the impasse continued unabated right down to 1914. Nowhere, perhaps, are they recorded more vividly than in the diary of Baroness Spitzemberg, an intelligent, well-connected South German lady who had the good fortune to die on 30 January 1914, and so to escape the war she so clearly foresaw. What her diary reveals is the rising crescendo, beginning in 1909, when her brother told her 'he almost wants war as an outlet for the unbearable tension', right through to 1913 when she was 'cheered up' (she records) because 'the young marines' were 'pining for a "fresh and happy war"' as soon as possible'. But in 1910 and 1911 the 'talk' was much more of revolution than of war, of 'the internal state of Germany, and particularly of Prussia, which at the moment is in a state of latent revolution'. This was the prevalent concern, the great overhanging threat, and it was her brother-in-law, the President of the Prussian Diet, who voiced the unmistakable reaction of the possessing classes: he wanted, she wrote, 'a bloody outbreak – and the sooner the better, so long as one can be sure of the military!' It was a German voice; but would it have sounded so very different if it had come from France or England?

*   *   *

Let us not try to prove too much. It would be unfair and misleading to saddle Bethmann-Hollweg, or even Kiderlen-Wächter, with the extravagances of the Pan-German extremists or of the Liberal ultranationalists. Kiderlen, indeed, expressed himself with characteristic Swabian forthrightness about the stupidity of these 'cattle'. But one thing seems certain, and that is that the internal situation made politicians more trigger-happy, not merely in the literal sense of a readiness to turn the troops loose on strikers, as Winston Churchill did with such gusto in Britain, but also in the sense of making them more willing to take risks from which in more normal times they would probably have shrunk.

More serious, perhaps, was the longing of the electorate, at least of the middle-class electorate, for a solution – indeed, for almost any solution. This was certainly the mood in Germany where the near total paralysis of the political machinery, the apparent impossibility of making any decisions, produced on all sides a deepening sense of frustration. But it was not much different elsewhere. In France the only policy of successive governments since 1906 appears to have been to have no policy, or at least to avoid action on all serious social issues, in particular the crying need for tax reform. In Britain, the Liberals, who had come to power with such a fanfare in 1906, had run out of steam. By 1911 they were a spent force, buffeted by pressures from all sides, from the working class, from Ireland, from the suffragettes. Nowhere was the government in control; nowhere did it have the answers – or, if it had them, did it have the power or will to put them into effect.

It was, above all, the feeling of uncertainty that was oppressive, that and the apparent deadlock on the home front which drove people to the desperate conclusion that the only way out was to cut the Gordian knot by a bold stroke of the sword. This also was common to all countries. 1911 was the year of reawakened nationalism, in Great Britain and France as well as in Germany, and statesmen – not least of all the German Chancellor – were appalled at the spectre they had called forth. Sir Edward Grey, who had no illusions about the likely consequences, declared at the end of the year that the world was 'in a fit of political alcoholism'. So it was. But, having called the sorcerer's apprentice out of the cupboard, they found to their horror that, in a new political constellation, where the masses demanded a voice and diplomacy was no longer the preserve of courts and cabinets, the apprentice refused to go back.

But it was not simply a question of the 'masses' (however they are defined). One of the most significant aspects of the Agadir crisis was the reaction of the banking fraternity, or of 'high finance', as it liked to call itself. It was they who, when the crisis reached its height, put pressure on the German government, and the reason – then, as today – was that uncertainty is bad for business, particularly for the money-lender's business. What hurt them was the 'unbearable strain' of 'prolonged crisis', of 'indecision' and 'expectancy' – in other words, exactly the things that were hurting most ordinary people and driving them to desperate, irrational remedies, the only difference being that they could make their views felt, and ordinary people could not. In 1911, as it turned out, the pressure of *haute finance* came out on the side of peace. But would it always work that way? Sir Eyre Crowe, the leading light of the British Foreign Office, summed up the position sombrely but realistically enough: the aim of 'high finance', he said, at any time of prolonged crisis, would be 'to bring about – not so much a peaceful – but *any* solution, peaceful or war-like'.

Here, in the words 'unbearable strain', 'prolonged crisis', 'indecision', we have all the ingredients of which wars are made – particularly if the blame or responsibility can be put upon someone else, English or Germans or (for preference) Russians. In 1911, as already noted, the equation worked out on the side of peace; but it needed only one or two other factors, such as the heightening of the strain until it literally became 'unbearable', to tip the balance in the other direction. For the moment, however, all it is necessary to see is that it was the situation at home, the 'unbearable strain' on the home front, the threat of revolution, and the apparent incapacity of the political leadership to cope, that were the decisive factors. What seemed imminent was a breakdown, which would lead either to revolution or to war – and the only question was which would come first. We know the answer; but no one in 1911 did.

5

The New Machiavellians

'Well,' I said, 'I want an aristocracy.' 'This,' she said, smiling, 'is the pick of
them.... They cost a lot of money, you know.'
'...Give 'um all a peerage when they get twenty thousand a year,' she
maintained.... 'You'll get a lot of loafers and scamps among 'um, but you'll
get a lot of men who'll work hard to keep things together, and that's what
we're all after, isn't it?'
H.G. Wells, *The New Machiavelli* (1911)

Who were the political leaders – prime ministers, foreign ministers,
ambassadors and diplomats – who were called upon (as they would
probably themselves have said) to cope with the situation in 1911?
How did they measure up to the task?

The first thing to say about them is that, by all standards, they were
very ordinary men. We should not exaggerate their individual importance. When things go wrong – and they certainly went wrong
between 1911 and 1914 – people look around for scapegoats on whom
responsibility can be pinned. Once upon a time it was the German
Kaiser, William II, who was denounced after 1918 as a 'war criminal'.
More recently there has been much argument about the role and
responsibility of Bethmann-Hollweg. Such controversies are not very
profitable. What we are dealing with are not the failures of individuals,
but the failures of a class. Everyone knows about the Kaiser's aberra-
tions and indiscretions, his bluster and irresponsibility; but the problem is not so much the man as the system which allowed and even
encouraged him to indulge in them. As for Bethmann, he was by all
standards a sensitive and cultivated man – the epitome, it has been
said, of the 'good German' – but he was the captive of a system in
which he had lost faith, but from which he could not liberate himself.

Let us, therefore, not spend too much time on personalities. There
was a sprinkling of colourful characters among them, like Kiderlen-
Wächter with his famous canary yellow waistcoat, a Christmas present,
the story went, from his mistress who had knitted it for him with her
own hand. But for the most part, they were colourless, often almost
faceless, individuals. They were also, most of them, honourable men
by the not very exacting standards of their day, though even Sir
Edward Grey, the austere British Foreign Secretary against whom no

word of scandal was ever uttered, was not above misleading, if not actually lying to, the House of Commons. The great exception in 1911 was Joseph Caillaux, who almost accidentally became First Minister of France only three days before the Agadir crisis broke on the world. We shall come back to Caillaux, who was lucky later on to escape a firing squad. But even of him it is safe to say that he almost certainly believed that his devious underhand dealings with the notorious Freiherr von der Lancken were in the best interests of France.

Caillaux apart, the charge against the principal actors is not that they were dishonest, but that they were men of narrow vision and limited ability, competent enough in the sense that they did a routine job (most of them at least) reasonably conscientiously, but incompetent in the sense that they were totally unfitted by character and upbringing to meet the challenges of a world in the throes of revolutionary change. Their minds were shaped by the assumptions and modes of thought of the late Victorian era, and they shared an intense distrust of the new forces struggling to find an outlet in their day. Even in 1911, there were individuals – Lenin, for example; or Mussolini, who made his first appearance on the stage of history at this very moment – who saw through the existing dispensation. But in 1911 they were outsiders. Within the ranks of the establishment – with the possible exception of Lloyd George, and he was an outsider who had climbed in – no one questioned the existing social and political order, or the established rules and conventions. That does not mean that their responses did not vary, only that their individual responses were constrained within a web of assumptions and preconceptions (or what today would be called an ideology), which conditioned all their thoughts and actions. Sir Edward Grey and Count Metternich, the German ambassador in London, might stand on opposite sides of the political fence, but they talked the same language, and it was not the language of Ben Tillett or Tom Mann.

We should not, perhaps, judge them too harshly. This was the age of the amateur, a time when it was tacitly assumed that a nodding acquaintance with Thucydides and the history of the Peloponnesian War were the best, or at least a sufficient, preparation for the conduct of twentieth-century politics. We should remember also that diplomacy, if not politics, was still the preserve of social standing and wealth. It was virtually impossible for any diplomat to live on his salary (attachés were not paid at all), and the upkeep of an embassy, particularly leading embassies such as Paris or St Petersburg, dug deep into the ambassador's pocket. Not surprisingly, a private income, set in Britain at a minimum of £400, and in Germany at 15,000 marks a year, was a prerequisite for entry. But far more important was social acceptability. Even after 1907, when reforms were introduced to put recruitment on a more competitive basis, it was still necessary in Britain for candidates to get the Foreign Secretary's permission to apply, and then to face a board of selection, which ensured, by personal interview, that they measured up to the requisite social standard. No wonder that competition was restricted to a narrow élite! 'Few men', it has been said, 'who did not conform to the generally accepted pattern applied, and fewer still slipped through the net.'

In these circumstances, it would be surprising if we were not confronted by what a foreign correspondent who knew them well called a set of 'amiable nonentities'. Kiderlen, who was nothing if not frank, wrote off most of the German ambassadors in Europe – Schoen, Tschirschky, Metternich and Lichnowsky – as 'lightweights'. A candid observer would have to say the same about most other representatives of most other countries. The Cambon brothers, Paul and Jules, French representatives in London and Berlin respectively, are commonly regarded as exceptionally able; but, except for their arrogance and ambition, it is hard to see why they have won such high reputations. On the English side, a typical lightweight was the ambassador in Vienna, Sir Fairfax Cartwright of Aynho Park, a magnificent country seat in Buckinghamshire, more of a poet than a diplomat, whose indiscreet remarks to an Austrian journalist caused a minor storm and a lot of trouble for Sir Edward Grey, and ended Cartwright's career. Of his predecessor, Sir Edward Goschen, promoted from Vienna to Berlin in 1908, the best that could be said was that he was 'a loyal servant', but no one had much belief in his ability.

The star in the British galaxy in 1911 was, or was reputed to be, Sir Francis Bertie, ambassador in Paris and younger son of the Earl of Abingdon, scion of a family of diplomats going back to the reign of Queen Elizabeth I, but petulant, bad-tempered and, as Lord Vansittart later wrote of him, 'wholly disinclined to scrape a second fiddle'. Bertie's career was typical of the aristocratic bias of the foreign service. Another example was Francis Villiers, packed off as minister to Lisbon in 1906 and still there in 1911 (a sure sign of mediocrity). Villiers was the fourth son of the Earl of Clarendon, and a member of another family with a long history of service in the diplomatic corps. The difference was that Bertie, in his early days, was an intimate of the Prince of Wales, soon to be Edward VII, and there is no doubt that Bertie's rapid rise owed a great deal to the king's influence. The situation in Germany was no different – Count Metternich, the German ambassador in London, and the amiable and elegant but lackadaisical Schoen, were favourites of William II, and Kiderlen-Wächter also had belonged to William's entourage, the Kaiser's companion on his various cruises, until his indiscretions resulted, in 1899, in his banishment to Bucarest, from where he only returned in 1910.

Influence, social connections, wealth, were the essential requisites in 1911 for entry into the charmed circle of the ruling élite. Arthur Ponsonby, son of Queen Victoria's private secretary, who embarked upon a diplomatic career and threw it up in disgust, put the matter in a nutshell: 'As it stands at present', he wrote, 'the Diplomatic Service can more accurately be described as a position, than as a profession.' More accurately still, perhaps, it can be described as a prerogative, a card of entry into good society. In France it was a little different. After 1890, or perhaps a little later, the aristocratic preponderance dropped sharply, from 88 per cent (it has been calculated) to a mere 7 per cent. Birth gave way to wealth. But it cannot be said that the conduct of affairs was noticeably affected. Indeed, if anything, mediocrity was even more firmly embedded. Who, even if his life depended upon it, could possibly paint a life-like portrait of such colourless nonentities as the French Premier, Monis, or his Foreign Minister, Cruppi? And of Cruppi's successor, Justin de Selves, French Foreign Minister throughout the Agadir crisis, it can safely be said that his only mark of distinction was his high-sounding name.

It has sometimes been argued that this did not matter very much, because the conduct of affairs was in the hands of their professional advisers – the Cambon brothers in Berlin and London; the permanent officials of the British Foreign Office, Nicolson and Crowe. But the permanent officials were, if anything, more rigid and hidebound than their superiors. No doubt they acquired a certain expertise in drafting treaties and scrutinizing despatches, but on any other level they were prisoners of the social and political system they inherited. They also belonged to the ruling élite in 1911, and their common attitudes are more important than their personal idiosyncracies. Despite their different backgrounds and nationalities their main concern was to ensure that the system went on functioning. Surprisingly, it did. In 1914 it looked as though they had bungled the whole operation, and indeed they had. But when the mists of battle cleared, and the slaughter was over, they were back with all their privileges, and the society they stood for emerged, not unscathed but substantially intact. Even Joseph Caillaux, released from prison in 1920 and amnestied in 1924, re-assumed his self-appointed role of saviour of France. He did not get far, but his return was symbolic.

*   *   *

On the fringe of this society – not part of it, but linked with it by characters such as Caillaux – was a second tier, a motley crew – almost a rogues' gallery – of adventurers, speculators, corrupt or corruptible politicians and journalists, and shady individuals from the underworld of international finance. We shall have more than one occasion to observe them at work. Except for Caillaux, ministers and diplomats viewed them with distaste and disdain, but it is necessary to take note of them and their activities because they were an integral part of the 1911 scene. Some historians have even argued that Europe was brought to the verge of war in 1911 on behalf of dubious financial interests in Hamburg, Paris and Berlin. That is certainly an exaggeration. But it is also true that we shall not understand the course of events unless we take account of the underhand, or undercover, activities going on behind the formal diplomatic exchanges.

This is no place to tell the whole shady story, even if it could be told. Morocco was one of their fields; another was the Congo. But they were also active – perhaps even more active – in Persia and China, and nearer home there were close and intimate contacts between the iron and coal magnates of eastern France and western Germany. There were interlocking shareholdings, and behind the whole operation were the interests of banking corporations, French and German (and British, Russian and American as well), which probably played a dominant part. The multinational corporation is not solely a phenomenon of our own time.

For our purposes it is sufficient to look quickly at Morocco and the Congo. In the former the troublemakers were the Mannesmann brothers, six in all, and 'all pushing'. We have already briefly encountered them. Earlier they had founded what soon became, and still is, a major German metallurgical company; but by 1911 their interests had shifted and they were busy promoting a Mannesmann Morocco Company they had established in Hamburg a few years earlier. The Kaiser, as we saw, described them succinctly and aptly as 'rogues'. An even bigger rogue was a certain Mestayer (no one seems to know his first name) who, even earlier, had secured a concession in the French Congo and floated an undertaking, the N'Goko Sangha Company, allegedly to exploit it. In reality, neither Mestayer nor the

Mannesmanns were interested in developing their interests. 'What', Mestayer is reputed to have said, 'is the point of stooping to the lowly business of selling cotton or raising rubber' when 'there was something more profitable to be done' – namely, to extract compensation for his alleged rights from the French government? Mestayer's main idea was 'to make fat sums of money easily and without working', and the Mannesmanns' minds moved on parallel lines. They were, in fact, still suing the German government when Hitler came to power in 1933.

The manœuvres and intrigues of the Mannesmanns and Mestayer were complicated as well as sordid. For the former the complication was that there already existed a rival organization in Morocco, the *Union des Mines*, a joint Franco-German undertaking, in which the leading industrialists of both countries, Krupp, Schneider-Creusot and others, were participants, and it had no intention of sharing the booty, if any, with the Mannesmanns. The complication for Mestayer was the existence, across the undemarcated frontier between the German Cameroons and French Congo, of a rival German company, the *Südkamerun Gesellschaft*, of which Semler, Vice-President of the German National Liberal Party and a close associate of the Deutsche Bank, was director, and this company (Mestayer alleged) was trespassing on N'Goko Sangha's territory. The question was how to get out of – or more accurately, how to profit from – these complications. The answer was to bring pressure to bear on their respective governments to support their claims, and it was in this way that Mannesmann's Morocco Company and N'Goko Sangha became involved in the wider question of Franco-German relations.

Today we are hardened to such things, and accept them as normal; what otherwise are governments for? In 1911 this perception of government's function was only beginning to break through. Theodor Wolff, editor of the *Berliner Tageblatt*, described the Mannesmanns sarcastically as 'the first German captains of industry who succeeded in turning their business into a matter of national concern', the 'pioneers of the new technique' of twisting the government's arm. It could, and did, backfire. When Mestayer seemed on the point of collecting an indemnity of 2 million francs from the French government this happy arrangement was blocked by public outcry, and instead he turned to negotiations with Semler for a joint undertaking for mutual profit – negotiations which soon spilled over into the political field. During 1911 Semler was forever on the move, back and forth between Berlin and Paris, carrying proposals for economic and political collaboration. The Mannesmanns, on the other hand, relied on other methods, posing as patriotic representatives of the national interest against the allegedly unpatriotic Franco-German consortium, and enlisting on their side the full blast of German National Liberal propaganda. And all, needless to say, had their agents and go-betweens, haunting the corridors of power and the ante-rooms of ministers. Most were shady and disreputable.

*   *   *

Let us look quickly at some of these characters, beginning with André Tardieu, the influential leader-writer of *Le Temps*, who claimed to be Mestayer's nephew and was certainly his most active agent. According to the British embassy, which surely had good reason to know, Tardieu was one of the most corrupt journalists in Paris, though needless to say by no means the only one. It was not only that he placed his influence and that of his newspaper behind Mestayer; he was also active as a go-between. It was Tardieu who took up, on Mestayer's behalf, negotiations with Lancken, the counsellor at the German embassy in Paris, who happened, in addition to his official duties, also to be unofficially Semler's business agent. The subject was the possibility of co-operation between N'Goko Sangha and the Südkamerun Company, or alternatively a project for a joint railway linking the Congo and the Cameroons. But the significant thing about the conversations between Tardieu and Lancken, which took place during a pleasant excursion on a bright spring day in 1910 in the forest of St Germain, is that they soon extended beyond this to the whole question of Franco-German economic and political co-operation in central and north Africa. Was this Tardieu's idea, or had he, as seems more likely, been prompted by other interests? We shall probably never know the answer; but what is important is the repercussions of these discussions. Relayed by Lancken to Berlin, they were almost certainly one source of Kiderlen-Wächter's idea, in 1911, of a trade-off between German disengagement in Morocco and compensation for Germany in the Congo. They were, in short, the overture to Agadir.

Tardieu was only one of the more or less disreputable characters involved in the backstage intrigues of 1911. Many other names crop up more or less frequently as intermediaries in the secret negotiations between Caillaux and the Germans, among them a certain Fondère, a speculator in African lands and concessions of about the same moral calibre as Mestayer, and a series of minor characters, including a

Russian-born fringe banker, Günzbourg, and a minor newspaper proprietor, Pierre Lenoir, whose son was shot in 1918 for treason. Fondère was undoubtedly Caillaux's most active agent in his underhand dealings with Lancken behind the back of the Quai d'Orsay; but what is all too evident is that Paris in the days of M. Fallières, President of France from 1906 to 1913, was not morally a very salubrious place. Corruption, intrigue and double-dealing are met with everywhere, even in Washington; but in Paris in 1911 they were the rule, and not the exception.

At the heart of this intrigue and double-dealing, like a spider in his web, sat Oscar, Freiherr von der Lancken-Wakenitz. We have already seen something of him, and shall see more. He arrived at the German embassy in Paris in 1907 and remained there until 1913. Often described as the Kaiser's 'confidential agent' (though I know of no reliable evidence for that assertion) and inordinately proud of his aristocratic lineage and military bearing, Lancken was in effect the member of the embassy staff who had the unenviable task of carrying out the disreputable, underhand negotiations, of which it was advisable that the ambassador should, at least officially, have no cognizance. Someone, no doubt, has to do the dirty jobs. The point about Lancken is that he did them so expertly that, after the outbreak of war in 1914, he was immediately sent to Belgium to take charge of espionage and counter-espionage, where he earned the unenviable reputation (against which he never ceased to protest) as the butcher of the nurse, Edith Cavell. At the same time he was in charge of espionage in France, where he lost no time in getting into touch (among others) with his old friend Joseph Caillaux.

Lancken is, on all accounts, one of the more distasteful figures on the 1911 scene. Herbert Hoover, who met him during the First World War when he was head of the American Relief Commission in Belgium, had nothing but contempt for him, and Poincaré described him as 'the typical Prussian rogue, overbearingly proud and wicked'. But it has also to be said that Lancken could not have conducted his underhand operations in 1911 if he had not found accomplices on the other side. Among these was Joseph Caillaux, who already as early as 13 December 1908, when he was Minister of Finance in the Clemenceau government, had entered into secret conversations with Lancken with regard to a Franco-German understanding over Morocco. What he began then, he continued in 1911. Caillaux – not, as is so often said, Kiderlen-Wächter – was the *éminence grise* of Agadir; and to Caillaux, so typical of the confusions of French policy in 1911, and before and after, we must now turn. It is not a particularly happy story, but it is a necessary one.

* * *

Historians have been kind – in my opinion, far too kind – to Caillaux, perhaps as they were all too kind to that other war criminal Albert Speer when he was released from Spandau. But anyone compiling a rogues' gallery of 1911 has not much choice, except to put Caillaux high up in the first rank. Clemenceau once said of him that 'he thinks he's Napoleon' (later he described him more succinctly as 'a bandit'), and this without much doubt was the basic flaw in his character. Madly ambitious, he was also, by all accounts, a foppish dandy, 'the Beau Brummel of the radicals'. He does not, with his glistening skull and piercing, pig-like eyes, look like it in any of the photographs I have seen, though he evidently had a fair measure of success with the female sex. But he was certainly arrogant, disdainful and absurdly confident of his own abilities. He had also (as Denis Brogan put it) 'too many friends in low finance', from whom he learnt how to cut corners, particularly where money was concerned. And this aptitude he carried over into politics, where he felt free to dispense with the ordinary scruples. Caillaux was by no means the only French politician to go behind the back of his Foreign Minister and negotiate surreptitiously with the Germans. Rouvier, Prime Minister in 1887 and again between 1905 and 1906, had done the same thing and, like Caillaux later, had been caught out when the cryptographers at the Quai d'Orsay broke the German secret code. But the result was that by 1914, when his underhand activities in 1911 were public knowledge, Caillaux had become the embodiment of everything a patriotic Frenchman despised and rejected. Hissed and threatened, he was rushed out of Paris by the police at the outbreak of war for fear lest, like Jaurès, he would be assassinated.

Caillaux is, on all scores, an unsympathetic character. On the other hand, at the time of Agadir, he almost certainly represented the views and wishes of his constituents, the prosperous farmers of Mamers, who stood by him through thick and thin, and perhaps even of a majority of Frenchmen. There was a long tradition of Franco-German understanding in the Third Republic, going back to the first Republican president, Jules Grévy, and there were plenty of people in France in 1911, particularly among the wealthy provincials who were the dominant voice in the Republic, who would have been happy to do a deal with Germany rather than risk war, another defeat, and its corollary, the Commune. The Commune of 1871, and the threat to property it was thought to symbolize, was still the dividing line, and Caillaux epitomized pretty accurately the fears and calculations of the Radical petty bourgeoisie. Furthermore, German industry was in need of an infusion of French capital, and most Frenchmen, given some sort of political *détente*, would have been only too glad to supply it. To this degree Caillaux saw right. His mistake – and it turned out to be a cardinal mistake – was to negotiate surreptitiously behind the back of his government. Not a few Frenchmen had reservations about the recent entente with England, and there was nothing basically wrong behind the idea of a Franco-German understanding in place of a Franco-British understanding – except, of course, that it would have made France a junior partner of the Reich and put paid (but few people cared about that) to any hope of recovering the provinces of Alsace and Lorraine, lost in 1871. But if such a policy were reasonable and certainly not unpopular, why did Caillaux have to pursue it in a clandestine way?

Caillaux's career casts a good deal of light on the history of the Third Republic from its beginning in 1871 to its end in 1940. He was the link – but certainly not the only link – between Thiers, the murderer of the workers in 1871, and his accomplice Ferry ('Ferry, the valet of Bismarck', as he was called) at the one end, and Pétain and Laval at the other. In fact, if he had not been too old and too worn out, Caillaux, rather than Laval, would probably have been the ideal leader of the collaborationists in 1940; that, after all, was the main thread of his political life. Instead, with his memories of disgrace and imprisonment, he cautiously stood aside. But he is said to have died in delirium in 1944, calling for a new Joan of Arc to 'kick the English out of France'. It is not for an Englishman to complain against that; it is an old French tradition. Caillaux's misfortune was that in 1911 it became, because of German pressure, a minority view. Kiderlen-Wächter could, with patience, almost certainly have got anything he wanted from him; but when he decided with typical Swabian *Plumpheit* to 'thump the table', he cut the ground from under Caillaux's feet. Thereby he got a great deal less than Caillaux was prepared to offer, and at the same time laid up a store of trouble for the future.

*　　*　　*

The story of Joseph Caillaux is the best evidence that nothing disqualified a man from a political career under the Third Republic, provided he had the means. Caillaux had. When, in the last years of the nineteenth century, his mother and older brother died he was left with a fortune of a million francs, by no means extraordinary wealth by the standards of the time, but putting him in the class – which was the only class that mattered – of aspirants to a political career and its perquisites. In this respect at least he was a typical product of the prevailing social system. This meant, among other things, that when he fell out of office in 1909 he had no difficulty in picking up director-ships in the Banco del Rio de la Plata, the Crédit Foncier Argentin and the Crédit Foncier Egyptien, which brought in a tidy and (in view of his various amatory adventures) much needed income of something like half a million francs a year.

If, as we shall see, imperialism in all its manifestations was a domi-nant element of the mentality of the well-to-do classes of 1911, the very names of these undertakings are significant. To cream off a little – or, if possible, more than a little – from overseas financial transactions was part and parcel of the perquisites Europeans expected from their colonial or semi-colonial ventures. Unfortunately for Caillaux his South American connections, which seemed like pure profit, got him into hot water. When in 1914 he visited Brazil and Argentina he immediately got involved with a number of dubious characters, in-cluding a certain 'Count' Minotto (needless to say, no count at all but an American adventurer) who turned out, as anyone but Caillaux would have known, to be a German agent. In Europe, on his return in 1915, he did no better. Lancken sent agents to him from Switzer-land, but even without Lancken's help he managed to surround himself with the political underworld of Europe. By 1917 he was a rallying point for crooks, spies and traitors, and when the axe fell it was only the fact that he was so obviously naïve and impressionable that saved his neck.

He also was unlucky in his marital and extra-marital affairs. Plenty of others were more notorious in an age when the art of love was part of the training of every young attaché – how otherwise would society ladies have spent their afternoons? Asquith (one of whose mistresses was a colourful figure in Oxford when I was an undergraduate) is said to have whiled away the tedium of Cabinet meetings writing to his girlfriends, and Kiderlen's private life was particularly flamboyant. The story of his relations with a certain Marina de Jonina, a double-agent who passed on his love-letters to the French (as almost certainly he knew she would), provided a fund of entertaining scandal, parti-cularly the episode when – in the middle of the Agadir crisis, at the very moment when France and Germany were supposed to be on the edge of war – he went off with her secretly for a weekend at Chamonix, only to be greeted on arrival at the railway station by the French Prefect and a guard of honour. Caillaux's exploits were less entertaining and a good deal more sordid, particularly the so-called 'Caillaux *affaire*', when his second wife shot at point-blank the editor of *Figaro* to prevent him from publishing the love-letters Caillaux had written to her when she was still his mistress. Mme Caillaux was, indeed, acquitted in the end in the face of all the evidence by a jury disposed, as French juries so often are, to side with the delinquent rather than the victim in crimes of passion. But the case, coming on top of the disclosures about his underhand dealings with the notorious Lancken and allegations that he had used his position to halt proceedings against one of his shady financial associates, provided still another handle for Caillaux's many enemies.

From this time on, Daniel Halévy says, he began 'to take on that outlaw look which was not ill-suited to his native insolence'. It remained with him for the rest of his life. When in 1925 he went to the United States to try to negotiate a settlement of war debts, Herbert Hoover (who had no more use for him than he had for Lancken) described him as looking like a 'roulette table croupier' in a second-rate casino.

*   *   *

The story of Caillaux is worth telling briefly because of the part he played in the events of 1911. It is also worth telling for the light it casts on the political atmosphere in 1911. Caillaux is, no doubt, an exceptional case, but he is also recognizably a denizen of what a contemporary sardonically called the *république des camarades* – the 'comrades' (or 'chums' or 'pals') being that fairly wide and elastic group of senators and deputies for whom a political career meant jobs and opportunities to make fortunes on the side, and who regarded the body politic as something existing for them to exploit and plunder. That this opened the door to a regime of graft, bribery, corruption and reciprocal favours is obvious enough, though there was also a sort of unwritten convention which most people observed about how far they should go.

Money and money-making were never far below the surface in the France of President Fallières. When the famous *Times* correspondent, George Saunders, was transferred to Paris towards the end of 1908 he said that what struck him most was 'the prevailing desire of pecuniary gain', adding significantly that in his view it was also a powerful factor in French foreign policy. Coming from a man who had spent the past ten years in Berlin, where money was certainly not without influence, this was a significant judgement. Without much doubt, a sharp deterioration had occurred in French political morality after 1906. For a few years, at the turn of the century, the Dreyfus affair had produced a genuine conflict of principles, around which political parties had crystallized. But after 1909, if not earlier, the victorious Radicals broke up into conflicting factions, divided only by personal rivalries and the scramble for the spoils of office, people for whom the 'supreme talent' (as Robert de Jouvenel once said) was 'to survive'. And so they did, moving from office to office, as one short-lived ministry (there were no fewer than nine between the fall of Briand in February 1911 and the outbreak of war in August 1914) was followed by another. Only Caillaux, too conceited and self-confident to play the game according to the rules, fell by the wayside, but even he did better than he had any right to expect.

By 1911, the political scene in France was back again somewhere where it had been in the 1890s, at the time of the notorious Panama scandal. The egregious Mestayer boasted openly that he had 200 Deputies in his pocket. Caillaux, who had made his name as a zealous advocate of tax reform, wrote proudly to his mistress (it was one of those unfortunate letters, signed '*ton Jo*', which subsequently became public) that he had 'crushed the income tax while seeming to defend it'. Both these stories give a taste, but only a taste, of the muddier undercurrents of French politics in and around 1911 – and this at a time when, as we have seen, the 'social question', and particularly the maldistribution of wealth, was crying out for a constructive solution.

The France of President Fallières, the *république des camarades*, is sometimes written off as a peculiarly French aberration. No doubt, there were special features such as the absence of a clearly defined party system, the existence of which in Great Britain produced at least the semblance of a conflict of principles. But if we wish to understand the political atmosphere in 1911, and the assumptions with which the political élite confronted the crisis, the common elements are more significant than the differences. Even in Imperial Germany, where an obsolescent aristocracy enjoyed artificially maintained prerogatives, the same factors prevailed. Princes, counts and barons might secure some of the perquisites of office; but the bourgeoisie, high and not so high, pulled the strings. If Mestayer had his clientele in the Chamber of Deputies, the Mannesmann brothers, whom no one in German official circles regarded as anything but upstarts and scallywags, had theirs in the Reichstag; and, characteristically, when the Agadir question was eventually settled, the settlement included some nice, and totally undeserved, benefits for them – no less than 30,000 gold francs in recognition of some of their 200 claims. 'Ouf!', the French ambassador in Berlin wrote to Kiderlen on 14 November 1911, expressing clearly enough their common opinion of the Mannesmanns. But the need to propitiate financial interests, however unjustifiable, had become part of the 1911 scene.

The English prided themselves on avoiding the financial scandals which so unhappily punctuated French political life; but, except perhaps in degree, England also was not so very different. As 1911 turned into 1912 the Marconi scandal suddenly erupted. It implicated (rightly or wrongly) Sir Rufus Isaacs (later Lord Reading), Herbert Samuel and Lloyd George, all ministers in the Liberal government. The *république des camarades* – in this case, British comrades – made sure, needless to say, that its reverberations did not go too far. The Tories were delighted to have an opportunity to blast Lloyd George's reputation, but they had no idea of blasting the system and, after a lot of damaging exposures, the whole affair was carefully brushed aside. Its interest, in the end, is that it shows the solidarity of the 'pals', the 'comrades', or the 'club'. What mattered was not your political label (in France it was as near as possible meaningless), but whether you had paid your entrance fee; and if you had – unless you did something very foolish, as Caillaux did and as Remington, the hero of the novel H.G. Wells published in 1911, also did – you were pretty safe. This even applied (except in Germany) to the socialists, a now growing number, provided they obeyed the rules of the game – and most of them did so willingly.

*   *   *

If we try at this point to draw the threads together, what do we see? The most obvious fact is that politics, in the usual acceptation of that word, were at a very low ebb in 1911. At a time when the rapid progress of industrialization had created an industrial democracy with democratic, parliamentary institutions (Prussia still stood out as a glaring exception, but even Austria and Bavaria introduced universal male suffrage in 1906 as Baden had done in 1904 and Italy was to do in 1912), political power in Europe was in the hands of a remarkably

54

small body of men – the notorious 1000 families – who made and executed all the important decisions; and the one thing they seemed oblivious to was the challenge of the time.

They varied, naturally, a little from country to country, not quite the same mixture in Britain as in France, or in France as in Germany; but what all had in common, rather like the feudal aristocracy of medieval Europe, was a consciousness, irrespective of nationality, of belonging by right, birth or prescription to a privileged ruling class. They were people (as H.G. Wells put it) who 'opaquely accepted the world for what it was' and who 'set themselves single-mindedly to make a place for themselves in it'; and their attitude to democracy and the forms and processes of democratic government – if they did not think of them (as quite a few Germans and a sprinkling of others elsewhere certainly did) as an obstacle to be swept aside – was to treat them as a means of keeping in their possession a power which in their view was theirs by right. That, and the preservation of the class and way of living to which their lives were attuned, were for the political élite of Europe what politics were about in 1911. Whether it was an adequate view in a world where the overriding issues were war and revolution and economic crisis is another question.

As a political élite it is easier to see than to define. But nowhere, perhaps, is it better seen (certainly not in the writings of Proust, and probably not in those of Anatole France, either) than in H.G. Wells' ambitious though curiously unsatisfying novel, *The New Machiavelli*, which he published in 1911. *The New Machiavelli* is a thinly disguised, perhaps slightly jaundiced review of the political scene at the moment when the great Liberal experiment, launched in 1905, was grinding into the dust, and the picture it paints is veracious enough; perhaps a little too veracious.

The world Wells puts before us – the little world of 'in' people who met together in country houses and at cocktail parties (just becoming, like ragtime, a feature of the day), a world which knew nothing, and wanted to know nothing, of the real world threatening to engulf it – is, alas, too near the reality of 1911 to be dismissed as a novelist's fantasy. And what do we see? First of all, its hero (if that is the right word), 'a rather shallow, rather vulgar, self-seeking careerist', picked out and propelled at the ripe age of twenty-seven by Sidney and Beatrice Webb into the House of Commons, who became the editor of a minor political weekly, which, 'before 1911 was out' (and that was its great achievement), 'went into all the clubs in London and three-quarters of the country houses where week-end parties gather together'. I don't know how far, when he wrote this, Wells had his tongue in his cheek (I suspect not at all); but, sarcastic or not, he put his finger on the essential factor – the 'complex of powerful people, clever people, enterprising people, influential people, amidst whom power is diffused today.' Were there not, his hero asked himself, 'big bold qualities about these people' – 'the wealthy and influential people' – 'that common men lack?' The answer, of course, is that there were not; and that is part of the tragedy (or, cynics might prefer to say, the comedy) of 1911.

If we look more closely at this élite – not only in England – the first thing to say is that, contrary to the prevailing view, it was in no sense an aristocracy, still less (as Proust, among others, argued) a caste. There was, of course, a fair sprinkling of aristocrats (that is to say of people who owed their position to noble birth and connections); but the fate of the elegant, aristocratic Arthur Balfour, nephew of the former prime minister, Lord Salisbury, who was deposed from the Tory leadership in 1911 by the dour, middle-class Scots-Canadian businessman, Bonar Law, is a warning not to exaggerate their influence. Bonar Law was, by any standards, more typical of the 1911 political scene that Balfour. But it was also in no sense a plutocracy. On the contrary, what stands out across a broader spectrum as its distinctive feature is neither business (its turn would come later, with the 'hard-faced businessmen' who flocked into Parliament after 1918) nor aristocracy, but the dominance of the bourgeoisie – that is to say, of the established, educated, well-endowed people of independent means who were called in France the *haute bourgeoisie*, and in Germany the *Bildungsbürgertum*.

This was true even in imperial Germany, reputedly the last bastion of aristocracy and autocracy. No doubt, the Prussian nobility still had a hold on the army (but not on the rising navy), and to a lesser degree on the diplomatic service. But for the rest the government was pretty solidly in the hands of the educated upper middle-class bureaucracy which had been the backbone of the petty German principalities before 1871, and continued to be the backbone of the Empire after 1871. The man who ran the Kaiser's civil secretariat for twenty years from 1888 to 1908 was nicknamed the 'apothecary', allegedly because that was his father's occupation. Bethmann-Hollweg himself came from a family of Frankfurt bankers, whose ennoblement went back a little further than some, though only to 1840, and the oracles of etiquette had to be consulted before William II in his youth was permitted to visit the Bethmann estate at Hohenfinow. There was, in short, far more social mobility in imperial Germany than is often supposed. The predicate 'von', or even a title, did not necessarily denote noble birth or long lineage. Freiherr von Schoen, Foreign Secretary before Kiderlen, and ambassador at Paris from 1910 to 1914, was a member of a well-known family of wealthy tannery owners at Worms. He 'smelled of leather' was the unkind comment of Prince Münster when Schoen first turned up as a junior member of his embassy staff.

In France, even the army by this time was thoroughly democratic and republican, and the aristocracy had withdrawn to sulk on its provincial estates or in the *salons* of the Faubourg St Germain. It was no longer a political force, as the career, or failed career, of Henry de Jouvenel, descendant of a famous line of Limousin barons which had entered history during the Hundred Years War, amply shows. Jouvenel was undoubtedly an able man, but he was better known for his private life (including marriage to the novelist, Colette) than for his public life, though his private life was public enough. In the Chamber of Deputies, the Count de Mun was a rare and distinguished exception, but he was surrounded there by the serried ranks of the bourgeois dynasties of the Republic; and Justin de Selves, Foreign Minister in Caillaux's administration in 1911, certainly owed more to his relationship with Freycinet, one of the legendary fathers of the Republic, than to his native ability. A mere inspection of the names of ministers in the various Cabinets between 1909 and 1913 is sufficient to reveal how strongly entrenched the bourgeoisie was.

Its core was the established upper segment, people with ample inherited wealth who did not have to work for a living, although (this was part of the bourgeois ethic) they almost always did; but it was also an open-ended – or at least relatively open-ended – élite. There were many ways of entry: the universities, the *Abitur* and *Staatsexamen* in Germany; the *baccalauréat* in France; a scholarship to Oxford or Cambridge in England; very frequently the law; or, like Wells' hero Remington, you could marry an heiress, live on her fortune, and devote all your time to furthering your political career. None of this opened the door very wide – the number of university students in the various European countries at this time averaged below 0.1 per cent of the population – but a glance around the political scene shows that it was wide enough. In England at least half a dozen members of the Asquith Cabinet were self-made men, including Lloyd George, 'an angry little solicitor from an uncouth, starved district of Wales', and the Prime Minister himself, a gifted lawyer who rounded off a brilliant legal career by marrying a famous society beauty. So, on the other wing, was F.E. Smith, later Lord Birkenhead, the rising star of the Tories (but a star which never rose), the son of a provincial lawyer, whose pranks and exploits as a Fellow of Merton College were still being talked about when I became a Fellow myself a whole generation later. Of F.E. Smith it was said that 'he learned at Oxford the infinite pleasure of spending money one does not possess'; and the lesson was not forgotten after he entered Parliament in 1906.

But if the system undoubtedly opened a career to talent – of a sort – it was not necessarily the sort of talent the situation needed. There were, to begin with, too many careerists 'on the make', of whom F.E. Smith was one, and Wells' Remington – a bright but entirely shallow young man who never did a real day's work – was another. Furthermore, the preponderance of lawyers, in Germany and France as well as in England, meant that politics was conducted in the spirit of the law courts, that is to secure an acquittal or a conviction, no matter what the merits of the case. In politics this meant that there were no principles requiring a firm stand. This does not imply that there were not exceptions – Jaurès in France was one, though he also made (usually disastrous) political compromises. But far more typical was the remark of the right-wing reactionary Charles Benoist to Poincaré: 'In sum, there is really nothing separating us!', or the familiar spectacle (familiar at least to connoisseurs of Spy's cartoons) of Asquith and Balfour sauntering arm-in-arm through London drawing-rooms. If we are to believe Lloyd George (which is not always wise), there were even serious negotiations in 1910 for a Liberal-Conservative coalition to dish the obstreperous Irish. True or not, the story illustrates faithfully enough the political temper of 1911. Political skirmishes were almost *de rigueur*, provided they were conducted, like a medieval tournament, according to the rules, and the various parliaments, assemblies and diets existed precisely for that purpose; but these were trimmings, and the essential fact was the solidarity of the possessors of power against intruders from outside. That was what the dominance of the bourgeoisie really meant.

The other essential fact in 1911 was the increasing attention paid to Guizot's old exhortation, *enrichissez-vous*! If £20,000 a year was the mark of success, the temptation to see a political career as a means of entry into the select few was not easy to resist. Even the socialist politicians whose arrival on the scene was a mark of the new century quickly succumbed to the lure of an assured place in society and a steady income.

Here again, there were exceptions – like dear old Keir Hardie, an incurably romantic, utopian socialist, whom the hard-headed trade union bosses were doing all they could to get rid of – but far more typical were John Burns, who had quickly switched from the role of a Labour agitator to that of a Liberal careerist, and Ramsay Mac-Donald, the inordinately handsome, leonine Scot whose proclivity for duchesses (in his case, snobbism not sex) quickly became a fable.

The entry of the socialist Millerand into Waldeck-Rousseau's Cabinet in France in 1899 – the first socialist to take office anywhere – was undoubtedly a turning-point; but a turning-point in what? By 1911 not only Millerand but also the fierce agitator Briand and Viviani, who, like Millerand, had built up a great practice at the Bar, were part of the machine and profited by it immeasurably. But it was not only the socialists who were affected. Lloyd George, the firebrand of 1909, was visibly softened by his contacts with the aristocratic milieu of Lansdowne House in 1910, and though he may not have had a villa in the south of France, as detractors and slanderers alleged, no one – not even Lloyd George himself – could seriously maintain that he came out of politics worse off than he went in. The tragedy, of course (if it was a tragedy), was that the people who had looked up to Lloyd George as their tribune – another Gracchus in another age singularly like that of the declining Roman Republic – were disappointed, Labour parties everywhere were discredited, and no one had an answer except to keep the machine ticking over. But after all was not that, as Wells' Lady Forthundred observed, 'what we're all after?'

*　　*　　*

A French writer defined a bourgeois, perhaps too cynically, as 'a man who has money and consideration and who always wants more money and more consideration'. Certainly, the *haute bourgeoisie* of 1911, less cynical than Lady Forthundred, regarded consideration as its right. It had created a world of affluence: what remained, but to perpetuate it? And who better qualified to do so than the bourgeoisie – suitably reinforced – which had created it? The word bourgeois did not have the pejorative connotations in 1911 it has acquired today. On the contrary, it was a matter for pride. They were the solid element in society, by comparison not only with the plebs below, but also with the flighty *haut monde* above, and the dubious financiers on the fringe.

But unfortunately this society, with all its achievements, was being assailed, not so much by the unrest of the workers, which it still was fairly certain it could contain, as by the unpredictable fluctuations of the economic barometer. Anyone who surveys the 1911 scene in this respect will quickly be struck by the sense of helplessness – as though faced by an act of God – which seems to have permeated it, and the total absence of any idea of what to do. It was not only a question of those who still were short of £20,000 a year, and were determined to make it; it was also a question in 1911 of those with £20,000 a year, who saw it being whittled away by inflation and the absurd demands of the working class for higher wages. To live on a fixed income, independent and untainted by gross calculations of profit and loss, was desirable – it kept one's hands clean, so to say – but how much longer would it be possible? The spider's web between business – upon which most well-born bourgeois still looked down – and bourgeois society was getting closer and tighter. And not only the bourgeois. Grey, an aristocrat if ever, had been chairman of the North Eastern Railway Company before he became Foreign Secretary and (it was rumoured) went on drawing his salary afterwards in flagrant disregard of established conventions; and in Germany the Junker aristocracy – still, in spite of tariffs on imported grain, unable to make a decent living (or a living at all) – was busy turning its rye into spirits in association with distinctly non-aristocratic financiers.

This blurring of the social frontiers is another characteristic feature of 1911. Most people – that is to say, most people who counted – still looked down on the business community. But how to get along without it? And how to keep it out? Particularly when one of the most favoured persons at the German court was the Jewish financier, Albert Ballin, and one of the most favoured persons at the Court of St James's was the Jewish financier, Sir Ernest Cassel. Neither Ballin nor Cassel, both men of integrity, belonged even remotely to the same class as the disreputable Mestayer, whose unappetizing career we have already touched upon, or even the Mannesmann brothers, who were not much better; but they all reflect, with different accents, the impact on European politics of the discovery of diamonds at Kimberley, and of gold on the Witwatersrand.

After 1886 financial interests, and with them the lure of quick profits, dominated the political scene. And since profits on a grand scale were to be found abroad, it was not long before the emphasis moved from domestic to international politics. The career of Cecil Rhodes in South Africa and the fortune he made from Kimberley diamonds and Transvaal gold pointed the way. So did the Jameson raid of 1895. There were, of course, other areas of profit – railway concessions in China and in the Ottoman Empire, for example. But the greatest area of profit seemed to lie in darkest Africa. Hence the fact that Morocco and the Congo – countries to which no one had given a thought fifty years earlier – suddenly emerged as bones of contention. Here, perhaps, was untold wealth – or at least sufficient wealth to keep the system going. And even if it turned out not to be true, the financial community would make a profit, and the costs could be charged up against the government.

It is, in retrospect, a sorry story, but it casts a good deal of light on the mentality of the new Machiavellions in 1911. As things got tighter at home – and they were visibly getting tighter – they looked abroad for relief. They were doing the same in 1980. That, in the end, is what imperialism is about, and what it signified in practice is revealed in one of Kiderlen-Wächter's more amusing and more instructive letters to Mme Jonina in Switzerland. It is the letter dated 18 October 1910, in which – exaggerating, perhaps, to impress her with his own importance – he tells her how would-be concessionaires queued up in his ante-room, soliciting the government's support for their undertakings. First in the line was the anglicized Dutchman, Sir Henry Deterding, later to be an enthusiastic supporter of Hitler, who arrived at 10 am and talked to him about petrol and petroleum concessions long after the appearance of the next appointment at 11 am. This was Paul Schwabach, head of the Bleichröder Bank, who had come to discuss a loan to Turkey. Then came a Swede; then, after some intermissions, Gwinner, the well-known director of the Deutsche Bank, who talked for a good hour about the Baghdad railway, a loan for Turkey, and a petrol monopoly. What is significant is that a Foreign Secretary's day could be taken up by such things. It casts some light on the state of politics in 1911 that these were the people he was condemned to listen to; but they were clearly too important an interest to ignore.

6

'The Potter's Wheel of Empire'

'It somehow shocks the sense of fairness of hard-headed White or Yellow people that semi-savages should be driving ill-bred sheep, scraggy cattle or ponies hardly fit for polo over plains and mountains that are little else than great treasure-vaults of valuable minerals . . . be turning this waiting wealth to no use, nor allowing it to circulate in the world's markets. Whatever a few poets . . . may pretend, the world at large is arriving at a pitch of intolerance of the lotos eater. It wants him to can or cask his lotos berries and ship them overseas in exchange for manufactured goods.'
Sir Harry Johnson, *The Backward Peoples and our Relations with Them* (1920)

Petroleum, concessions, monopolies, a loan to Turkey, the Baghdad railway: what all this shows is the hold of imperialism over the minds of those directing policy in 1911. Our history books tell us that the era of the 'new imperialism' was the last two decades of the nineteenth century. But on any closer inspection that is not true. After the Boer War, imperialism was under a cloud in England; but the cloud soon lifted. By 1911 imperialism and its concomitants in the form of trading privileges, concessions, and the inborn right to pillage the four quarters of the globe, were a basic element in the minds, thoughts and calculations of the ruling classes everywhere. It was no longer the imperialism of the 1890s, of Chamberlain and Rhodes – 'the vulgar and bastard imperialism of irritation and provocation and aggression', as the Liberal leader Campbell-Bannerman called it – but an imperialism tailored to fit the needs and interests of the dominant bourgeoisie. The day of the pro-consuls, of Cromer and Curzon, was past, and imperialism was, in 1911, in all essentials a middle-class ideology.

It is true that imperial propagandists made strenuous efforts to widen its appeal and to win over the working classes in Germany, France and Italy, as well as in Great Britain. It may be that they had a limited success with the accredited working-class organizations (the German Social Democrats, for example). Were not jobs involved? But they failed to bamboozle the workers, though they certainly bamboozled themselves. The mystique and cant of empire, with its unique mixture of oratory and half-truths, was probably never more potent than in those palmy days before the First World War – palmy for imperialist entrepreneurs of all sorts, including the little man who invested his life's savings in rubber plantations in Malaya. Once again Wells' Remington, who was won over to the imperialist cause in 1908, is worth citing. A vague, cloudy, emotional imperialism – 'the idea of Imperial patriotism' as a 'wide, rough, politically acceptable expression of a constructive dream' – became thenceforward his guiding light. Needless to say, he never stopped to define what he meant, but in that respect and others he was typical enough of his class and generation.

More significant, because this was reality and not the novelist's imagination, was the conversion of *The Times* to the imperialist cause. As its historian observes, it was 'hesitant and non-committal' at first, but it was already strong in 1911 and became definite and full-blown when Dawson became editor in 1912. The adhesion of *The Times* gave the cachet of respectability and acceptance to the 'new imperialism', successor to the old imperialism which had perished in the holocaust of the Boer War. In 1903 imperialism as a creed or ideology seemed to be a lost cause, not only in England but also in France and Germany. By 1911 it was back again, stronger than ever, but with different assumptions and different motivations.

*   *   *

There has been much argument about the roots and character of modern imperialism, about the role of sentiment and prestige, of gain and profit, of national interest, security and strategy, even of a civilizing mission. This is a thorny path, beset with brambles, and there is no need to pursue it here. What is beyond doubt for anyone prepared to follow in detail the diplomatic correspondence of the year is the importance of the economic component in 1911. This may not always have been the case. In the 1890s, before and after he became Colonial Secretary, Joseph Chamberlain had made great efforts to persuade industry and finance to invest in the tropical colonies, particularly in tropical Africa. He had little success. Capitalists, German as well as British, had no interest during the years of depression in boosting the out-put of raw materials for which demand was at best uncertain. Around 1903, the year of Chamberlain's resignation, the atmosphere changed abruptly. By now the boom was in full swing; demand shot up; shortages developed; the search for new sources of raw materials redoubled; and the scramble for concessions was on, more heated than ever before. This explains the character of imperialism in 1911, and its almost mystical hold over people's minds: it was by now entwined in the very fabric of bourgeois society, particularly its economic fabric.

This is not meant to suggest that other components of imperialist ideology had faded from the picture. No conceivable economic motive lay behind the Italian decision to invade and annex Libya, though the Italian Prime Minister, Giolitti, managed to convince himself there was one. In reality, his motive was simply the fear that Italy's 'prestige' and its standing among the powers would be irreparably damaged if it failed to match the French advance in Morocco, and similar calculations were operative on the part of Spain, still smarting from its defeat at the hands of the United States in 1898. It is also true that there were still people in the ruling class who were not bewitched by the imperialist ideology. Clemenceau, for one, was sceptical whether it was in France's interest to get bogged down in colonial adventures when the real test would come in Europe. And in Germany, also, some of the Junker nobility, anxious always about the 'Russian colossus', took a similar line. But by 1911 the trend everywhere was in the opposite direction.

Ever since 1906 the imperialist tide had been visibly mounting. The new Liberal Cabinet in Britain was undoubtedly hostile to colonial adventures of the sort in which Rhodes had indulged; but its leading lights were Asquith, Grey and Haldane, all imperialists of the new school, and their influence rapidly grew, particularly after Asquith succeeded Campbell-Bannerman as prime minister in 1908. In the United States the turning-point came in 1909 when Roosevelt – an imperialist, indeed, but an imperialist of the old-fashioned sort – was succeeded by Taft, under whom 'the forces of industrialism', represented by Edward H. Harriman, the chairman of Union Pacific, were 'in the seat of command'. In France the change may be dated from the fall in 1909 of the Clemenceau government, cautious and conservative in all colonial matters, or perhaps from 1908 when Tardieu first placed his pen and the influence of *Le Temps* at the service of Franco-German colonial entrepreneurs. In Germany, where the meagre results of Bülow's intervention in Morocco in 1905 had produced a sharp revulsion against colonial adventures, the appointment of Kiderlen-Wächter as Foreign Secretary in 1910 denoted – and was meant to denote – a return to a 'forward' foreign policy. A new, more active phase was beginning.

The outstanding characteristic of this new phase of imperialism was the importance of big business. When France and Germany signed an agreement about Morocco in 1909 the negotiations which led to its conclusion had taken place initially not between the two Foreign Offices but between the financiers and manufacturers of both countries. Between its lines could be read an understanding in which Krupp in Germany and Schneider-Creusot in France played an important part for a joint development not only of Morocco but of the whole of North Africa, and joint action not only in North Africa but also in Turkey. This, in 1911, was what imperialism was about. In Turkey, Persia and China, as well as in Morocco, governments were increasingly responsive to business interests. Given the climate of opinion it could hardly have been otherwise. The first necessity in the case of a backward country, said Lord Elgin, the British Colonial Secretary, is 'to attract capital'. If that meant anything – and it did – it meant a working agreement with capitalists. If Cecil Rhodes had personified the imperialism of the preceding decade, the personification of the new imperialism was Sir William Lever, the soap king and founder of the great multinational conglomerate, later to be renamed Unilever, who began in 1907 to prospect in Africa for facilities for the large-scale farming and processing of palm oil.

Governments, it is true, believed that they could control business interests and co-ordinate and discipline them to serve as instruments of national policy. But could they? Certainly, businessmen did not always get all they wanted, as we have seen in the case of Mestayer; and Lever, refused a concession in British West Africa, moved in 1911 to the Belgian Congo, where the authorities were less concerned with safeguarding the rights and welfare of Africans. But, in a competitive world, once a country was involved in the scramble for raw materials and concessions it was virtually impossible for the government to stand aside (though on occasion it did) on the grounds that what was involved was a purely private commercial transaction. Once business had a foothold it felt entitled to demand at least protection against 'unfair competition' and the maintenance of the 'open door'. The Mannesmanns had no friends in the German Foreign Office; but, said Langwerth von Simmern, one of the under-secretaries, Germany could not deny them support 'up to a certain degree'.

This was why, in 1911, diplomacy in Morocco and elsewhere revolved round the question of equal opportunity and the 'open door'. The German Kaiser was genuinely sincere when he said he desired trade, not territory, and there is little evidence that any major business interest (the notorious Mannesmann brothers apart) had any serious interest in territorial acquisitions. But everyone knew, though few people wished to say so, that there was more to it than that. What the Germans feared (and, for that matter, the British also) was that, if France secured a protectorate in Morocco, it would proceed to cut them out. And, of course, they were right. When, at the end of 1911, the French Foreign Minister announced the settlement of the Agadir crisis, adding that France had acquired no special economic privileges in Morocco, a Deputy jumped up and interposed: 'Well then, what use is the protectorate?' But it was Giolitti, defending the Italian attack on Libya who, as usual, let the cat out of the bag. Before the Turkish revolution, he said, there was no need to 'have recourse to military measures' because Italy could always obtain concessions that would ensure its interests against any other country. After the revolution the Turkish government had offered concessions to other powers with the object of 'putting obstacles in the way of our economic supremacy in Libya'. In this way it had destroyed the possibility of 'peaceful penetration' and forced Italy to take military action.

Sir Edward Grey, or even Kiderlen-Wächter, would never have spoken in those terms; but Giolitti's statement represents fairly enough the mental attitude of the ruling class in 1911. Magnified, no doubt, and strident, it is the authentic language of imperialism in its bourgeois phase.

*   *   *

It was a language with a vocabulary of its own in which the governing word was 'get'. 'To get Morocco as she has Tunis' – to get it, that is, 'in fee simple' – 'would be a great step for France,' wrote Grey. But, he added, she would have to 'pay a good price for it'. No one, in a world dominated by big business, expected to get something for nothing. Hence the second governing word, 'compensation'. This was a key concept in the ethic of imperialism implying that the charge for disinterest in one part of the world was reciprocation in another. Whoever got something somewhere had to pay someone else somewhere else. This was the way the diplomatic game worked, and it had many peculiar results. One of the more bizarre occurred when England and France agreed to divide the spoils of North Africa in 1904 ('spoils' is another prominent word in the imperialist vocabulary) and England had to 'compensate' Russia by promising not to set up a protectorate in Tibet.

Compensation figures large in the diplomacy of 1911. Germany would agree to France setting up a protectorate in Morocco; the question was where Germany would obtain compensation and how large it would be. This was the question that brought Europe to the verge of war, but it was only a beginning. Once it looked as though

France and Germany were nearing agreement the British Foreign Secretary immediately pointed out that 'we should want some compensation' too. He also told the French that Spain 'must get something'. The French, on the other hand, argued that Spain owed 'compensation' to them for the 'sacrifices' they had made to Germany to get a settlement in Morocco.

The vocabulary of imperialism casts a great deal of light upon its unspoken assumptions. For what exactly, for example, was Grey demanding compensation? What had Britain done, or refrained from doing, to require compensation? The doctrine that an agreement between two powers in Africa required compensation to a third in remotest Asia may have made sense to diplomats in 1911 but it does not make much sense of ordinary uninitiated people today. Still less does Grey's assertion that it would be 'a great step' for France to 'get Morocco'. Just why he does not ask, and evidently sees no reason to ask; the assumption is, or seems to be, that acquisition of territory anywhere is a feather in any imperialist country's cap. The reality, as we know, was very different. When it took over Morocco in 1912, France laid up for itself forty-four years of strife, resistance and costly warfare, with minimal, if any, profit. Perhaps it was 'a great step', but if so it was a step in the wrong direction.

More significant still is the fact that Grey never appears to have questioned the right of France to 'get Morocco' at all. Nothing, perhaps, better illustrates the imperialist assumptions of the day. 'We merely proposed to conquer Libya,' wrote Giolitti, as though it was the most natural thing and there was no question of right or wrong involved. But Giolitti (nicknamed 'the Minister of the Underworld' because he governed Italy like a Chicago gangster) was not much troubled by moral scruples. Grey, whose moral standards were beyond dispute, is a different case; and yet even Grey never asked, or thought of asking, what Moroccans – or Libyans, or any other subject people – desired, still less whether they should not be left alone to conduct their affairs by themselves as they thought best. Rather, he took for granted – as practically everyone took for granted in 1911 – that the higher standards of civilization which white people had developed (or, more truthfully, claimed to have developed) had conferred upon them (in Lord Curzon's words) 'a general right of entry to the darker places of the earth'. Others, less portentous and more in harmony with the commercial spirit of the time, simply asserted that no country's resources – for example, the iron ore of Morocco – should be allowed to go to waste through the ineptitude of its inhabitants when other countries could use them.

This was the ethical justification (though very few people in 1911 considered any justification was needed) for the exploitation of one people by another. Thousands, hundreds of thousands, of Africans were handed over without asking from France to Germany, and no one thought more of it. The assumption was that the world was at the disposal of the white powers, to be divided up between them as they thought best; and the business of diplomacy, what it existed for and was paid to do, was to sort out the differences and arrange compensation so that everyone (except the victims) shared in the benefits. In this it had the virtually unanimous support of the bourgeois electorate, for whom the maintenance of the privileged position of the metropolis was the very foundation of its prosperity.

It was a Machiavellian doctrine, but it was accepted without question by even the most honourable people of the age. Grey, for example, knew that the Italian invasion of Libya in September 1911 was an act of blatant aggression. But he argued that 'neither we nor France should side against Italy' for fear it would be driven over into the arms of Germany. There was, in other words, one morality for individuals and another morality – or lack of morality – for states and governments. When the French marched into Fez in May 1911, Grey was well aware that it was the first move in an action to take over Morocco, but he accepted the assurances of the French Foreign Minister to the contrary. All this, his biographer observes, 'was pure *Realpolitik*'; and so it was. But it casts a bright, and not very flattering light on the moral standards of the age, and in particular on those of the ruling class. Prevarication, half-truth, double-talk, and a double standard of morality, were other characteristics of the imperialism of the time, and they were not confined to the less scrupulous characters on the fringe of politics.

It is easy to attack this attitude on ethical grounds. The other question is whether the naked pursuit of national self-interest, 'with but faint regard' (as Sir Eyre Crowe, one of the leading professionals in the British Foreign Office, put it) 'to the ethical character of the means involved', was likely to produce the desired results, even within its own terms of reference. What the ruling classes in Europe in 1911 wanted above all else was a stable international environment in which to pursue their interests; and this was the function of the balance of power, which was supposed to iron out differences between and maintain the relative standing of the different powers, and so ensure peace and stability – provided everyone obeyed the rules. But suppose someone broke the rules, as Austria did in 1908 when it overtrumped

Russia and annexed Bosnia and Herzegovina without paying compensation? Suppose, in other words, all ethical considerations apart, that the assumptions of the ruling classes were false, and that the machinery of the balance of power, instead of sustaining the existing order, was placing it under a steadily increasing strain?

The dominant, almost single-minded, concern of the privileged classes in 1911, whether in France, England or Germany, was the perpetuation of their own interests and the maintenance of a social order which played into their hands. That, as they saw it, was what politics was about, and they were aware – or at least the more intelligent of them were aware – of a common interest of the possessing classes. This, apart from sheer self-interest, was what people like Caillaux and Tardieu had in mind in promoting joint Franco-German undertakings to exploit the underdeveloped countries. There was, from their point of view, more to be gained from co-operation than from conflict; and the same was true of the diplomats. Aristocrats for the most part, they viewed international politics from a different angle from that of financiers and businessmen. But they also had something like a common aim; namely, to preserve the peace of Europe, and therewith the existing social and political structure, without endangering the security and interests of their own country.

What no one seems to have perceived was the incompatibility of these aims. By 1911, as the economic cycle reached its peak, economic stability – or, more crudely, profitability – came more and more to depend on the gains that could be extracted from the countries on the periphery; and though, in theory, this might have been better done by co-operation, in fact it resulted in a collision of interests and a division into rival and hostile blocs. In theory, according to Joseph Schumpeter, imperialism should be a force making for co-operation and peace; in practice, it makes for competition and war. It has sometimes been argued that the peace of Europe in the generation before 1914 was purchased at the expense of Africans and Asians. In reality, rivalry in Africa and Asia – the search for exclusive concessions and spheres of interest – poisoned the relations of the European countries, and made them more aggressive and less accommodating.

This is the reason why, when there were so many far more serious problems in the world, the question of Morocco came to dominate the scene in 1911. There was not much reason in it; but for the moment it is sufficient to see how profoundly imperialist assumptions coloured the attitudes of the ruling classes in 1911. This is, perhaps, the most telling commentary of all. The situation in 1911, both at home and abroad, required imagination, or at least an ability to adapt to a new and challenging situation. Instead it got the traditional – and, in the end, disastrous – answers. Wrapped up in its own affairs, busily promoting its own interests, the prisoner of its own assumptions, the European élite could not see beyond the end of its nose. But what élite ever could?

7

'The Moroccan Wasps' Nest'

'There are two things in colonial policy: first the joy of conquest, then the bill to pay. . . .

Among the dangers of colonial expansion are those everyone sees and those which people do not see. What everyone sees are the sacrifices in men and money. . . . What people do not see are the international complications. . . . "Who has land has war", it is said. But the proverb applies as much to colonies as to the metropolis, perhaps even more.'

Baron Paul d'Estournelles de Constant, 8 December 1899

There was plenty of combustible material in the world in 1911. Imperialism, in the form of concessions, privileges, government support for ventures overseas, and the like, was ingrained in the mentality of the ruling class. But why should the flash-point have been Morocco? There were imperialist pressures and rivalries no less serious in the Ottoman Empire and in Persia than in North Africa; in fact, Morocco was by any standard a small fish in the muddy colonial pool. There had, it is true, been a first Morocco crisis in 1905, but it had apparently been settled by the Franco-German agreement of 1909; and in any case it might have been thought that the very fact that there had been a crisis in 1905 would have been a warning against reopening the 'Morocco question' in 1911. Unfortunately, the French government did not see it that way. On the contrary, it appears to have thought (though the text scarcely bears out such a view) that its 1909 agreement with Germany gave it a free hand in Morocco; and in the spring of 1911 the Monis Cabinet, which took office on 2 March, acted accordingly. When, during April, it authorized the despatch of a military expedition to the Moroccan capital of Fez – though, through the usual bungling and incompetence, it did not arrive there until 21 May – it set in motion the chain of events that led to the Agadir crisis.

Historians, almost without exception, have attributed responsibility for the crisis to Germany, and more specifically to the new German Foreign Secretary, Kiderlen-Wächter. This is arguable, but only if it is assumed that Germany should have stood aside while France violated the treaties guaranteeing Moroccan independence and brought the country under French control. This was inherently unlikely, particularly as it ran contrary to the established conventions of imperialist diplomacy and its underlying principle of compensation. In fact, it was perfectly normal by the recognized standards of the day for Germany to react against the French march on Fez. On the other hand, the nature of the reaction – that is to say, the despatch of the *Panther* to Agadir – offended current conventions by its brusqueness, and to that extent Kiderlen may be held accountable for the severity of the crisis. But if we wish to trace the source of the crisis, we shall discover it not, as historians have been inclined to do, in some deep-laid fault in German national character, but in the history of French imperialism and, more broadly still, in the development of nineteenth-century imperialism as a whole. The Agadir crisis is a comment on the imperialist ethic which, unfortunately, has not ceased to be valid today.

*   *   *

A full account of the origins of the Agadir crisis would take us back to the year 1830, for from one point of view it was the culmination of an imperialist thrust which began in that year when French troops landed at Algiers and began the conquest of North Africa. France, the French ambassador in London told Lord Lansdowne in 1902, saw Morocco as an extension of Algeria, and Algeria as an extension of France. This, in a nutshell, was the underlying assumption of French imperialism in Morocco. It was reinforced after 1881 when French troops invaded Tunisia and set up a protectorate. From that time forward the belief that France, at some opportune moment, would seek to 'Tunisify' Morocco and so round off its empire in North Africa, was never far from statesmen's minds, and what came to be called 'the Morocco question' soon became an issue of international diplomacy.

But eighty years and a great deal of history separated Agadir from the French occupation of Algeria, and so far as the immediate antecedents of the crisis of 1911 are concerned it is unnecessary to go much further back than 1903, when Great Britain, jolted out of its dream of 'splendid isolation' by the experience of the Boer War and still more by German naval building, entered into the negotiations with France which resulted in the conclusion of the Anglo-French entente on 8 April 1904. The signature of the entente was little short of a diplomatic revolution. Hitherto both commercial and strategic interests had pitted Great Britain against France in Morocco, and at least twice, in 1892 and in 1901, it looked as though Britain might establish some sort of protectorate. It was the British who, by threat of naval action, had forced the Sultan in 1856 to open his country to foreign commerce, and in 1904 they still had by far the largest share of Moroccan trade. Strategically, they were concerned about the security of Gibraltar and free passage through the Mediterranean to the Suez Canal, both of which might be threatened if France took over Morocco. And in their opposition to France they could count on the support of Spain, which had old established claims which it feared the French would extinguish if they could, and of Italy, whose ambitions in Tunis had been thwarted by France in 1881. The obstacles to a French occupation of Morocco were still formidable when the new century began.

It was the fundamental aim of Théophile Delcassé, who became French Foreign Minister in 1898, to remove these obstacles, and the Anglo-French agreement of 1904 was the keystone in the structure he built with that in mind. Delcassé believed that, unless something were quickly done, time was running out for France in Morocco, and his whole policy was directed to making sure that this did not happen. In 1901 and 1902 his fear was of being out-manœuvred by the British, and this, in view of the activities of Sir Arthur Nicolson, the British minister in Tangier, was not entirely imagination. By 1903, he had convinced himself that Germany was planning to seize Morocco and that France must act by 1906 at latest if it were to forestall these designs. This was pure fantasy. His first reaction to the British threat was to angle for German co-operation against Britain. When this came to nothing, he turned to Italy, and here he scored his first success. In December 1900, Italy agreed to French freedom of action in Morocco in return for French agreement to Italian freedom of action in Tripolitania. It was a classical imperialist deal, and it set the tone for the sequel.

Delcassé next turned to Spain, proposing the partition of Morocco on very favourable terms; but Madrid, well aware that partition behind the back of Britain had little chance of success, turned down his overture. Oddly enough it was this failure that finally convinced Delcassé of the need to come to terms with the British, and the result was the Anglo-French agreement of 1904. In effect, it was the Franco-Italian deal of 1900 writ large. France agreed to disinterest itself in Egypt, England to disinterest itself in Morocco. It was – though no one, of course, put it in those terms – a partition of North Africa from the Sinai desert to the Atlantic, with *pourboires* for Spain and Italy if and when the opportunity came to cash them. One result of the Anglo-French agreement was that Spain came to heel, accepting in 1904 terms much less favourable than those offered by Delcassé in 1902 for fear that it would be left out in the cold.

The Franco-Spanish agreement of 3 October 1904, completed – or so he thought – the structure Delcassé had been building since 1899, and opened the way for a French protectorate in Morocco. Hitherto he had proceeded with circumspection in his dealings with the Moroccan government. In 1904, having cleared the way with Italy, Spain and Britain, he calculated that the time had come to brandish the sabre. A 'programme for the military, economic and financial reconstruction of Morocco' under French tutelage was quickly drawn up, and when the Sultan demurred, a scarcely veiled threat of force brought him to heel. On 29 January 1905, a French mission arrived in Fez to put the programme into effect, and what Lord Lansdowne had described four years earlier as the 'plundering of Morocco by the French' began in earnest. It had, of course, been prepared in advance.

* * *

If one aspect of the diplomacy of imperialism is to neutralize the other powers, the other aspect is to soften up the victim by disrupting the government, stirring up trouble, and creating pretexts for intervention.

Here, also, there were well-known rules and gambits, but in the case of Morocco it did not prove easy to put them into practice. For one thing, nineteenth-century Morocco had a series of able rulers who knew how to hold the European powers at arm's length. Even before the commercial treaty with Britain in 1856, a number of countries, including the United States, had agreements with Morocco; but trade was confined until 1880 to only two ports, Tangier and Mogador, and even when four more ports were opened in 1880 the effects were very limited. Morocco had little need of European imports, and the government refused to permit construction of modern communications and utilities. By and large, Europeans were confined to the ports, and were few in number. As late as 1904 there were only 780 French residents in Morocco, and European investment was correspondingly small: British capital investment, largely advances to Moroccan middlemen, was no more than £1,000,000 in 1892, French only half as big.

What is sometimes called 'the imperialism of free trade' had, therefore, surprisingly little impact on Morocco. It had, of course, some. In particular, the recognition of foreign consular jurisdiction and the exemption of protected persons from the ordinary legal processes were a derogation from the Sultan's sovereignty. But European rivalries checked the indiscriminate extension of protection, and in 1880 the eleven European countries with commercial interests in Morocco, together with the United States, agreed to regulate their claims. The Madrid convention of 1880 recognized the right of all signatories to most favoured nation treatment, which meant little in practice in view of the restricted nature of foreign trade. But it also established the right of foreigners, hitherto denied, to hold property in Morocco; and this proved to be a significant precedent for the future. It was a second breach in the Moroccan defences against imperialist penetration.

The first breach had occurred earlier, in 1860, when Spain, with the scantiest of excuses, had attempted to occupy the whole of northern Morocco, only to be defeated by British opposition. But, characteristically, Morocco was held responsible for the costs, and saddled with a bill for 100 million francs, which (as also was intended) it proceeded to fund by a loan, at exorbitant charges, from European (in this instance British) banks. Here, in the opening of the country to foreign property-owners (more likely to be great corporations seeking mineral rights than smallholders interested in farming) and in the control of the economy by foreign banking interests, we have the origins of the 'new imperialism' which prevailed after 1900. Trade was no longer the issue; it was, in the American idiom, 'peanuts'. What mattered now were property rights, mineral rights, mining rights, but above all else financial control, for loans meant the right to control the wherewithal to repay the loans, which usually was customs duties; and this meant foreign – which in Delcassé's view meant French – control of the customs finances, and perhaps also the right to insist on new taxation to provide the means to service the loans. And if, as was only to be expected, new taxation produced unrest and even revolt, that also would create a pretext for intervention which could only be welcome.

These, a little crudely – but not too crudely – were the motivations and calculations of imperialism, and specifically of French imperialism in Morocco, when Delcassé became Foreign Minister in 1898.

*　　*　　*

Morocco was, no doubt, by European standards a 'backward' country. It did not want railways or tramways, or even the *Grands Magazins du Printemps*, which already had a branch in Tangier. A rigidly orthodox Moslem people necessarily had a system of government and laws which did not comply tidily with European preconceptions. But, left alone, it worked reasonably well in accordance with Moslem preconceptions. Morocco was, and always had been, an anomalous country in so far as the Sultan's authority over the Berber tribes in the south had rarely, if ever, been more than indirect; but until around 1900 this arrangement had caused no serious problems. For the strictly orthodox Moslem tribesmen of the south, it was 'infidel' pressures at Fez, with their demand for 'reforms' – particularly tax reforms – that were the cause of trouble.

They were almost certainly right. Later, the Germans blamed French interference for the uprisings in Morocco, and they also were not wide of the mark. Whether the French deliberately set out to stir up trouble with the intention of profiting from it is a more difficult question; but that this was the result of their intervention is not a matter of doubt. The so-called 'Moroccan question', which played so large a part in European politics after 1904, was a European invention. Left to itself Morocco would have managed not perhaps magnificently, but well enough. But European imperialism was not content to let well alone; and the result was that Morocco – like Afghanistan today – became a bone of contention and division between the powers. No one, except possibly the French, cared much about it on its own account; but it became the touchstone of the comparative standing of the great powers.

It is unnecessary to follow in detail the devious manoeuvres of the powers after 1900 to assure control in Morocco. There were, needless to say, a number of special interests involved, business, banks and, in the case of France, the French army in Algeria. There were also propaganda organizations, in France the *Comité de l'Afrique Française*, which founded an off-shoot, the *Comité du Maroc*, in 1903, in Germany the *Marokkanische Gesellschaft*, founded in the same year with Pan-German and colonialist support. It would be easy to exaggerate their influence. So long as governments wished to keep them under control they had no difficulty in doing so; this applied even to the army. In 1900 Delcassé told the Algerian generals that 'the question of Morocco must not at any price be opened by an incident on the Algerian frontier'. In 1899 he refused to sanction a proposal by the giant Schneider-Creusot iron and steel combine to open a branch in Morocco, and in 1902, when he finally agreed to the formation of a trading company by Schneider and other associates in French heavy industry, he made it clear that it was 'the government which will say when the era of concessions is to begin'.

But by now Delcassé's position was beginning to change. With the appointment of Lyautey (later to become the French governor-general of Morocco) to an Algerian command in 1903, 'the discreet penetration of Morocco' by Algerian forces began. At the same time concern at the growth of British and German business activity in Morocco led to a stepping up of French economic involvement. In 1902 the consortium of French business interests was formed which, in 1903, became the *Compagnie Marocaine.*

✓Even now, these were secondary and subordinate issues, merely preparations for the future, as Delcassé told Schneider. The decisive factor, as everyone knew, was control over Moroccan public loans, and therewith over Moroccan finances, and this was the issue to which Delcassé addressed himself after 1902. His basic aim was to eliminate foreign competition since he knew that, so long as the Moroccan government could obtain loans from England or Spain, or conceivably Germany, it could play off the one against the other and thus maintain its independence; and in this, step by step, he was successful. The factor which helped him most was the decision of the British government, after the opening of the negotiations which led to the *Entente Cordiale,* to discourage British banks from making loans to the Sultan, and to use its influence at Madrid in the same direction. This was the financial counterpart of the political agreement, and it implied recognition not only of the preponderance of French finance in Morocco, but also of the political leverage financial preponderance bestowed.

The process began in 1902 and was completed with the French loan of 1 July 1904, which was used to buy out the British and Spanish creditors. After 1 July France was in control, and the British banking consortium led by Sir Ernest Cassel had to content itself with a minority participation of 12½ per cent. Delcassé immediately began to exploit his success. The security for the French loan was the Moroccan customs revenue, 60 per cent of which was earmarked for a period of thirty-five years, and among the main proposals of the mission which was sent to Fez in January 1905 was the appointment of a French financial controller to ensure that the terms were carried out. This was – and is – a classical, time-honoured tactic of predatory imperialism.

At the same time, steps were taken to prepare for the occupation of Morocco once the softening-up process was complete. A military railway was built from Oran to the outpost of Bechar in Morocco, which Lyautey had occupied in 1903, and other bases were established on both sides of the Algerian frontier. The time was not yet ripe for military action; but France was ready for action when the occasion arose, and the demands which the French mission took to Fez in January 1905 made it pretty certain that it would arrive sooner rather than later. Already in 1902, the necessity of imposing new taxes to pay for European loans had led to a serious uprising with pronounced anti-European overtones. Might it not be said that Morocco was falling into anarchy, that European interests were in danger, that intervention was an unavoidable necessity, and who, if not France, was to intervene?

This, again, was an established imperialist tactic. No one asked whether it was not, in fact, European intervention that was responsible for the unrest; it was sufficient to have a pretext to intervene. In fact, the pretext was not used in 1902 and 1903 because France was not yet ready. But in 1911, as we shall see, a similar situation provided the pretext for the French advance on Fez, which was the prelude to the Agadir crisis.

*　　*　　*

By the end of 1904, Delcassé seemed to be well on his way to establishing for France in Morocco a position at least equivalent to that which England had possessed in Egypt for the previous twenty years. Unfortunately, from his point of view, he reckoned without Germany. The result was the first Morocco crisis of 1905. It was the great mistake of his career, and he had to pay for it dearly.

Delcassé, as we have seen, had taken great pains to buy off England, Spain and Italy. Why he failed to do the same with Germany remains one of the mysteries of history. It was certainly not due to lack of advice from his colleagues. One and all, friends and foes alike, warned him that it would be 'prudent' at least to seek a Franco-German agreement about Morocco. Apparently, with the talks at Fez going well in January and February 1905, Delcassé saw no need to make concessions to Germany to get his way. If this was his calculation, events quickly proved him wrong.

He had, it is true, approached Germany at an earlier stage, seeking a Franco-German line-up against Britain. The German answer was that its interests in Morocco were, in Bülow's words, 'trifling and insignificant'. But that did not mean that they were non-existent. Germany, in 1905, was probably not seriously interested in Morocco itself; its object, under the influence of the sinister Holstein, the dominant personality at this time in the German Foreign Office, was to use French ambitions in Morocco to further its own wider interests. But Germany was one of the signatories of the Madrid Convention of 1880 which, as we have seen, guaranteed equal rights in Morocco to the twelve signatories; and it had only to recall the precedent of Tunis to know that, if France succeeded in establishing control, these rights would not, in practice, be worth the paper they were written on. The same thought had not escaped the British government, which therefore took care to write into its 1904 agreement with France a specific guarantee of equal commercial rights for a period of thirty years. In March 1904 Delcassé rather vaguely offered a similar guarantee to Germany, but he did nothing to follow it up. On the contrary, he even failed, contrary to diplomatic protocol, to communicate the text of the Anglo-French agreement to the German government.

The result was foreseeable, even if it was not foreseen. On 20 March 1905 it was announced that the Kaiser would call at Tangier in ten days' time, which he very unwillingly did. Even at this stage it is as certain as certain can be that Germany had no territorial ambitions in Morocco. Its object was the maintenance of the *status quo*, which France was clearly setting out to undermine. With this in view, three main propositions were placed in the Kaiser's mouth: first, the maintenance of the sovereignty and independence of the Sultan of Morocco; secondly, the integrity of his realm; thirdly, a Morocco 'open to the peaceful competition of all nations, without annexation or monopoly'. In addition, he advised the Moroccan government – with obvious reference to the proposals put forward by the French mission to Fez at the end of January – to be careful about any 'reforms' they introduced.

The Kaiser's visit to Tangier was the first demonstration that the German government was going to put a spoke in the French wheel. The second was its decision, much to the consternation of Great Britain, France, Spain and Italy, to convoke a conference of the signatories of the Madrid convention of 1880, which met at Algeciras in January 1906. Meanwhile, to show the way the wind was blowing, a German bank had been persuaded – not very willingly – to make a loan to Morocco. Clearly, the Germans were not prepared to stand idly by while France acquired complete financial control.

The conference of Algeciras is usually regarded as a defeat for Germany. That may be true so far as any larger objectives Holstein may have had in view are concerned. So far as Morocco is concerned, it is anything but true. First of all, there is no doubt that the Franco-Spanish plan to partition Morocco with British connivance had been defeated; hence the irritation of all three powers at the reconvention of the Madrid signatories. The minor powers, on the other hand, who saw their commercial rights being snuffed out, welcomed the Algeciras conference, though they were not prepared to give active support to Germany. Secondly, Algeciras placed Morocco, for the first time, under an international guarantee, something the Moroccan government had been striving for unsuccessfully since 1884. This, admittedly, was only a paper guarantee; if the signatories did not stand up for Moroccan independence – and it was certain that Great Britain, Spain and Italy would not – it was no real safeguard against renewed French pressure. In this respect all depended on Germany, the only great power likely to stand out against France.

It depended also on the practical measures taken to make international control effective. These were spelled out in great detail in the 123 articles of the Act of Algeciras; but their practical implementation was more difficult. Theoretically, control was in the hands of the diplomatic corps at Tangier which had to approve all measures taken. In practice, this meant that there was no effective supervision. The two decisive points were control of the state bank, which the Act set up, and control of the police. In both France secured a preponderant influence. This, certainly, was a defeat for Germany, which had hoped for a genuinely international police force. However, it is important to note that the jurisdiction of the police was limited to the eight open ports; it did not, as is often believed, confer on France a right to interfere anywhere and everywhere 'to maintain order'. It was also limited, in the first place, to a period of five years.

Finally, the Act guaranteed all nations 'economic freedom' in Algeria 'with no inequality whatsoever'. This was something it was much harder for France to evade, since tangible, concrete rights were involved, and in fact it was only after the setting up of the French protectorate in 1912 that it began to do so. Moreover, the economic equality proclaimed in the Act went far beyond trade, the 'open door' and the old 'most favoured nation' principle, and was clearly intended to apply to any kind of economic activity, including public works, exploration and mining. The result was the beginning of a new phase of imperialism. After 1906 the scramble for concessions got under way. This was the time, in particular, when German finance and industry began to play an active role.

*   *   *

After Algeciras France had, in effect, to make a new start in Morocco. In 1905 the Rouvier government had made one last attempt to salvage the wreck of Delcassé's policy. First, it dropped Delcassé himself, whom it regarded as the main obstacle to agreement with Germany. Then it offered Germany compensation elsewhere if it would fall into line with

Britain, Spain and Italy and recognize French supremacy in Morocco. It was too late. The Algeciras conference had already been convened, and the Germans were not ready to back down. 'It is out of the question', Bülow declared, 'that the conference should result in handing over Morocco to France.'

He was right. As far as could be done so on paper, Algeciras prevented the 'Tunisification' of Morocco. The French position was still strong, both in Morocco itself and otherwise. Holstein and Bülow had hoped that the crisis of 1905 would weaken Anglo-French relations. Instead it strengthened them, and France could still count on Spain and Italy, the other two members of the robber-band. But after 1906 two new factors had entered. First, it was now abundantly clear, as it should have been to Delcassé in 1904 and 1905, that any resumption of the French advance was dependent on a satisfactory arrangement with Germany. Secondly, new methods were necessary. After Algeciras the time-honoured strategy of financial penetration was no longer sufficient. In short, French policy had to be adapted to the new situation created by the Act of Algeciras, and this was what happened in 1907. It ushered in the last period of French imperialism, running from 1907 to 1912 (after that, it was little more than an increasingly desperate rearguard action), and its method was now predominantly, though not exclusively, military.

There is no need to follow the evolution of French policy in Morocco step by step from 1907 to 1911. It is, in more ways than one, a paradoxical story. For one thing, colonial adventures were not, and never had been popular in France, and the unhappy outcome of Delcassé's schemes made them even less so. The Clemenceau administration, which came to power in 1906, was concerned above all with the internal situation in France, where the onset of recession had led to serious industrial unrest, and was not interested in pushing French claims in Morocco. Clemenceau himself, twenty-five years earlier, had denounced the French occupation of Tunisia as the work of sinister back-door interests whose only object was to 'make money on the Stock Exchange'; and his attitude towards Morocco was little different. It was he who coined the phrase, 'the Moroccan wasps' nest', and his attitude was reciprocated in Berlin. In a famous statement in October 1908 William II declared that 'the wretched Morocco business must be wound up as quickly as possible'. But this was an area where facts spoke louder than thoughts. It was easier to get into the wasps' nest than to get out. Once intervention with all its consequences had begun, once the machinery of European control had been set in motion, it went on under its own momentum. This was another characteristic of imperialism, leading by inexorable though unpredictable stages to catastrophe.

Just as, in 1878, the Congress of Berlin had provoked the first stirrings of Turkish nationalism, so in 1906 the Algeciras conference sparked off an outburst of resentment and anti-European agitation throughout Morocco. There had, as we have seen, already been trouble in 1902 and 1903. The unrest which came to a head in 1907 was on a much larger scale, and comprised two separate movements which eventually coalesced. The first, at the end of July, was a spontaneous uprising at Casablanca, now being turned into a great port and centre of European influence, where a native mob killed three Frenchmen and six other Europeans working on the construction of the harbour. The second was a revolt, supported by the southern tribes, against the weak Sultan Abd el-Aziz, who had lost all popularity as he passed more and more under the influence of the Christian powers. There were other incidents, including the murder of a French doctor at Marrakesh, and the agitation at Casablanca quickly spread to the port of Mazagan, some 100 kilometres to the south. But the anti-European uprising in Casablanca and the revolt of Mulay Hafid, the brother of Abd el-Aziz, the representative of Moslem resistance to the infidel incursion, were the decisive events. They made it possible for France to resume its advance, this time in the guise of the disinterested defender of the Algeciras settlement.

The immediate French reaction to events at Casablanca was to despatch two cruisers, the *Galilée* (appropriately named) and the *Forbin*, which proceeded to bombard the city – an action which the Germans, not unreasonably, regarded as excessive, though perhaps the Germans, who had reacted equally ferociously to the murder of two German missionaries in China in 1897, were hardly the people to protest. But which of the imperialist powers, including the United States, was in a position to throw stones? Had not the British bombarded Alexandria in 1882 with even less provocation? In the long run these were actions none of the peoples of Asia and Africa would forget. In the short run more significant was the French decision to land troops to 'maintain order'. The international police force stipulated in the Act of Algeciras had still not been set up when trouble arose in Casablanca. Who, in those circumstances, could question the right, if not the duty, of France to take action as a temporary, emergency measure? It would only be a force of around 3000 men, the French announced at the beginning of August, and 'no advance into the interior' was 'contemplated'. Six months later, according to the British representative on the spot, they had 'about 14,000 men there'. As Eyre Crowe noted in his minute on this report, 'the French are not acting straightforwardly'. He was quite right.

The French occupation of Casablanca was the beginning of what soon became known as 'the policy of the drop of oil'. It was extremely effective. From Casablanca the oil spread out north, south and east, until by May 1908 an area of 12–13,000 square kilometres, reaching almost to Marrakesh and Rabat, had been occupied. At the same time, French forces from Algeria were advancing westward, beginning in March 1907 with the occupation of Oujda, the pretext being the necessity to pacify the dissident tribes on the eastern frontier.Once the two movements met at Fez – and that was the obvious objective – French control would be assured. Meanwhile, following the precedent of 1860, it was taken for granted that the Moroccans would have to bear the cost of the French occupation of their country. That was another hallowed convention of imperialism. Morocco, everyone was agreed, would have to pay an indemnity for the Casablanca uprising, otherwise France would 'refuse to evacuate the country behind Casablanca till her just demands had been met'. But France would be reasonable: 'probably not more than 50 millions would be asked'. In fact, the bill was set at 70 million francs. The result, as the British representative in Tangier remarked, was that the 'Moorish government' was 'absolutely crippled'; but that also was part of the intention. Loaded with debt, it would have to turn to France for a loan – on French conditions. This was what happened in 1910.

The revolt of Mulay Hafid caused the French more difficulty. If the French protégé were displaced by a Sultan unfriendly to France, might not the concessions Abd el-Aziz had been forced to make be repudiated? Unfortunately, from the French point of view, there was no doubt about Mulay Hafid's popularity. He had proclaimed himself Sultan on 17 August. Within a month he had been recognized throughout the whole country, except in the Chaouia province which was in French occupation and, on 5 January 1908, his accession was formally endorsed by the mullahs at Fez. Nevertheless, France continued to support Abd el-Aziz, with money and otherwise, even after his defeat in August 1908. Germany, on the other hand, supported Mulay Hafid almost from the start. Whether or not the Germans knew of the onerous terms, including exclusive French control of Moroccan finances and the Moroccan army, secretly imposed on Abd el-Aziz as a condition for French help, their aim, without much doubt, was to reverse this situation or, as Eyre Crowe rather crudely put it, 'to be first in with Mulay Hafid'. Hence their decision to send a representative to Fez without consulting the other powers and before they had formally recognized the new Sultan. He arrived there at the beginning of September 1908 and immediately pressed Mulay Hafid to consult Germany 'in all matters', only to act upon German advice, and in particular to take no decision about any French demands without first consulting the German government.

The result was a sharp deterioration in Franco-German relations, and there was talk of a new crisis, similar to that of 1905. German disgruntlement is understandable. The new French policy of sheltering behind the Algeciras agreement and pursuing its aims in Morocco under its cover placed Germany in a difficult position. It could not easily object to actions carried out allegedly to ensure implementation of the Algeciras decisions, but it also could not fail to see that these actions were changing the whole situation in Morocco in favour of France. Bülow informed the French that, so long as they and Spain 'acted in conformity with, and within the limits of, the Algeciras Act', they could count on German support. Admittedly, the despatch of a military force to Casablanca was an infringement of the Act; but it had been unavoidable in the circumstances, and the German government (the British ambassador in Berlin reported) 'accepted this explanation'. The fact remained that the French occupation of Casablanca, the Chaouia and Oujda continued, in spite of French protests that it was 'temporary' and 'provisional', and instead of the promised withdrawal of troops there was a steady build-up. Even the British admitted by the spring of 1908 that the French were getting themselves in a position where it would be hard for them 'to justify their respect for the Algeciras Act'.

The situation was made more tense in September 1908 when the French authorities in Casablanca arrested some deserters from the Foreign Legion who were being put on a German ship by a member of the staff of the German consulate. Nevertheless, the expected crisis did not materialize. Instead, there was a Franco-German reconciliation. The initiative seems to have come from Caillaux, at this time Minister of Finance in the Clemenceau Cabinet, who broached the subject in a private conversation – the first, so far as we know, of a long and increasingly compromising series – with von der Lancken, though it seems likely that he was acting on this occasion in agreement with Clemenceau and with the French Foreign Minister, Pichon. He found plenty of interest on the German side. No doubt, considerations of general policy played a part (the Bosnian crisis was at its height); but so also did the situation in Morocco. Once the French had reconciled themselves to recognizing Mulay Hafid, the weakness of the German bargaining position was only too obvious. As the French ambassador in Madrid rather crudely but perfectly correctly put it, France's 'naturally strong position as a neighbouring power' – in other words, its ability to use force at a moment's notice – meant that Mulay Hafid would have to follow French advice whether he liked it or not. By the end of 1908 the Germans had come to terms with this fact. The German mission in Tangier was told to stop making difficulties for France, and a Franco-German agreement was signed on 9 February 1909.

It was not long – a mere matter of two years – before it became evident that it had changed nothing; but at the time it was certainly a shock to the British, who saw themselves being left out in the cold. Just as Germany, in 1904, refused to believe that France and Britain could come to agreement, so in 1909 the British were shocked to find that France could do a deal with Germany behind their backs; and there was something very hollow in the congratulations they showered on the French and German governments. But those, as everyone knew, were the hazards of imperialist diplomacy. Nevertheless, the lesson guided the British through the vicissitudes of 1911. As the French could certainly not be trusted to maintain the *Entente Cordiale*, Britain would have to do so. That is why what began as a Franco-German colonial dispute, ended as an Anglo-German confrontation. But the real lesson is that, in an imperialist world, no one trusts anyone, and everyone is ready to stab everyone else in the back.

8

'The Dash to Fez'

'I am afraid the French have got too deeply in to get out and they will have to go through with a partition of Morocco, in which there will be some difficult and rough water to navigate.'
Sir Edward Grey, 9 June 1911

The Franco-German agreement of 9 February 1909 was the last milestone on the road to Agadir. The only outstanding obstacle to the establishment of a French protectorate in Morocco, it seemed, had been cleared away. On the one hand, Germany recognized France's political predominance and undertook to do nothing to interfere with it; on the other hand, France promised not to interfere with German commercial and industrial interests and where possible to associate businessmen of both countries in joint enterprises. It looked like a counterpart of the Anglo-French deal of 1904, and promised to have the same effects. Spain, it is true, had certain claims in the north, arising from the 1904 agreement; but that was a minor complication. Otherwise France's position in Morocco seemed assured.

For a time the agreement worked satisfactorily. In October and again in November 1909 von Schoen, the German Foreign Minister, expressed his satisfaction at the loyalty with which the French were carrying it out, and in February 1910 the German Chancellor re-affirmed his country's decision to place no difficulties in France's way. But there was one crucial difference between the Anglo-French agreement of 1904 and the Franco-German agreement of 1909, and that was that the one preceded and the other followed the Act of Algeciras. Historians assume for the most part that the 1909 agreement gave France a free hand in Morocco, and some Frenchmen at the time, particularly in colonial and military circles, may have made the same assumption. It was not true. France and Germany could not, even if they had wished, ride roughshod over the Act and the rights of the other signatories which it established; nor could they ignore the principle of the sovereignty and integrity of Morocco, which it enshrined.

This was later pointed out by Schoen, who had conducted the negotiations of 1909 on the German side and who claimed, almost certainly with complete sincerity, that the Franco-German understanding over Morocco was his proudest achievement. Nevertheless, Schoen pointed out, the obvious intent of the signatories of the Act of Algeciras was that Morocco should not fall under the control of any single power. The Act admittedly foresaw European support for the Sultan, 'but in specific areas and within specific limits'. Germany had recognized France's special political rights and interests, but always on condition that it respected 'the broad lines' of the Act.

There is no doubt that these limitations were recognized by the Clemenceau and later by the Briand governments in France, and that they governed and defined their Morocco policy during 1909 and at least until the middle of 1910. Pichon, who was Foreign Minister in both administrations, took every precaution to remain within the limits set at Algeciras; but that did not mean that French pressure on Morocco relaxed. On the contrary, the aim, ever since the recognition of Mulay Hafid in January 1909, was to force him into a French orbit, to compel him to rely on France, and to surround him at Fez with French officials and advisers whose pressure he could not resist. If French influence in Morocco were exercised on behalf, and at the request, of the Sultan – if, for example, he asked the French to reorganize his army – it could not be said (or at least could not easily be said) that France was overstepping the limits of the Algeciras agreement, and least of all by the Germans who, in a secret supplement to the 1909 declaration, had agreed that they would not put up in competition with France candidates for 'posts susceptible of having a public character', and more specifically 'instructors in such services', among which the army was outstanding.

It was a Machiavellian policy (but Pichon had previously served in China, where Machiavellism was the rule), but it succeeded to no small degree. It was also a complicated policy, extending over the whole field of military, financial, industrial and commercial affairs, and it would take us too far to follow it in detail. The central point, upon which all else hinged, was the loan which Mulay Hafid, forced as a condition of his recognition to take over the debts of his predecessors, was compelled to negotiate with France. This was the handle which Pichon used to impose French control over Morocco. The aim, as Allain has demonstrated, was nothing less than the systematic 'degradation' of Mulay Hafid's financial status. The terms of the loan were such that it was doubtful, to say the least, whether the revenues of Morocco could conceivably satisfy them. France would, therefore, require some guarantee. Hence the political clauses that were written into the financial agreement. For Mulay Hafid signature meant that France would evacuate the Chaouia and eastern Morocco; for the French it meant that they would remain in occupation until the loan had been redeemed – which meant, in fact, until Doomsday or beyond.

It is, by any account, a sordid story. Mulay Hafid, who knew perfectly well what was happening and what was intended, struggled hard to keep his freedom, refusing to sign the draft agreement which had been concluded in Paris on 14 January 1910. He was brought to heel by a forty-eight hour ultimatum. According to one version he had already signed the agreement on 8 February before the ultimatum; according to another, it only reached Paris on 21 February; according to yet another, it was concluded only on 4 March. The date scarcely matters. What was significant, as the British ambassador in Madrid observed, was that the convention, whenever it was signed, 'confirmed triumphantly the ascendancy of France'. After March 1910 Mulay Hafid, who had come to the throne as the embodiment of resistance to westernization, was tied hand and foot to France. The position was summed up, brutally enough, by the French consul at Fez, Henri-François Gaillard, in an interview with the son of the Grand Vizier, Mokri, on 24 April. 'Have no illusions,' he said.

> What we understand by collaboration is not promises but facts. .... International agreements have given France a special position in Morocco which it would prefer to acquire with good will, but which it has made up its mind to acquire anyhow. The Moroccan government has neither an army nor money and its international administration is not much better than brigandage; with this system it is facing imminent ruin. We will co-operate with you, but only if we can intervene in the army, in finance and in administration in order to improve them, while respecting the principle of the Sultan's sovereignty. That is what we mean by collaboration.

*   *   *

This crude, threatening and intransigent statement indicates in the clearest possible manner the fundamental change of attitude which was the mark of French policy after the capitulation of Mulay Hafid. Caution was not thrown to the wind, but changes were visible almost immediately. Hitherto at least the outward forms of diplomatic courtesy had been maintained in dealings with the Moroccan government. Now, although still in law a sovereign power, it was treated with the brutal disrespect colonial governments usually reserve for subject peoples. That is the measure of the change in French policy after March 1910.

The immediate aim was to put through the financial, administrative and military reforms which Gaillard had specified. The first step was to introduce what the British ambassador in Madrid only too correctly described as 'a new system of financial supervision', nominally under joint French and Moroccan control, but actually entirely run by France. A little later, beginning in the autumn, the French military mission at Fez (by now effectively the only foreign military mission in the country) was reconstructed and rapidly expanded in order to equip it, under the direction of Major J.E. Mangin, to embark on a thorough reform of the Moroccan army, now reorganized entirely on the French model, down to the familiar red and blue uniform. Finally, there was a continuous infiltration of Frenchmen into all the public services – debt, customs, police, harbours, telegraph – as well as the various international commissions. By the beginning of 1911 Gaillard's programme was pretty well completed.

It was also done in such a way as to make it difficult for the other signatories of the Act of Algeciras to complain; that is to say, the 'reforms' were carried out in the name of the Sultan, often at his voluntary or involuntary request, and technically without derogation of his sovereignty. Was it not perfectly legitimate for France to provide help and co-operation when it was asked for? But it was clear by the beginning of 1911 that citizens of other countries were being systematically squeezed out. As Seckendorff, the German minister at Tangier, wrote in February 1911: 'one cannot escape the feeling that one is living in a purely French colony.' And this, as the Belgian minister observed, was directly the result of 'the last loan'. Since then, he said, 'a swarm of functionaries', Gascons and Provençals, had descended on the land like a cloud of locusts – 'You run into them at every street corner in Tangier.'

Parallel with the build-up of French administrative personnel there was also an unmistakeable intensification of military activity. The new financial agreement with Mulay Hafid had legalized the position of the French military both in the Chaouia in the west and in the Algerian-Moroccan borderland (the so-called Confins) in the east. The generals, Moinier in the west and Toutée, who succeeded Lyautey as High Commissioner in 1910, in the east, were quick to see the possibilities. But this was nothing new; the army had long been pressing for action. What was new was the attitude of the government in

Paris. Pichon, it is true, still exercised some control: 'I will not allow myself to be drawn by the military into a policy which is not and never will be mine,' he told the German chargé d'affaires on 29 June 1910. But when Moinier, without authorization, launched an expedition deep into Moroccan territory he was not dismissed, as Drude had been dismissed in 1908 and d'Amade in 1909, but was simply recalled to Paris, instructed not to exceed his competence, and sent back to his command. It was a clear intimation – and one not lost on the military and on the colonial lobby in the Chamber of Deputies – that the army was being given a new degree of latitude.

In the west, it was still important to go carefully for fear of inter-national complications. In the east France's legal position was more clearly defined, and here there is not much doubt that the French advance was officially planned and inspired. Two important develop-ments clearly pointed in this direction. The first was the decision, made known in December 1910, to carry through a complete admin-istrative reorganization of the Confins. Seckendorff was quick to see its significance. It was not just a question, he said, of the French occupation of the territory, which was already a long-established fact. What it showed, rather, was that France was setting up a permanent system of government and (contrary to the undertakings made to Mulay Hafid) had no intention of getting out. This was confirmed, if confirmation were needed, by the second decision, which, signifi-cantly, dates from March 1910. This was an ambitious programme of railway development, which eventually, if all went as planned, would extend from Marnia on the Algerian frontier via Oujda and Taza to Fez, and there link up with Casablanca. Such a railway system would serve not only immediate military needs, but would also in the longer term be a means of exercising control over the whole country and, indeed, over the whole of North Africa. With a continuous railway network from Tunis to Casablanca under its control, France would be in an unassailable position.

The railway programme, pointing unambiguously at Fez, is the key to French policy in Morocco in 1910. Invested from both sides, east and west, the capital was bound sooner or later to fall; it was only necessary to have patience, not to push too hard or too fast. This, essentially, was the point at issue between Pichon and the generals. But it was also vitally important that control of the railway should be exclusively in French hands, and here the government in Paris was as adamant as the generals on the spot. The problem was the restraints imposed by the 1909 agreement with Germany and the other inter-

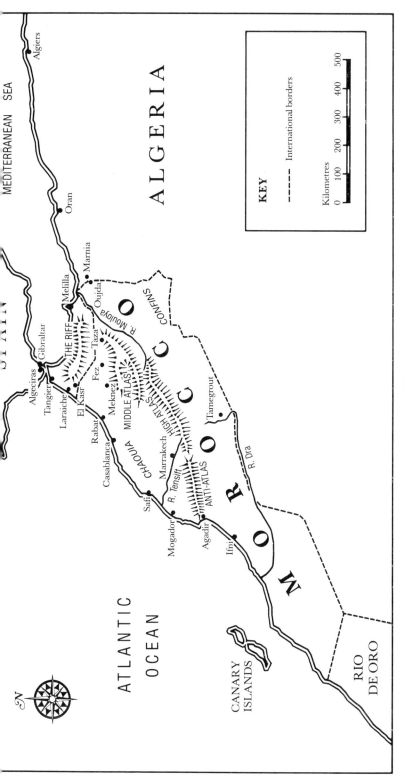

MOROCCO 1911

national commitments, which laid down that all construction projects should be available for open tender. At the end of 1910 and in 1911 the government in Paris tried to get round this restriction by arguing that the railways in question were being constructed by the army for purely military purposes, and were therefore exempt from public competition. It was an ingenious subterfuge, but it deceived neither the Germans nor the British, who knew perfectly well that it was (as Eyre Crowe observed) part of 'a general scheme for acquiring a railway monopoly in Morocco'.

This was not the only area in which France was trying to go behind the Franco-German agreement and the Act of Algeciras. There was also the question of mining rights, which led to trouble with Germany in May 1910 and later to an open breach with Holland. But the railways were the test of French intentions, and here it was obvious that the aim was to squeeze out the other European nations. The British were indignant. It was, they said, a 'flagrant example of the vicious policy which the French government are pursuing in Morocco', but they concluded that 'it would probably be difficult to object to such a purely military measure'. In Germany, Kiderlen-Wächter, who succeeded Schoen as Secretary for Foreign Affairs in June 1910, took a similar line, but he also made it clear that he regarded the question as a test-case for the future of Franco-German relations.

*   *   *

The evolution of French policy in Morocco in the second half of 1910 is remarkable. Fundamentally, it denoted a shift away from negotiation and co-operation with the other powers, in particular Great Britain and Germany, to military expansion and a policy of 'go it alone'. This change of direction, it seems possible, reflected the growing influence at the Quai d'Orsay of an imperialist group which had never reconciled itself to the Franco-German agreement of 1909, and which now, with the active support of Regnault, the French minister at Tangier, believed the time had come to brush aside the international agreements and take over Morocco by direct action. What is evident, in any case, is the growing reliance on military measures. In the Confins they had full government support; in the Chaouia they were undertaken, often against orders, on local initiative. But it is noticeable that, though insubordinate generals might be reprimanded or even dismissed, the territory they had won was rarely evacuated. Here also the area of French penetration and control was steadily advancing.

By the beginning of 1911, therefore, all the indications are that the French were ready to pounce if and when occasion arose. Furthermore, Moinier's campaigns in the Chaouia and beyond – and his success in getting away with them – had aroused an outburst of imperialism and chauvinism in bourgeois circles in Paris, particularly in the bourgeois press, which put the not very strong or secure Briand government under considerable pressure. Nevertheless, Pichon still counselled caution and avoidance of the risk of international complications. 'Time, with our help, is working for France in Morocco,' he wrote on 25 January 1911. 'If the military do nothing stupid, our influence will continue to increase and our presence there will be consolidated.' But then two things happened which changed the whole situation. First, the Briand government resigned on 27 February, and Pichon, who had been Foreign Minister for the last five years, was out of office. Secondly, almost simultaneously serious and widespread unrest broke out in Morocco, a direct response to the financial and military measures introduced by France during the preceding twelve months. Was not this the opportunity for which imperialists had been waiting, the signal to clear up the 'Morocco question' once and for all? France had never been better prepared, militarily or otherwise. Had it not now the excuse it needed to intervene without the risk of hostile reactions from the other signatories of the Act of Algeciras?

We do not know what Pichon's answer would have been if he had remained in office. He also, by the spring of 1911, had moved, by design or under pressure, a long way down the road leading to a military solution. It would be a mistake to draw too sharp a contrast, as some historians have tended to do, between him and his successor. By March 1911 the line dividing the choices was razor thin, and Pichon also might very well have decided that the moment for direct action had arrived. This, in any case, was the decision of the new Foreign Minister, Jean Cruppi. It has been suggested that Cruppi, who had no previous experience of foreign affairs, let himself fall into the hands of the military, and in particular of Berteaux, the Minister of War. Whether or not this is true, it is an insufficient explanation of the subsequent course of events. There are, no doubt, differences between the Briand administration and the Monis administration which followed it. But the essential difference was the new situation in Morocco. Now, if ever, the opportunity had come to carry the ambitions of French imperialism to their logical conclusion and complete the conquest of North Africa. Hence 'the dash to Fez', the decisive move in the train of events which led to Agadir.

The new factor in 1911 was the decision in favour of a military solution. It carried with it, obviously, the risk of international complications, but this was a risk the French government accepted, gambling perhaps – as other governments have done, before and since – that it could get away with a *fait accompli*. What is clear, in any case, is that the international crisis which followed was initiated by France. It was the last fling of an imperialism which was already outdated and for which, ironically, the great majority of Frenchmen and Frenchwomen had no sympathy. But in 1911, when the bourgeoisie still dominated the political scene in Paris, making and unmaking Cabinets with impunity, what the majority of Frenchmen and Frenchwomen wanted had little political significance. Certainly not for the Monis Cabinet, the epitome of bourgeois self-esteem, which took over on 2 March 1911, and led France – and, with it, the rest of Europe – to the very edge of the precipice.

*   *   *

We shall, of course, never know the thoughts and calculations of the new government which took over in France on 2 March 1911. Probably there was no immediate change of direction, no thought of introducing a new policy. But almost immediately two facts made their influence felt. The first, hardly unexpected, but by now increasingly urgent, was that the mandate conferred on France and Spain in 1906 by the Act of Algeciras to exercise police authority in Morocco for a period of five years was on the point of expiring. What would happen if it were not renewed? Secondly the new Monis government was confronted by a sudden deterioration of the position in Morocco. Already in January the first signs of trouble had appeared when a small French detachment, advancing without orders beyond the recognized boundary of the Chaouia, was ambushed with heavy losses. During February the disaffection spread rapidly and in March reached the region of Fez. Taken together, these two events shaped French policy after the beginning of March.

Even Pichon must have been aware of the possibility of the French police mandate running out. This, perhaps, explains the heightened tempo of French policy in Morocco during the second half of 1910. What is certain, in any case, is that France would prefer the risk of a new international crisis rather than surrender the police rights upon which its whole position in Morocco had been built ever since the Casablanca incident of 1907. Nor could it afford to see Mulay Hafid toppled from his throne, as now seemed likely. Already at the beginning of March, just when the new government was taking over in Paris, rumours of unrest in Fez itself, as well as in the surrounding countryside, reached Tangier, and when a column sent out from the capital under a French officer, Captain Brémond, suffered a serious reverse on 26 March all the tribes surrounding the capital, including those traditionally loyal to the Sultan, joined in. This was the situation at the beginning of April, and on 4 April the French ambassadors in London, Berlin, St Petersburg and Madrid were instructed to inform their respective governments that, in view of the situation at Fez and the potential danger to Europeans in the capital, the French government might find it necessary to take military measures. This communication, and a second which followed on 6 April, marked the opening of the diplomatic crisis which culminated in the despatch of the *Panther* to Agadir on 1 July.

In view of the state of communications in Morocco, it was – and is – difficult to decide how far, if at all, the French apprehensions were justified. In normal circumstances it took four days for a courier to reach Tangier from Fez, but two or three days more if there was unrest on the route, and by the time the news had been passed on to Paris it was often out-of-date. Was there, in fact, any threat to the handful of Europeans in Fez at the beginning of April? We shall never know for certain. But what we do know is that most other countries – Britain, Belgium and Switzerland, as well as Germany – viewed the French claims with considerable scepticism. 'The reason for the whole movement', the British minister at Tangier reported to the Foreign Office on 2 April, 'is undoubtedly hatred of the Grand Vizier', el Glaoui, and his exactions: 'there appears so far to be no anti-Christian feeling.' But the situation was, in reality, a little more complicated than that. Resistance to el Glaoui, which quickly turned into resistance to Mulay Hafid himself, sprang in the last analysis from his subordination to France. The exactions which inflamed resentment were a consequence of the heavy financial burden France had imposed in 1910. A second factor, no less inflammatory, was the new military discipline imposed by Major Mangin. He, according to Seckendorff, was 'the only Christian against whom there is popular resentment'. Certainly, one aim of the rebels was to get rid of the French military mission, and this could turn easily into an anti-French and eventually into an anti-European movement. But there was no sign of this happening at the time when Cruppi and the Monis government in Paris decided on military intervention. All the evidence indicates that the alleged threat to Europeans in Fez was a pretext – and not the reason – for French action.

Already in January Moinier had asked authorization for a punitive expedition against the Zaer tribe which had ambushed the column of Lieutenant Marchand. He was refused by Pichon, and again in March by Cruppi. But the latter authorized the reinforcement of the French forces at Casablanca. Even earlier Mangin had prepared plans for a mobile column to march on Fez should the occasion arise. The immediate question was whether it should advance from the east or the west. The decision went in favour of the west, but Toutée, in command in the east, was ordered to build a bridge across the River Mouloya, the boundary between the area of French occupation and independent Morocco, and hold his forces ready for action. The first clear indication of an intention to intervene militarily came on 3 April – one day before Cruppi sent out his notification to the four main European governments – when Moinier was ordered to report how long it would take to occupy Rabat, and march on Fez. Meanwhile more reinforcements were sent to Casablanca. By 19 April the decision had been taken. On 25 April Moinier was officially placed in charge of operations between the Chaouia and Fez, and on the following day the advance began. The powers had already been notified of the impending campaign on 19 April.

If hitherto the pretext for intervention had been France's duty to protect Europeans endangered in Fez, the excuse now was an urgent appeal for aid from Mulay Hafid. This also (this is, perhaps, the most important of the new facts established by Jean-Claude Allain) was not true. There was no appeal from the Sultan for the despatch of French forces and no one, probably, was deceived. But it was necessary, to justify French action in the eyes of the other signatories of the Act of Algeciras, to fabricate an appeal, and finally, on 4 May, Mulay Hafid was induced against all his better feelings to request the support of the French government and the help of its troops. The letter was antedated 27 April, but did not reach Tangier until 12 May, and had obviously no bearing on the French decision, taken on 17 April, to launch French troops on Fez. When, two months later, Kiderlen-Wächter sent out an urgent appeal to German industrialists to ask for government intervention on their behalf in Morocco he had a good precedent; the only difference was that he did it before the event, not after.

*   *   *

What, from a French point of view, was serious about the unrest in

Morocco in the spring of 1911 was that, if Mulay Hafid were deposed, with him would probably go the rights and privileges he had granted France since March 1910, and then it would be back in the position it had found itself in after the deposition of Abd el-Aziz in 1908. This, probably, was the consideration which weighed most heavily with the Monis government – or rather with Cruppi and the Minister of War, Berteaux – when it faced up to the situation in April 1911. The new Cabinet was, in any case, more favourably inclined to a forward policy in Morocco than the Briand government which preceded it. The return of Delcassé as Minister of Marine after five years in the wilderness could certainly be interpreted in that sense, though in the event, chastened perhaps by his experience in 1905, Delcassé consistently opposed the risk involved in a military solution of the 'Morocco question'. More important was the influence of finance and banking, represented by Monis himself, by Cruppi, and by the new Minister of Finance, Joseph Caillaux – an influence which had always, since the days of Jules Ferry, favoured an active colonial policy, in co-operation with Germany, as a means of restoring French prestige after the disasters of 1870 and 1871.

These tendencies were inherent in the Monis Cabinet of 1911. Whether they would have come out into the open without the challenge of the Moroccan revolt no one can say. By April 1911, on the other hand, the threat to the position France had won in 1910 was manifest; and Cruppi and Berteaux reacted accordingly. From their point of view it was, in a sense, now or never – for how long would the police authority given to France under the Act of Algeciras still remain in existence? – and on Easter Monday, 17 April, the necessary decisions were taken. Previously France had held back for fear of international complications; now, under pressure of events, the risk was deliberately taken, and Moinier was given the authorization to go ahead.

The moment was opportune. President Fallières, accompanied by Delcassé and another minister, was away on an official visit to Tunisia. Other ministers, including Caillaux, were absent from Paris for the Easter holiday. The Chamber of Deputies, as both the British and the German ambassadors observed, was prorogued until 23 May. If the military action could be completed by then (as, in fact, it was), might it not be accepted without opposition?

The decision, so far as we can see, was taken by Monis, Cruppi and Berteaux alone. Caillaux (if we are to believe him, which is rarely wise) rushed back to Paris when he heard the news and insisted on a full meeting of the Cabinet, which took place on 22 April; but its outcome, true to form, was to endorse the decision already taken. Both the British and the German ambassadors in Paris noticed immediately the change of tone and atmosphere in the French press. Schoen's conjecture was that the Monis Cabinet had embarked on a 'prestige policy' to offset the growing discontent over its economic failures. Sir Francis Bertie noted simply the launching of a press campaign 'to accustom French public opinion to the idea of an expedition to Fez'. What was clear, anyhow, he said, was 'that the point of view in France as regards intervention in Morocco is undergoing a complete change'. He was not, of course, referring to the great working-class majority, which, as always, was sceptical and indifferent, but to the bourgeoisie. Here, without doubt, the influence of the nationalists, colonialists and imperialists was on the rise.

After 17 April the French military action went forward according to plan – or, as is usual with military actions, nearly according to plan. In fact, bad weather held up Moinier's operations, and the expedition to Fez only left on 11 May. French diplomats protested unceasingly that the whole operation was within the scope of the Algeciras agreements and that there was no intention of transgressing them. No one believed them, though even Kiderlen-Wächter politely pretended to do so. In London, Grey observed pointedly that 'we are already skating on very thin ice in maintaining that the Act of Algeciras is not affected by all that has happened.' He was certainly right.

Even now France still kept up the pretences so far as it could. When, on 21 May, the French column reached Fez, it took good care to remain outside the city walls. It had achieved its object which was to keep Mulay Hafid, by now the symbol of French domination, on the throne. But the reaction of the other powers was less than enthusiastic, to say the least. Nicolson in London told the French ambassador point-blank that the advance of the French troops would probably 'create a fierce agitation ... and possibly precipitate a general catastrophe'. He also said that, if the French object was to keep the Sultan on his throne, 'they would never be able to leave the country and what was intended merely as a temporary measure ... might develop into a more permanent and far-reaching proceeding.' Nicolson, of course, knew that it was not intended to be a temporary measure at all. But the British, their hands tied by the 1904 agreement with France, could do no more than expostulate gently. Not so the Germans. As for Mulay Hafid, he himself said, according to the Italian minister in Tangier, that he had sunk to the level of the Bey of Tunis – the only difference being that he had come out of the operation financially better off. He was undoubtedly right. After 21 May Morocco was in fact, if not in name, a French protectorate.

*   *   *

But did Cruppi and the Monis government really believe that they could get away with their military action without international repercussions? They had certainly good reason to suppose that the British, however alarmed they might be about possible complications, would raise no objection. But what about Germany? There was also the question of Spain which, not without reason, had been anxious ever since the Franco-German agreement of 1909 about the observance of its rights or claims under the Franco-Spanish agreement of 1904. The 'dash to Fez', it soon became clear, far from solving the 'Moroccan question' once for all, as the French apparently hoped, had instead stirred up the 'Moroccan wasps' nest'.

Even before the Cabinet meeting on 22 April, Cruppi must have been aware, if only because of what had happened in 1905, that there could be no question of ignoring Germany altogether. If he did not, he had plenty of warning both from the German ambassador in Paris and from Jules Cambon, the French ambassador in Berlin. As early as 14 April Cambon urgently recommended his government 'to be *very* careful' – advice it had already received independently from Sir Francis Bertie, the British ambassador in Paris, who emphasized how important it was 'not to give the German government any opportunity to make objections and difficulties'. The soundness of this advice was immediately apparent when Cambon saw the German Chancellor on 19 April. He would neither encourage nor discourage France, Bethmann-Hollweg said; but he then pointed out that any such action as the occupation of Fez which resulted in the Sultan's loss of independence would 'lead to the reopening of the whole Morocco question'. The warning could scarcely have been more explicit.

So far as can be seen these warnings had no effect on Cruppi. Had he, perhaps, convinced himself and the rest of the French Cabinet that the Franco-German agreement of 1909 removed all danger of the German government raising difficulties and objections? Certainly this was the impression he tried to convey to Schoen on 19 April, and repeatedly thereafter. If so, it was, as Schoen said, an 'illusion'. Germany had, indeed, recognized France's special interests in Morocco, but how far that recognition extended was a matter of interpretation.

Cruppi also made a great show of acting in agreement with Berlin. 'No significant step', he told Schoen on 22 April, 'would be taken without a previous exchange of views.' But almost simultaneously he decided that notification, rather than consultation, would be enough, the excuse being that consultation would take up too much time in an emergency; and in fact there was no consultation during the whole period from 17 April to the arrival of Moinier's forces at Fez on 21 May.

Cruppi's position was summed up in the instructions he sent to Cambon in Berlin on 26 April. The 1909 agreement, he said, had given France a right of intervention in Morocco going beyond the 1906 convention. For this reason it was inadmissible for Germany to join any international protest against French intervention. Cambon was instructed to put Germany in its place. It was enough for it to be notified of French intentions; there was no ground for promising not to occupy Fez; above all, he should not yield to German intimidation 'to obtain concessions from us contrary to our rights and our duties as a great nation'.

These were brave – perhaps foolhardy – words, and it soon became clear that they could not be maintained. Cambon had the good sense to tone down his instructions before presenting them to the German Secretary of State on 28 April. Their effect, nevertheless, was to produce the first explicit statement from Kiderlen that, if France occupied Fez, Germany would regard the Act of Algeciras as void and would 'resume complete liberty of action'. In case the lesson was lost he then, two days later, placed a statement to the same effect in the *Norddeutsche Allgemeine Zeitung*, well known to be an organ of the Foreign Office. The fact that Germany would not stand idly by was now public knowledge.

The effect was dramatic. Hitherto there had been no sign at all that the French government was prepared to pay more than lip-service to German interests, and that, to all appearances, was still Cruppi's position. But the declaration in the *Norddeutsche Allgemeine Zeitung*, which got worldwide attention, caused alarm and dismay in Paris. Was Cruppi leading France into a quagmire? There were even rumours that Germany was on the point of invading France. They were wide of the mark, but their effect was quickly seen. On 7 May the French Minister of Finance, Joseph Caillaux, approached in all secrecy the notorious counsellor at the German Embassy, von der Lancken, suggesting that, if Germany would recognize without reserve French interests in Morocco, France would gladly make concessions to Germany elsewhere. Similar suggestions also appeared in a number of Paris newspapers.

* * *

Caillaux's secret conversation with Lancken on 7 May opened a new chapter in the Agadir story. As we have seen, he had already engaged in backstage negotiations with Lancken in 1908, and the contact he now made would run like a red thread through Franco-German negotiations until the final agreement on 4 November.

We have already seen a good deal of Caillaux's activities, and we shall have to come back to them, so far as they affected the course of events after 1 July. At present it is sufficient to note that it was his intervention on 7 May that first raised the possibility of a settlement on the basis of colonial compensation for Germany. On the other hand, it is important to note that this was entirely a private and unauthorized initiative behind the back of Cruppi. There is not the slightest indication that Caillaux was speaking on behalf of the government; on the contrary, his repeated demand for strict secrecy makes it clear that he was not. What we do not know is how Caillaux intended to put his proposals into effect, still less why Schoen and Kiderlen took them seriously. Was he planning the fall of Monis and perhaps to put himself in his place? Certainly, there were powerful financial interests in Paris which would go to any length to avoid a breach with Germany. But there is no indication at this stage that the Monis Cabinet, and particularly Cruppi, was thinking of a deal with Germany. That came – very half-heartedly – later. For the present, at the beginning of May, it was certainly counting on absorbing Morocco lock, stock and barrel, for France. There was, indeed, the question of Spain; but there was no intention of sharing the loot with Germany.

On the German side, also, there was no immediate pressure. No one knew that Kiderlen had, on 3 May, prepared a plan for eventual German intervention at Mogador and Agadir for submission to the Kaiser. German policy was to wait until the results of the French military action were known. This was reasonable enough, and Nicolson in London (who was no particular friend of Germany) was forced, on 1 May, to concede that the attitude of the German government was 'quite correct'.

After the arrival of the French military expedition at Fez on 21 May the situation began to change. Cruppi's defiance of the Germans – the word is hardly too strong – had rested on the expectation (or, more correctly, the hope) of openly declared British and Russian support. Faced with the solidarity of the Triple Entente, the Germans would have no choice except to back down. But Cruppi's expectations soon proved unrealistic. The Russians, indeed, supported the French position on paper – they could scarcely do otherwise – but they also made clear that they were not ready to go to war in support of a colonial adventure in Africa. The reaction on the British side was even more galling. Cruppi had tried in April to extract a statement from the British government indicating that there was a military agreement between the two countries. Grey refused point blank, intimating that any suggestion of the sort would cause 'a row in Parliament' which might result in the fall of the government. The result was a change in the French attitude to Germany. It was slow, reluctant and half-hearted, but it was inevitable. Perhaps it was reinforced by the growing disillusionment in France about the impasse into which Cruppi's policy seemed to be leading. The result, in any case, was a realization that it would be necessary to come to some sort of arrangement with Germany. The question was what sort.

The question had, very tentatively, been raised on the German side at the end of April when Zimmermann, the Under-secretary in the German Foreign Ministry, had suggested to Cambon that it might be a good idea to discuss the situation which might arise if France, contrary to its expressed intentions, was prevented by circumstances from evacuating Fez. But it was only at the end of May, after the French military action had been completed, that Cruppi took up the suggestion. It seemed to him, he told Schoen, that Berlin was not disinclined 'to talk'. But beyond that he did not go until 15 June – and neither did the Germans. The intention, obviously, on both sides was to wait for the other to make the first move. Finally, on 15 June, discussing the project of a Cameroon-Congo railway – an enterprise in which, as we have seen, Tardieu and Caillaux were deeply implicated – Cruppi suggested that it might be the basis for 'an exchange of ideas about the whole of North Africa' – provided that France could be sure that 'Germany was ready for a friendly compromise in other North African questions'. What he clearly had in mind was Morocco.

What seems evident from these interchanges is that Cruppi was still hoping to buy the Germans off by commercial concessions. If so, he was seriously deceiving himself. The Congo-Cameroon railway, Schoen replied, was a purely private undertaking and had nothing to do with the Morocco question. Kiderlen-Wächter and Bethmann-Hollweg in Berlin took the same line. By this time, French diplomacy was in disarray. In Berlin, Jules Cambon was talking, apparently on his own initiative, about compensation 'in the colonial field'; but even in July all his emphasis was on economic enterprises – Turkish railways and, more generally, the enormous advantages German industry would gain from French financial support. In mid-May, Kiderlen went off to take a six weeks' cure at Bad Kissingen, observing ominously that, by the time the six weeks had elapsed, 'a very serious situation would have developed'. What he meant, as Nicolson in London correctly surmised, was that in that time France would have 'plunged herself up to the neck in Moorish affairs' and that the moment would have arrived for 'Germany to step in and demand her price'. Precisely that was what happened.

Meanwhile a bombshell had fallen in the form of the Spanish occupation of Laraiche and El Kasr on 8 June. Spain got a bad press – particularly from the British – for this act of blatant aggression. But it is hard to criticize in terms of the peculiar ethic of imperialism. Once the French advance on Fez was under way the Spaniards had every reason to think that the intention was to go back on the Franco-Spanish agreement, not perhaps to squeeze them out altogether, but to force them back to the tenuous footholds (the so-called Presidios) they had held ever since the sixteenth century. They were almost surely right; certainly at a somewhat later stage Caillaux's intention was to get compensation from Spain for the concessions he was forced to make to Germany. Nevertheless, the result of the Spanish action was to open one more breach in the Algeciras agreements. Madrid had feared a deal between Paris and Berlin which would cut Spain out. Now it looked as though France and Spain would carve up Morocco, cutting Germany out altogether.

The reaction in Berlin was immediate. Already at the beginning of May, as we have seen, Kiderlen had submitted a plan for German intervention to the Kaiser, and got his general approval. But this was contingency planning, and it would be a mistake to suppose that it signified a definite intention to send German warships to Moroccan waters. After 8 June it was different. The Spanish action seemed to indicate that time was running out, and a new scheme, more detailed and specific, was drawn up by Zimmermann on 12 June and submitted to Kiderlen at Kissingen. On 16 June he wrote to Zimmermann giving his approval.

Even now, Kiderlen left the door open. He did not, he told Zimmermann, really think that Germany would get any acceptable proposals from France unless it took independent action; but he was ready for one more try. Cambon was due to visit him at Kissingen on 20 June before leaving for Paris: perhaps, Kiderlen said, I shall hear something from him. What led him to believe that this was likely? Had Caillaux, after his first contact with Lancken on 7 May, made further proposals, perhaps through his go-between, Fondère, whom he sent to Berlin in May? It seems likely, but we do not know for certain. In any event, if Kiderlen thought that Cambon was coming with an offer from Paris he was quickly disillusioned. When the meeting took place on 21 June, Cambon immediately announced that he was not authorized to make proposals, only to give assurance as to an early evacuation of Fez. In any event, there could be no question of handing over part of Morocco to Germany: 'If that is what you want, it would be better not to open a conversation.' But, he added, 'one could look elsewhere.'

It was the first official suggestion of territorial compensation, and Kiderlen was quick to take it up. 'But you must tell us', he added, 'what you have in mind.' That was impossible, Cambon replied, 'because these are new ideas'; but he promised to submit them to his government when he went to Paris. 'Bring us something back from Paris,' was Kiderlen-Wächter's last word.

*   *   *

What judgement are we to pass on this famous Kissingen interview, or, perhaps more important, what judgement did Kiderlen pass on it? Was it, from his point of view, a success that the accredited representative of France had finally come out with a proposal for territorial compensation? Or was the proposal to refer the 'new ideas' to Paris just a subterfuge to keep negotiations going until it was too late for Germany to intervene? Had Kiderlen been led by Caillaux to believe that definite proposals would be forthcoming, and was he disillusioned when they weren't? Should he, in any case, have waited to see what Cambon brought back from Paris?

These are questions it is impossible to answer. All we know is that preparations to send warships to Morocco went on irrespectively – a sign, perhaps, that Kiderlen did not find the results too encouraging. The day following the interview with Cambon Kiderlen left Bad Kissingen for Berlin. On 26 June he and Bethmann-Hollweg went to Kiel and got the Kaiser's authorization for the *Panthersprung*. The following day he was in touch with the naval staff, and, on 1 July, as we know, the *Panther* anchored off Agadir.

Kiderlen's action has been condemned on all sides. Bülow called it 'deplorable', and others have described it as 'ill-considered', 'miscalculated' and 'mistimed'. If it was intended to put pressure on France to make concessions, it is said, its effect could only be the opposite. Cambon himself, when he returned to Berlin, complained that, just when he was about to make positive proposals, the German action had made his position impossible. Bertie in Paris wrote of 'the brigand-like proceedings of the Germans', Buchanan in St Petersburg of 'this sudden display of the German mailed fist', and Crowe in London of another instance of Germany's 'well-tried policy of blackmailing'.

In the event, as it turned out, all these criticisms were true. Kiderlen's action *was* miscalculated, and certainly had consequences he neither foresaw nor desired. But is that not true of all Machiavellian political calculations? What diplomatic planning and military planning fail to take into account, with surprising regularity and consistency, is the impact of the fortuitous and unexpected. That was also the case in 1911. Kiderlen's calculations looked watertight until they were overtaken by an accident no one could have foreseen. There is, perhaps, a lesson there which should not be forgotten today.

Why did Kiderlen decide, as he himself put it, 'to thump the table'? Crowe, who was certainly no friend of Kiderlen or of Germany, provided the answer, honestly enough, in 1912 when most of the dirty linen had been washed and laundered. The answer was the secret, underhand manoeuvres of Caillaux. Crowe recalled how Admiral von Holzendorff, who actually had disapproved of the despatch of the *Panther*, had told him that, 'if I only knew what had preceded the Kissingen interview, the impatience of the German government with France . . . would have become quite intelligible'. What had preceded it, of course, were Caillaux's unauthorized advances. So long as these were unknown the despatch of the *Panther* 'seemed singularly inopportune'. When Caillaux's treasonable actions became known – but that was not until the end of 1911 – Kiderlen's calculations became credible. 'Having', as Crowe put it, 'M. Caillaux's concessions as it were in his pocket', he decided that 'the despatch of the ship would make an impression in Paris sufficient to strengthen M. Caillaux's hand in getting his cabinet to accept the policy of a general understanding with Germany.' It was, Crowe conceded, a perfectly reasonable calculation. But then, ironically, the caprice of God, that unpredictable gambler, Who delights to confuse the schemes of mice and men, took a hand in proceedings. At a great demonstration at the parade-ground of Issy-les-Moulineaux, designed to show how far France was ahead in the new branch of air warfare, an aeroplane lost control and dashed into the crowd killing on the spot the War Minister, Berteaux, co-author with Cruppi of the Moroccan adventure, and seriously wounding the Prime Minister, Monis. The crippled administration struggled on for a month, but was obviously failing. On 23 June it resigned, and was followed on 28 June by a new ministry under Caillaux.

The irony of the situation cannot have been lost upon Kiderlen, who by now was caught in a web of his own making. The preparations for the Agadir *coup* had gone too far to be countermanded, and a manoeuvre intended to help Caillaux worked instead to make his position more difficult. His aim was still to do a deal with Germany, but could he bring it off in view of the public agitation caused by the *Panthersprung*? For Kiderlen the question was how much he could save of his original plans in a situation he had never envisaged. These were the questions which were put to the test, with more than one threat of a European conflagration, between 28 June and 4 November 1911.

* * *

What is noteworthy in all this is that never once in the whole long drawn-out process of mutual bargaining and recrimination is there the least sign of any consideration of the interests or wishes of the peoples involved. When the Spanish threatened to disclose (which they did) the secret terms of the Franco-Spanish agreement of 1904 the British, not without reason, objected that such a disclosure – which implied a partition of their country – would 'have a deplorable effect upon the Moors'. Everyone knew, though not everyone was prepared to say, that the cause of the trouble in Morocco was the French. The Kaiser was apt to be erratic in his comments, but when in April 1911 he said that 'the state of anarchy and warfare' in Morocco during the past six years was due 'entirely to French intervention', he was not far from the truth. The 'dash to Fez' served only French interests – or supposed French interests, for no one, with the experience of Algeria and Tunis behind him, could possibly say that real French interests, calculated in terms of lives and money, were involved. On the contrary, the French taxpayer, who had already paid nearly one billion dollars for the Algerian adventure, was again going to have to foot the bill.

What, then, lay behind this policy? One answer is prestige. France,

Pichon told the German chargé d'affaires, could not let itself be 'pushed around by the nose' – that would be 'a renunciation of France's position as a great power'. The same considerations were obviously strong in Kiderlen-Wächter's mind. 'Bring us something back from Paris,' he said to Cambon – anything to show that Germany had not been ignored. But opinion in Germany was less easily appeased. As newspapers like the *Post* observed, Germany already had 'as much as she can stand of unhealthy tropical colonies'. A mere 'something' would not satisfy German ambitions; but what more could Kiderlen offer?

But the governments were not concerned primarily with what they did, or did not, gain in Africa, but with their leverage against each other in Europe. If France, Germany or Spain failed to get its way in Morocco they would have to face the repercussions at home: this was the issue in 1911. So far as we can see, the electorate nowhere cared deeply – or even cared at all – about the outcome in Morocco. This was at best an issue within a limited sector of the middle class. But the outcome, though from any national point of view of minimal importance, was a criterion of the ability, or inability, of the government involved to justify itself.

That is why, from 1 July 1911, the 'Moroccan question', as it was called, became a test of strength. It had little to do with Morocco or with Africa, but a great deal to do with Europe. Any country that failed the test in Morocco would feel the consequences in the European balance of power. Whether the Monis government, which began the advance in Morocco in April 1911, foresaw this outcome we do not know. It seems unlikely. But this was the result, foreseen or unforeseen, of the 'dash to Fez'. The question – almost miraculously postponed in 1911, but not settled – was no longer Morocco, but who would dominate the European balance of power. That question was not settled until 1918 – and, as we now know, was not even settled then. The answer, it would seem, is that it is easier to open questions than to close them. When, after forty-four years, Morocco recovered its independence in 1956, it was still undecided.

9

'Thumping the Table'

'Anyone who declares in advance that he will not fight, cannot achieve anything in politics.'
Kiderlen-Wächter, 17 July 1911

The arrival of the German gunboat at Agadir heralded the final act in the Moroccan drama. If the French were prepared to throw down the gauntlet and risk an international crisis to get their way in Morocco, Kiderlen-Wächter was equally ready to pick it up. The result was a situation of extreme complexity. After 1 July the scene of action moved from the periphery to the centre. What mattered now was no longer the course of events in Africa but what the next step would be in Berlin, Paris, London, and in the other European capitals.

And yet the crisis that followed – a crisis which more than once seemed to threaten the peace of Europe – was by any rational standard an unnecessary crisis. Morocco, King George v told the German ambassador when they met at Balmoral in September 1911, 'was not worth a war', and he was certainly right. So far as Morocco and central Africa were concerned there were no serious obstacles to a settlement, and both France and Germany were anxious to find one. The French, in particular, knew perfectly well that they would have to pay a price, probably a stiff price, if they were to bring Morocco under their wing. Moreover, there was nothing new about the idea of a revision of the map of colonial Africa. Once the fever of the 'scramble for Africa' died down, as it did to all practical intents after the Fashoda incident of 1898, the colonial powers had begun to take stock of the miscellaneous territories they had picked up on the way, and they were not always too pleased with what they saw. Hence, from the beginning of the new century, the idea of a more rational redistribution of the African spoils was never far below the surface, particularly as the possessions of Portugal and Belgium, both too small to count, could be brought into the pool and used, if necessary, to smooth over any conflicts of interest among the major powers.

There was, therefore, nothing unprecedented, certainly nothing contrary to the political morality of the day, about Kiderlen's demand for compensation for German acquiescence in the establishment of French control in Morocco. The possibility of bartering the French Congo (or part of it) for Morocco had, in fact, first been ventilated by the French themselves during the crisis of 1905, and from that time forward a whole series of schemes and projects for colonial exchanges and rectifications littered the desks and cluttered the archives of the Quai d'Orsay and the Wilhelmstrasse. In Paris, according to Caillaux's confidential agent, Fondère, 'the great idea' during the whole period of the Monis administration was to 'juggle with the colonies' in order to create a more efficient and unified empire. Cruppi, the Colonial Minister Messimy, Berteaux and Caillaux were all involved, and one aspect of this juggling, as all were aware, was negotiation with the British, Spanish and other interested parties, but particularly with Germany.

These schemes, discussed at length but not yet spelled out, undoubtedly lay behind Caillaux's secret overture to Lancken on 7 May. He was, as usual, jumping the gun; but except for a characteristic lack of caution and common sense, he was probably not very far in intention from his colleagues in the Monis administration. Moreover, their discussions were certainly no secret – how in Paris could they be? The German banker, Dr Ludwig Delbrück, returning from Paris to Berlin, told the Kaiser that he had been informed there that 'we could ask whatever we wanted in the way of colonial cessions and we would get it straight away, provided we did not cause them trouble in Morocco.'

If that was the case, and all indications are that it was, why did Kiderlen's action produce a crisis of first magnitude? That is the first question and perhaps the most important one, because it tells us a great deal about the way an international crisis comes about – now as well as then.

*   *   *

The simple answer, and the answer usually given, is that the crisis which began on 1 July was a result far less of Kiderlen's aims than of his methods. 'We are dealing', the British Foreign Secretary said, 'with people who recognize no law except that of force.' Grey's reaction is understandable, but it was also exaggerated. The *Panther*, with its two guns and 125 men, could not by any stretch of the imagination be described as a demonstration of force. But what Grey had in mind was, of course, not the presence of the *Panther* at Agadir, but the devious, provocative and unpredictable character of Kiderlen's diplomacy. Oddly enough, William II, who had begged Kiderlen at the very start to put his cards on the table and make 'a regular offer' to the French, took much the same view. 'This kind of diplomacy', he grumbled in despair, 'is altogether too sly for my understanding!'

There is no doubt that Kiderlen's devious diplomacy laid up a store of trouble which more straightforward methods might have avoided. When Bethmann-Hollweg brought Kiderlen back from Bucarest in 1910 to take charge of the Foreign Office in Berlin, the Kaiser warned him, prophetically, that he would soon find he had a flea in his ear. But it is not sufficient to blame the crisis that followed on Kiderlen's Swabian temperament or the taste for Byzantine intrigue he had acquired during his years of exile in Bucarest. Kiderlen's policies certainly heightened the suspicions which hung like a dense pall of thundercloud over the international scene in 1911. But the suspicions were already there, poisoning the atmosphere; and it was these suspicions, together with an almost infantile preoccupation with prestige and an ingrained habit of secrecy and prevarication, that turned a colonial clash in a region about which no one seriously cared into a confrontation no one seriously wanted.

In the end, the cause of the crisis lay in the system itself. Just occasionally, usually when they were depressed (and as a group they were singularly neurotic and therefore frequently depressed), statesmen seem to have had an inkling of this fact. Both Bethmann-Hollweg and Grey saw themselves involved in a sequence of events in which the pressure of circumstances, not their own plans or actions, would determine the outcome. They were prisoners of the system, tied into it by all the myriad strands with which the Lilliputians entangled Gulliver; but they were willing prisoners, and they played their hands according to the rules of the game, which usually meant close to the chest. Indeed, the complaint against

Kiderlen-Wächter, the immediate cause of suspicion, was that he was a bit too much like a card-sharper, ready to stretch the rules, if not to break them, if nobody was looking. That, for a man like Grey, was the ultimate sin. If the rules were ignored the system would collapse, and the result would be anarchy.

In reality, the international situation in 1911 *was* anarchy – a sort of regulated anarchy, but anarchy nevertheless – as historians later on were not slow to point out. Stability based on fear, suspicion, and an illusory balance of power, was essentially unstable, at the mercy of any incidental shock or tremor, and precisely such a tremor shook the system in 1911. The French 'dash to Fez' stirred sleeping dogs all over Europe. The complex, interlocking network of secret treaties and agreements which regulated the relations of the powers, and which was supposed to ensure a balance, meant that any change in the *status quo* at any point was bound to have repercussions along the whole line; and, needless to say, it did.

That had already been seen in June when Spain, not to be outdone by France, invoked its rights under the secret Franco-Spanish agreement of 1904 and occupied Laraiche and El Kasr. It was to be seen even more dramatically in the aftermath when first Italy and then Russia sought to cash in what they regarded as their justifiable claims under their secret treaties of 1900 and 1909. Except for France, which was determined at all costs to establish a protectorate, and for the Spaniards who feared the French would do so at their expense, no country was vitally interested in Morocco. But when the crisis occurred they saw it as an opportunity to promote their own interests, or what the small circle of professional diplomats and politicians in charge of policy deemed to be their interests; and no one was quicker off the mark than Kiderlen-Wächter.

Hitherto events in North Africa had followed more or less a course of their own. They had been watched with a certain amount of apprehension by people like Grey, but it had been possible to keep them in quarantine. Now they became involved with all the other conflicts brewing in Europe, not least of all the explosive Anglo-German naval rivalry. The dash to Fez was the catalyst which fused them all together. That was why an episode in the long history of European imperialism, discreditable enough in itself but no more discreditable than many others in the imperial ledger, brought the nations of Europe perilously near to war. North Africa in 1911, like the Persian Gulf in 1980, was a touchstone of international relations, a symbol of discords and suspicions embedded much deeper in the threadbare fabric of a faltering international order. Suspicion and distrust, irrational fears and a pervading sense of insecurity, lay at the heart of the crisis.

* * *

Nowhere were suspicion and distrust more rife than in the Foreign Office in London. Its officials suspected the French; they suspected the Russians; but above all they suspected the Germans. In histories of pre-war Europe written a generation ago the British come out almost as pure and clean as new-shorn lambs. Today, few people would still maintain that view. Possibly the fears and suspicions of people like Crowe and Nicolson reflected an obscure realization that the assured position Great Britain had enjoyed in the nineteenth century was slipping. What is certain is that they contributed substantially to the international tension; indeed, it could almost be said that the crisis of 1911 was made in Britain. But that, too, would be an exaggeration. Everyone had a finger in the pie, and there is no doubt that Kiderlen-Wächter, by thumping the table too often and too hard, went a long way to justify British fears and apprehensions.

What, indeed, was Kiderlen's game? That was the question in everyone's mind on 1 July when the German ambassadors in the various capitals formally notified their respective governments of the arrival of the *Panther* at Agadir. The British Foreign Office was never in two minds about the answer. Even before the dash to Fez, Crowe, still only a senior clerk but rapidly rising to eminence, had predicted that 'Germany's game' would be to 'frighten France by threatening armed intervention' and 'undermine the position of the Triple Entente'. After 1 July his tone and that of his superior, Sir Arthur Nicolson, became shriller and more apprehensive. Germany, he now wrote, was 'playing for the highest stakes'. Kiderlen had embarked on 'a trial of strength' with 'the purpose of testing the solidity of the *entente* between England and France'. Hence the necessity, as Nicolson concluded, 'to range ourselves alongside of France, as we did in 1905 and 1906, and show a united front to German demands.' Otherwise 'the whole Triple Entente would be broken up', England would be faced by 'a triumphant Germany and an unfriendly

France and Russia, and our policy since 1904 of preserving the equilibrium and consequently the peace of Europe would be wrecked.'

The Foreign Office diagnosis was plausible enough, and is still generally accepted, but the evidence to support it is remarkably slender. No doubt Kiderlen had only himself to blame if his actions were misinterpreted. The secrecy and abruptness of his move, still more his refusal to disclose his aims, were bound to cause suspicion, and what was known of his antecedents and temperament was not reassuring. But that does not mean that he was as Machiavellian as the Machiavellians in the Foreign Office in London chose to believe. Paradoxically, it was Nicolson who, in one of his less alarmist moments, put his finger on the essential point: 'I am pretty sure', he surmised, 'that he thought he saw an opportunity for playing a big card and improving his reputation.' That is probably as near the truth about Kiderlen as we shall ever get.

Certainly his aims were much less calculating and malevolent than those the Foreign Office experts in London attributed to him. The reason Bethmann-Hollweg brought Kiderlen back from Bucarest in 1910 was his need to placate his Conservative and National Liberal supporters who were chafing at what they called the 'stagnation' of German policy. He needed a more energetic and forceful Foreign Secretary than Schoen, who went off happily to the comparative tranquillity of the Paris embassy; but above all else he needed a success which, as Kiderlen said, 'would make people forget the earlier fail-ures', and Kiderlen was picked out as the person most likely to produce one for him. There is almost certainly no need to look further than this for the mainsprings of his policy. His aim, quite simply, was to score a success, naturally the bigger the better. What neither Beth-mann nor Kiderlen could have foreseen was that the French would so quickly create an opportunity for him. When their 'stupid and dis-honest' policy in Morocco (as Grey's private secretary called it) gave him his chance, Kiderlen jumped at it; but all he wanted was to make the biggest splash possible and parade his success in triumph before an admiring Reichstag.

Kiderlen was, as Nicolson surmised, essentially an opportunist, not a schemer with deep-laid plans. No doubt he would have been happy enough if, in the haggling over Morocco, British support for France had wavered and the Franco-British understanding had foundered. That would have been an extra bonus. But it was not what he expected or planned. Even before he despatched the *Panther* to Agadir, he said he was convinced that Britain would stand by France as it had done in 1905, if only so as not to 'endanger the *entente cordiale*'. The implication could hardly be clearer. If Crowe and his colleagues believed he was hatching some deep-laid scheme to disrupt the Triple Alliance and make Germany supreme in Europe, they were deceiving themselves.

Nor was Kiderlen gambling on the German navy. Tirpitz might do that, and the Kaiser too. Kiderlen, who was an old-fashioned continental politician – a throwback, almost, to the age of Bismarck – had too much sense. His calculations, as revealed in the documents, were altogether simpler; in fact, they were the stock arguments of prestige, standing and influence, common to all statesmen in all countries in the age of imperialism. 'If we don't play our trump cards' while we can, 'if we stand aside while France lays hands on a large new colony', it will be a major 'diplomatic defeat'; 'our international credit will suffer permanent injury' and 'we shall be without political influence in the world for years to come.' Such language may sound old-fashioned in our own more sophisticated day – though who could put his hand on his heart and say he has not heard it, or something very like it, during the last twelve months? – but it was well understood at the time. Unlike the hawks and hardliners in the Foreign Office who believed that Germany must be resisted lock, stock and barrel, Sir Edward Grey shared and sympathized with Kiderlen's view that Germany had every right to compensation. Grey himself, after all, took care, almost as soon as the crisis broke, to lay down that Great Britain also would require compensation, though he was hard put to say why or what.

Nevertheless, Grey largely shared the obsession of the Foreign Office with the alleged German menace, and it was this obsession, more than anything else, that brought about the rapid deterioration in the situation after 1 July. Crowe and his colleagues were right, of course, in thinking that the German naval programme was a threat to Great Britain, though a lot of people in the Liberal Party and in the Liberal Cabinet disagreed with them. But there is no doubt that they overreacted to Kiderlen's rather puerile *coup*. The situation in 1911 was very different from that in 1905, and even if he had wanted to emulate Holstein's devious plot to break the entente, Kiderlen was in no position to do so. The thread Crowe and Nicolson drew between 1905 and 1911 may have looked logical, but it was a logic that had more to do with their sense of insecurity than with the facts. On the other hand, their assumption that a localized colonial dispute between

France and Germany in Africa somehow involved and affected the European balance of power was neither logical nor plausible; and yet it was this assumption that turned the question of Morocco into a trial of strength.

*   *   *

The Foreign Office in London also miscalculated the French position, though in this case they may, like Nelson, have been turning a blind eye to signals they did not like. They could, perhaps, hardly have been expected to know that Caillaux and his friends in financial circles in Paris were looking far beyond Morocco to a settlement of all outstanding differences between France and Germany and a 'lasting, friendly and loyal' agreement between the two countries. But it is hard to believe that they were unaware of the secret Franco-German negotiations before Agadir. According to my old friend, Frank Nielson, at that time Liberal MP for Hyde, London was full of rumours, and the Irish MPs, John Dillon and Swift MacNeice, had the facts at their fingertips. Lord Loreburn, the stormy petrel of the Liberal Cabinet, who resigned in despair in 1913, appears also to have been well informed. But when he told Grey of rumours of secret negotiations and complained that the French were not being straightforward in their dealings with Great Britain, Grey brushed the story aside as 'obvious romance'. This is not the only occasion when one is left wondering whether Grey was speaking the whole truth and nothing but the truth.

If the Foreign Office chose not to believe the rumours of Franco-German negotiations behind their back, it was almost certainly because they did not wish to believe them. As they saw it, the Anglo-French entente had become the sheet-anchor of British security. This, of course, was not true. As Hardinge, Nicolson's predecessor as permanent under-secretary, more realistically pointed out, the real guarantee of British security was the navy. But what it meant, from the perspective of Nicolson and Crowe, was that, if the French government looked like wavering – as it did under both Monis and Caillaux – it must be held in place. This was the predicament of British policy throughout: how to hold France to the entente, and yet at the same time not to give it sufficient support to encourage it to adopt an intransigent attitude which might lead to war. There was not much concern for France about this (as the French were aware), but a great deal for Britain and the possibility that it might be left to face Germany alone. When, on 3 July, Grey told the German ambassador that he was preoccupied 'with purely British interests', not with 'obligations to France', he was certainly speaking the truth.

From a British point of view there was good reason to be suspicious of France and what Loreburn called its 'tinpot government'. French policy throughout the crisis was devious in the extreme. The French point of view, or at least the point of view of the not inconsiderable number of Frenchmen who thought like Caillaux, was different. They had the Germans on their doorstep, and the British navy, whatever its other virtues, could not fight on wheels. There is no reason to think that they intended to desert the entente, certainly not Monis, and probably not Caillaux either: for France it was an invaluable reinsurance. But there is no doubt, either, that they were not averse, if they could bring it off, to doing a deal with Germany behind Britain's back. Why not? It might suit the British if, as Bertie the British ambassador in Paris hoped, Morocco remained 'an open sore between France and Germany': but it was less obvious what France had to gain. Caillaux's protestations that he was a man of peace were not entirely hollow, even if he was thinking mainly of the financial benefits which could flow into his pocket and the pockets of his financial friends from Franco-German co-operation. France and Germany were, after all, continental powers, with different attitudes and interests from insular Britain. Was it really necessary, forty years after the Franco-Prussian War, that they should be at each other's throats? Must the question of Alsace-Lorraine, which, after all, had been indubitably German until Louis xiv's wars of aggression in the seventeenth century, stand for ever in the way of a mutually beneficial reconciliation?

Not all Frenchmen took this view; but it goes far to explain the attitude of the French government during the Agadir crisis. Like Kiderlen, it wanted bilateral Franco-German negotiations, cutting out the other signatories of the Algeciras Act, including Great Britain, and it was only its panic when Kiderlen thumped the table and sent the *Panther* to Agadir that forced it to change course and rush to London for support. In that sense, it has often been said, Kiderlen's brilliant *coup* was a disastrous mistake. But that view is not altogether borne out by the reactions either of the French press or of the new French government. The panic, it soon turned out, was brief and temporary. After the first shock the attitude of the Parisian press (no doubt under pressure from the government) was to minimize the affair and treat it as 'a temporary move to induce the French government to hasten negotiations with Berlin' which, of course, was exactly what it was. Caillaux, for his part, quickly took control, countermanded the first hasty request of the new Foreign Minister, Selves, for a joint Franco-British naval demonstration, and by 7 July was again deep in negotiations with Berlin. It was only 15 July, when Kiderlen characteristically thumped the table too hard and demanded the whole of the French Congo, that French opinion was aroused. Even Caillaux was outraged.

Even then, Franco-British relations were often strained and seldom harmonious. Each side suspected the other of trying to drag it into war in order to pick its own chestnuts out of the fire. The French were shocked and angered when Grey informed them that Britain would have no objection, under safeguards, if the Germans obtained a port on the west coast of Morocco; they were equally annoyed by his repeated exhortations to be more liberal and conciliatory in the negotiations over Morocco and the Congo. In the end Caillaux angrily told Bertie, the British ambassador in Paris, that 'France could have come to more satisfactory terms with Germany without the *entente*'.

The Agadir crisis has often been depicted as a trial of strength between the Triple Alliance and the Triple Entente, and that may have been the outcome. But it was certainly not the case at the start. What the crisis revealed in the first instance was disunity, cross-purposes and disarray. Austria had no intention of being led by Germany into a situation which might end in war, and Russia's attitude to France was similar. Furthermore, the Russians, at loggerheads with England in Persia, saw the crisis as an opportunity to reach an agreement with Germany at British expense; which they did on 19 August.

We may see this, if we wish, as a measure of international morality in 1911, but it had its own rationality. Why should a million Russian peasants die an unhappy, agonizing death in order that the French should ensconce themselves in Morocco, where they had not a shadow of a moral right to be? Instead, common sense dictated, put your finger in the pie, and hope to pull out a plum. What no one seems to have considered is that they might, in reality, be pulling out a poisoned barb. But in that respect statesmen and politicians in 1911 were not unique. And in the end many more than one million Russian peasants died; and Germans, French and English, as well. They were a sacrifice – no less grim than the human sacrifices practised by the Aztecs in Mexico – to a system of international relations which could not work, and did not work. But it is a system which the world has still not outlived.

* * *

The Germans were not wrong in supposing that it was easy for the British, who had acquired the world's largest empire in a fit of absent-mindedness, to preach the virtues of international morality. They were the beneficiaries of the *status quo*, with nothing to lose and a great deal to gain. Sir Francis Bertie told Grey in a moment of irritation that he had not noticed, on the British part, 'any readiness to divest ourselves' of the colonies, and Count Metternich rather pathetically told Nicolson that whereas, in the last forty years, 'England had added hundreds of thousands of square miles to her vast empire', Germany had 'acquired nothing but a few isolated localities of little or no value.' Small wonder, given the assumptions of the time, that Kiderlen decided to thump the table! His calculations were neither very deep nor very sinister; but he was deeply conscious of 'the storm of indignation which would rage in Germany' if the French swallowed Morocco and the Reich came away empty-handed. Ever since 1904 German policy had been a record of failure: he was determined to score a success. This, neither more nor less, was the explanation of the Agadir *coup*.

But thumping the table is a risky procedure, more likely to arouse hostility and stiffen resistance than to achieve the intended results, unless you are quite sure you have the means and the will to follow it through. For all his brave words Kiderlen had neither. When the Kaiser made it clear that he was not prepared to risk war, Kiderlen got on his high horse and threatened to resign; but he quickly climbed down. He did not mean, he lamely explained, that Germany should actually 'draw the last consequences' and fight, only that others should think it would. This was a policy of bluff and bluster. Kiderlen, it has often been said, would have achieved more by patient diplomacy; and this may well be true. The trouble was that he needed a quick, spectacular victory to appease German opinion, not the more solid but less photogenic fruits of patient diplomatic negotiation.

Furthermore, it must be said in his defence that he had waited long enough to hear what the French had to offer and still, at the end of June, had no reply. This is one of the mysteries of the situation. Sheer common sense, one would have thought, would have told the French that the sooner they stated the price they would pay for Morocco the better for them. We can only surmise why they prevaricated, but it is not altogether surprising that Kiderlen lost patience and thumped the table.

But Kiderlen also, so far as we can see, had no clear notion of what he wanted or the price he intended to exact. Did he, as the British Foreign Office suspected, intend to partition Morocco with France, with or without Spain? The answer usually given is No. But the more likely answer is that he was waiting to see what the French had to offer, and had not made up his mind. What we do know is that, as early as April, he had approached Heinrich Class, the leader of the Pan-Germans who were campaigning for the establishment of a German sphere of interest in western Morocco, urging him to launch a large-scale press campaign 'to force the pace of the empire's foreign policy'. It may be, as Kiderlen later cynically implied, that he had no intention of supporting the Pan-German demands. If so, it was a dangerous policy to unleash a vicious dog and then refuse it a bone, and Kiderlen discovered this later in the year when, to his discomfiture, it bit him in the leg. There is, in fact, no reason to think that Kiderlen was disinterested in Morocco if anything was to be had there without too many complications. But basically his policy was a typically opportunist policy of stirring up trouble and then fishing in troubled waters. Unfortunately for him, all he caught was a minnow.

July was scarcely halfway through before it became clear that Kiderlen's ambitious schemes had miscarried. Nowhere is the impasse in which he found himself better revealed than in a letter he wrote to Bethmann-Hollweg on 17 July. A German occupation of southern Morocco, he now wrote, was out of the question because 'it would bring us into direct conflict with England as well as France'; in any case, 'I do not know where we should find the resources for such an undertaking.' Therefore the only thing left was 'tough negotiation', so at least as 'to get something by way of compensation'. This was the cry of an opportunist and gambler whose gamble had not come off; and though in the event Kiderlen got 'something', it was so much less than he had led Germany to expect that the result was to compound the existing frustration and discontent.

In launching the Agadir *coup*, Kiderlen made two fundamental miscalculations. The first was to underestimate French sensitivity about Morocco. Delbrück, as we have seen, had said that Germany could get anything it wanted from France 'provided we did not cause them trouble in Morocco'. Kiderlen would have done well to heed his words. For the French, Morocco was to be the final component of the Mediterranean empire they were intent on building, the keystone of their new imperial planning, the one area where they would brook no competition; and yet here was Kiderlen striking directly at what they had come to regard as the jewel in their imperial crown. It was a bad tactical error, and even Caillaux was repelled. But an even more serious mistake was Kiderlen's misjudgement of the British response.

He did not, as we have seen, expect Great Britain to stand aside, but he certainly underestimated British reactions. The British, he told the Kaiser, 'are bound to squeal anyhow; whether they'll squeal a little louder doesn't matter.' This cynical remark was typical of the man, and as usual was wrong. In the event, it mattered a great deal. After 21 July, if not before, what had started as a not very serious Franco-German colonial dispute turned into an Anglo-German confrontation, and from this moment Agadir became a threat to peace, the potential cause of an armed conflict involving all the European powers.

The other, inevitable result of Kiderlen's tricky diplomacy was that no one, in particular the British, knew what he was up to. He could not divulge his objectives, partly because he had no specific and concrete objective to divulge, partly because an essential feature of the game of poker he was playing was to keep the cards close to his chest and not let anyone guess how weak his hand was. If he admitted that he had no intention of setting foot in southern Morocco (supposing, as he later said, that such was the case), no one would worry much about the sudden arrival of the *Panther* at Agadir and the demonstration would go off like a damp squib. Hence he had to keep quiet about his intentions, though silence inevitably bred suspicion that they were more sinister than they were. In the game he was playing, you did not put your cards on the table; if you did, you might lose a couple of tricks you would otherwise have picked up. In this respect, of course, Kiderlen was not abnormal. It was the way everyone played the game, and explains largely why the French had made no offer of compensation; but the uncertainty it fostered certainly increased the international tension.

There were other considerations. In particular, after the unhappy experience of the Algeciras conference, which had certainly given Germany far less than it had anticipated, the last thing Kiderlen wanted (or the French, for that matter) was to see Morocco hauled once again before an international tribunal. Nothing worried Kiderlen, or Selves or Caillaux, more than Grey's threat, if the worst came to the worst, to reconvene an international conference. For the French it meant that all their gains since Algeciras, particularly their gains at Casablanca and fanning out from Casablanca, would be called into question. For Kiderlen it meant that a comfortable bilateral Franco-German deal would become impossible which, of course, was exactly what Grey intended; hence his insistence that negotiations should be conducted *à deux*, between France and Germany alone. Hence, also, the deliberate ignoring of London, the long silence of which Grey complained when he told Metternich on 27 July that he had received no communication from the German government for three critical weeks, from 3 to 24 July. He might have added, if he had been less polite, that he would almost certainly have received none even then but for the shock administered in Berlin by Lloyd George's famous Mansion House speech on 21 July.

Kiderlen's gamble might have come off on one condition: speed. This, at least, was something William II understood, and though his comments, when nothing had happened by 10 July, are characteristically shrill, they are also to the point. By allowing Franco-German negotiations to drag on, he told Kiderlen, he was making it certain that other countries would put a spanner in the works. Here again Kiderlen had miscalculated. He was misled, perhaps, by the secret *pourparlers* in May and June, which gave him a false impression that the French were ready for an immediate deal. But this time his miscalculation was fatal. When, by 21 July, he had still got nowhere at all, the only expedient left to him was to get out with the least possible loss of face. 'Germany is seeking the way for retreat!', minuted an exultant Crowe on 2 August. This time he was right. Thumping the table might conceivably impress or even cow the neighbours, but all Kiderlen managed to do was to bruise his own fist.

Half a Duck's Beak
and Two Elephant Tusks

'Has anyone the face to maintain that Germany's affairs are today in a more comfortable state than they were before the arrival of this Messiah from Swabia? . . . A man who does nothing and only smiles is far less dangerous to the State than a man of conspicuous ability who stirs up trouble in the hope of gaining personal prestige.'

Maximilian Harden, in *Die Zukunft*, August 1911

The obvious conclusion, and the conclusion immediately drawn, when the *Panther* arrived off Agadir was that the Germans intended to establish a foothold in southern Morocco. Whether or not this was the case hardly matters, for Kiderlen could not disavow the possibility without destroying the credibility of his move. The French must at least believe it was possible if they were to be induced to make worthwhile concessions. This was the threat hanging over their heads, and it had to be made to look real. That was why, when Schoen was asked point-blank on 6 July whether Germany intended to establish a firm territorial foothold in Morocco he did not deny it, but simply said that it would depend on what was offered in the way of guarantees for economic opportunities and compensation.

It was not a very deep game, but it appeared to have worked. Caillaux, who was, of course, fully cognisant of the preceding secret negotiations, may not have been taken in, but the new and inexperienced French Foreign Minister, Selves, whom Caillaux had perhaps put in as a figurehead while he himself pulled the strings, took the threat seriously. So did Grey and the British Foreign Office. For Britain, the future of Morocco, with its strategic position on the Mediterranean and Atlantic coasts, had always been a sensitive issue; and it was the strategic aspect, to begin with, that exercised the Foreign Office most. Did the Germans plan to secure a foothold athwart the British line of communications along the coast of Africa? This was the point at which Kiderlen-Wächter's policy seemed, at least to the suspicious minds of Crowe and Nicolson, to tie in with Tirpitz's naval challenge. Not surprisingly Grey immediately characterized the situation created by the German move as 'very serious'.

What made it still more serious was Kiderlen's evident intention to exclude Great Britain from the negotiations. The situation in Morocco, he insisted, was purely a matter between France and Germany; and the French, Selves as well as Caillaux, all too often seemed to take a similar view. If the Germans pressed too hard, they leaned on Britain; but they had no intention, if it could possibly be avoided, of recognizing British (or anyone else's) interests in Morocco. Crowe was right when he warned Grey, on 15 July, not to place too much reliance on 'French openness'; they would, if it suited their book, 'barter away' British interests without turning a hair. That was why, when Selves announced on 8 July that he was proposing bilateral negotiations with Germany, Nicolson told the French ambassador, Paul Cambon, that 'he did not quite comprehend M. de Selves' procedure'; his impression was that Britain and France would first agree about the line they would follow with Germany and 'then address themselves together to Berlin'. It explains, of course, still more Grey's insistence from the very start that Great Britain could not be 'disinterested' in Morocco. 'We could not', he told Metternich, 'remain passive spectators.' His protest was directed to Berlin because the Anglo-French agreement of 1904 made it difficult to protest in Paris; but the warning extended equally to both sides.

The first phase of the crisis, therefore, centred on Morocco, and German and French intentions in regard to Morocco. It was bound to do so until Kiderlen made it clear, which he did on 9 July, that he was ready to barter whatever rights Germany had in Morocco (which were tenuous enough) against 'compensation' elsewhere. Even then the suspicion persisted that he intended to remain there. When, on 15 July, he demanded as compensation the whole of the French Congo, the conclusion immediately drawn was that he was setting his claims absurdly high in order to bring the negotiations to a halt and have an excuse for establishing a permanent German settlement at Agadir.

The French undoubtedly took the threat seriously. The one thing about which political circles in France were agreed was that, whatever compensations might be given to Germany, they must on no account be given in Morocco. That, as Paul Cambon said, was 'a condition *sine qua non*'. Morocco was to be an exclusive French preserve, and there is not much doubt that the scheme to bring that about had been drawn up, at least in outline, well before Agadir. Germany could be bought off with compensation elsewhere; England could be discounted because of its obligations under the 1904 agreement; and France would recoup itself for whatever it handed over to Germany by squeezing Spain and taking over the Spanish zone in northern Morocco.

This was certainly the solution Caillaux had in mind, and probably most other leading French political figures as well, including Delcassé, Cruppi, Etienne, the influential leader of the Colonial Party, and the two Cambons. It was a package that could be taken to the Chamber with every confidence that it would be greeted as a major diplomatic success. Did it not round off the French colonial empire and set the seal on the much discussed programme of reorganization and consolidation? Would it not be possible to say that France had come out of the crisis better off than before, exchanging territory of dubious value in the tropics for a secure well-rounded empire on the Mediterranean?

Unfortunately for Caillaux, the package came unstuck at two critical points. The first was the arrival of the *Panther* at Agadir and the implicit threat that Germany might demand its pound of Moroccan flesh. The second was the refusal of the British to sell out Spain. If any European power was to be on the African coast facing Gibraltar they obviously preferred that it should be Spain, rather than Germany or France. The British refusal to go along with his scheme, just when he had squared Kiderlen, was particularly galling for Caillaux. It meant that instead of going before the Chamber with the whole of Morocco in his pocket, a worthy equivalent for the 'sacrifices' made to Germany, all he had to offer (as an angry Deputy told him) was 'a Morocco decapitated and mutilated', 'a Morocco bereft of all its Mediterranean ports, but with a magnificent view of the Sahara'! No wonder that, in the end, it was on Britain, not on Germany, that Caillaux vented his rage.

*   *   *

In the first place, however, the problem was Germany. Selves' immediate reaction on 1 July was to propose that France and Britain should reply to the German move by each sending a ship to Agadir or Mogador – a suggestion Grey appears to have entertained, but not for long. When the Admiralty was consulted it reported, to the consternation of Crowe and Nicolson, and of Bertie in Paris, that it saw no serious threat to British naval interests, and at a Cabinet meeting summoned to review the situation on 4 July it was decided not only not to despatch a British warship to Agadir, but also not to oppose the German acquisition of a port on the Atlantic coast of Morocco, provided it remained unfortified. In Paris, also, there were second thoughts, helped by the fact that Selves went off with the President on a state visit to Holland, and Caillaux took over in his absence. Caillaux's first act, on 4 July, was to send a telegram to Paul Cambon in London cancelling Selves' proposal for a joint Anglo-French naval demonstration. Nothing, he realized, was more likely to disrupt his own plan which was still, as it had been all along, to settle the Morocco question by direct Franco-German negotiations. Accordingly, as soon as President Fallières returned from Holland, Jules Cambon in Berlin was instructed to stop recrimination and reopen discussions. Two days later, on 9 July, he called on Kiderlen and picked up the threads of their Kissingen conversation. One week after Agadir it was almost as though nothing had happened.

Almost, but not quite. Even at this late date, and in spite of the despatch of the *Panther*, both Caillaux and Cambon still thought that Germany could be bought off by economic concessions. Kiderlen's first objective at the interview on 9 July was to disabuse them on this score. His and Cambon's accounts of the meeting differ on a number of points. According to Cambon, it was Kiderlen who brought up the possibility of compensation for Germany in the French Congo; according to Kiderlen, it was Cambon. Cambon also maintained that all that was discussed was a 'rectification' of the frontier, whereas Kiderlen says he told Cambon he would require 'substantial concessions'. In the end the differences do not, perhaps, matter much, because Cambon agreed to put the question of the Congo before his government and seek further instructions.

The Congo was now definitely on the bargaining table. From his point of view this was certainly a success for Kiderlen; from the French point of view it was a success for Paris. France, Caillaux told Bertie, would make almost any sacrifice to keep Germany out of Morocco. Why not in the Congo, if that was what Germany wanted? Now that Germany was no longer insisting on territorial compensation in Morocco and had turned its sight on the Congo, Selves told Schoen on 12 July, agreement should be easy. Jules Cambon, perhaps patting himself on the back, also thought the outlook 'favourable'. And in London Grey's reaction was one of evident relief. There was not, he knew, the slightest chance of Britain fighting to hand Morocco over to France, nor any reason why it should. If the French and Germans could reach agreement in some area where British interests were not involved nothing would suit him better. When, on 10 July, the French ambassador asked him, on instructions from Selves, whether he had any objection to Franco-German talks about the Congo, he replied that he 'did not see how there could be any objection on our part'. Thereafter, his main object, in spite of German suspicions to the contrary, was to persuade the French to make sufficiently generous concessions to bring the crisis to an end. His role, henceforth, was to be that of honest broker. Unfortunately, neither the French nor the Germans had much confidence in his honesty.

Nevertheless, by mid-July it looked as though the crisis had been a storm in a teacup, and that an amicable solution was in sight. Kiderlen might look and act like a bull in a china shop, but so far he had broken no porcelain. But after 15 July two events occurred – or three, perhaps, if an inexplicable and irrational French obduracy is taken into account – which threw everything back into the melting-pot. This, not 1 July, was when the real crisis began – the crisis which more than once threatened war – and 15 July marks the opening of the second act in the drama. In the first act the protagonists had taken up position; the second act sees the action; and in the third act, as we so often discover to our disappointment when we go to the theatre, the action peters out, and we are left with a weak and unsatisfactory ending.

*   *   *

The second act opened with a second interview between Jules Cambon and Kiderlen on 15 July of which Kiderlen has left us a dramatic, perhaps over-dramatized, account. France, Cambon hinted, might be willing to hand over a piece of territory on the border of the French Congo and the German Cameroons. What did Kiderlen want? Kiderlen's answer was to send for a map of Africa and point to the whole of the French Congo from the River Sangha to the ocean. Cambon, according to Kiderlen's account, 'nearly fell over backwards'. The German demand was totally impossible and could only lead to the breakdown of the negotiations; France was ready to make large compensations, but could never consent to the loss of a whole colony. Nevertheless, Cambon agreed to refer Kiderlen's proposal to Paris and ask for further instructions: the door was still open.

The German demand, nevertheless, caused consternation. It was totally unexpected – as unexpected as the despatch of the *Panther* to Agadir – and everyone, even those who believed Germany had a right to compensation, agreed that it was out of all proportion. To make matters worse, the whole story was leaked to the French press and

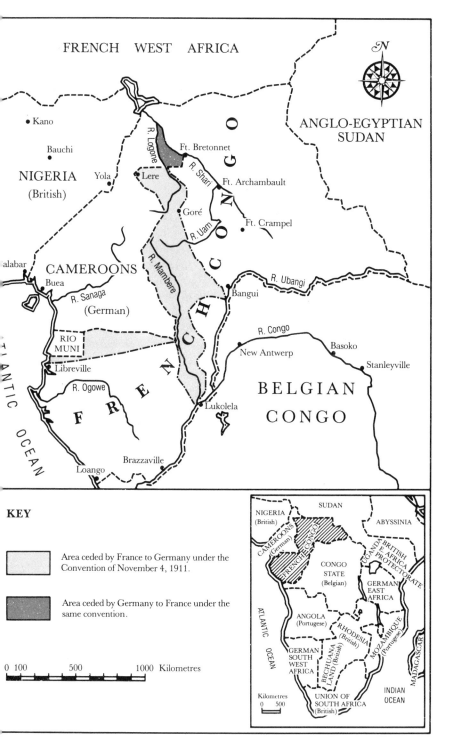

CENTRAL AFRICA AND THE CONGO

then to the London *Times*, which came out on 20 July with a thundering leading article, a detailed map of the territory claimed by Germany, and a threat that Britain would, after all, despatch a warship to Agadir. The source of *The Times*' disclosures is not known, though it may well have been a deliberate leakage by one or other of the pro-French and anti-German officials in the Foreign Office. In any case its dramatization of the situation added to the mounting sense of crisis. No one expected the French to give way and accept the German demand *in toto*; but what then?

It is also uncertain what Kiderlen had in mind. Probably, as usual, nothing definite. Bethmann-Hollweg told the Kaiser that he had asked for the whole French Congo 'in the first instance', implying that this was only a bargaining position which could be modified later. But he may have said this simply to calm William's nerves. In any case, the wildest rumours flew. The most common, much in favour in the Foreign Office in London, was that the Germans wanted to halt the negotiations before they had even begun in order (as Nicolson put it) to 'settle themselves permanently at Agadir'. Paul Cambon, who happened to be in Paris, and Bertie concocted an even wilder rumour, probably to frighten Grey and drive him into the arms of France. According to them, Kiderlen had conceived a deep-laid plot to build a great German empire stretching across central Africa from coast to coast. Once they were in possession of the French Congo, the Germans would absorb the Spanish settlement of Rio Muni lying between it and the Cameroons, then the Portuguese colonies, half promised to Germany by the British in 1898, and finally the Belgian Congo when, 'as M. Cambon considers it probably will before long', it came on the market. Then they would be poised to challenge the whole British position in South Africa – a frightening prospect, indeed!

Both rumours appealed strongly to those who like to see plots and plotters everywhere; but there happened not to be a word of truth in either. At a later stage, when he was under attack in Germany and needed to justify himself in the Kaiser's eyes, Kiderlen tried (not very successfully) to impress William II by drawing a glowing picture of a great future German African empire. He probably had his tongue in his cheek. On 15 July nothing of the sort was in his mind. Ironically, it was Grey, who was supposed to be frightened by the prospect, who picked up the hint and put (or tried to put) the Belgian Congo and the Portuguese colonies on the scales. Grey's object, once the possibility of a Franco-German deal in the Congo was broached, was to keep the negotiations going and deflect them from Morocco. This, for him, and here he was quite right, was the danger point, and the point at which Britain, owing to the obligations it had entered into in 1904, could be directly involved. The Congo was an entirely different matter. Hence his idea, which he telegraphed to Bertie on 20 July for transmission to the French government, that 'admission of Germany to a share in French pre-emption rights of Belgian Congo might be a possible element of bargain'. In this way Kiderlen might be persuaded to modify his demands. The next day he put his idea to Metternich, who relayed it to Berlin. Kiderlen was not enthusiastic: was it not, he wondered, a subtle move intended to stir up trouble between Germany and Belgium? Germany, he told Metternich, had no intention whatever of acquiring rights over the Belgian Congo. Once again, we do not know whether his disclaimer is true; but it rings true.

The other factor which is hard to explain is the attitude at this point of the French government. Why was it so adamant in its refusal to consider bartering its Congo colony? The possibility, as we have seen, had already been canvassed for a number of years. Furthermore, Kiderlen was willing to make concessions. He realized, he told Cambon, that no French government could make a unilateral surrender of territory. Though Germany would demand the lion's share, the transaction must take the form of an exchange, and he was prepared to offer the northern Cameroons, providing a corridor between the French colonies to north and south, and Togo. One of the mysteries is why the French refused even to consider this offer until too late. Togo was not a negligible quantity; its acquisition would have increased the size of the neighbouring French colony of Dahomey by half. Furthermore, it was one of the few African colonies which paid its way, whereas the resources of the French Congo, like those of the Belgian Congo, had been exhausted by merciless exploitation, and the population was restless and rebellious. Grey at least thought it would not have been a bad deal and was astonished at, and alienated by, French obduracy. 'The French', he told Bertie on 20 July, 'have drifted into difficulties without knowing which way they really want to go', and it was now up to them to 'make counter-proposals'. So far as Great Britain was concerned, it just didn't matter 'who owns tropical territory that we do not want for ourselves'. On the assumption that Germany would eventually get Portuguese Angola, which Britain had already given it by secret agreement, 'it wouldn't make any difference to us if she had the French Congo coast too'.

This was Grey's answer to the firebrands in the Foreign Office, and shows clearly enough the distance that separated London and Paris.

The French, in the view of Grey and the British Cabinet, were being unreasonable and must not expect Britain to bale them out. Nevertheless, it was soon evident that this time Kiderlen had thumped the table too hard. The worst shock, from his point of view, was the Kaiser's refusal of support, his intimation on 17 July that he would not contemplate any measures that might lead to war. Though he was almost certainly not contemplating war, this, more than anything else, took the wind out of Kiderlen's sails. The second setback was the change of attitude in Paris. In spite of Agadir, Selves had still been willing to negotiate a settlement. Now he reluctantly agreed that, in the last resort, he 'would not put aside the idea' of the British calling together an international conference. Though that could hardly help France, it might at least ditch Germany. Finally, though Grey was certainly not going to let the French drag him into an unwanted war, there is no doubt that Kiderlen's demand for the whole of the French Congo heightened British suspicions and increased British resistance. Grey had pinned his hopes of a peaceful outcome on some sort of a compromise in the Congo, and had stood aside so long as that seemed possible. Kiderlen's excessive demands seemed to have killed that hope, and the time had come for Britain to make its presence felt.

The climax came on 21 July when the British Cabinet met in Downing Street to review the situation. Grey pointed out that 'seventeen days had elapsed without any notice being taken by Germany of the British statement of our position', and asked authorization to arrange a meeting with the German ambassador. The interview with Metternich took place later the same day. It was followed the same evening by Lloyd George's speech at the Mansion House. Together, they gave a new turn to events; but it was Lloyd George's speech that brought the crisis to a head. Before 21 July there had been no real threat of war; afterwards, for six weeks, the threat was real. It was, perhaps, a warning not to conduct international negotiations publicly through after-dinner speeches over cigars and a glass of port.

*   *   *

Grey's communication to Metternich was deliberately informal and, by itself, would hardly have caused a crisis. Britain, he said, had so far stood aside in the hope that France and Germany would reach a settlement in the Congo. But if the negotiations now broke down on account of Kiderlen's excessive demands, and Morocco came back into the foreground, he wished it to be clearly understood that Great

Britain would insist on participating in any discussions and would take all necessary steps to safeguard its interests. This was little more than a reiteration of what he had said at the very beginning, and was not in itself particularly inflammatory. What, in German eyes at least, gave it a new and more sinister meaning was the fact that it was followed, almost without pause, by Lloyd George's speech at the Mansion House. Jules Cambon had complained bitterly to Kiderlen that, within days of their confidential discussion at Kissingen, Kiderlen had thumped the table by sending the *Panther* to Agadir without waiting for a reply. Kiderlen could equally reasonably complain that, within minutes of Grey and Metternich's interview, and without waiting for a reply, the British government had thumped the table by turning Lloyd George loose. If it wished to make its point of view heard, he said, it might have been expected to do so through the usual diplomatic channels. Lloyd George's speech was only comprehensible on the hypothesis that it wanted 'a violent explosion'.

The antecedents of Lloyd George's famous Mansion House speech have been much discussed and still remain enigmatic. According to Nicolson, it was 'no sudden inspiration', but 'carefully thought out'. According to Grey, 'it was entirely Lloyd George's idea', and he knew nothing about it until the afternoon of 21 July when he was suddenly told that Lloyd George wanted to see him. It certainly was a surprising step, for up to this moment Lloyd George had been a prominent advocate of understanding with Germany, and it is not altogether impossible that the explanation for his sudden change of attitude lies less in any new development in the international situation than in his own need to bolster his flagging reputation by a resounding statement that would put him back in the limelight. But the question is not very important, because what mattered, as Kiderlen told the British ambassador, was not the motive for the statement but its effect; and this, it can safely be said, was uniformly bad. Perhaps the most mysterious aspect of the question is why Grey not only sanctioned it but (so he tells us) actually welcomed it. It was an uncharacteristic error of judgement.

As befitted the occasion and his own reputation as an orator, Lloyd George's speech was a magnificent rhetorical exercise which soon had his listeners thumping applause on the table, but which, read more soberly after the event, seems a little short on substance and content. Great Britain, he said, was a great nation, which had won its place and prestige among the powers 'by centuries of heroism and achievement' and would 'at all hazards' maintain that place and prestige.

She could not be treated 'as if she were of no account in the Cabinet of Nations ... peace at that price would be a humiliation intolerable for a great country like ours to endure.'

Unfortunately, this piece of bravura reverberated round the world as though the age of radio and television had already arrived. Who, one might soberly ask (and some alarmed Liberals did soberly ask), was treating Great Britain 'as if she were of no account'? Quite clearly the speech was aimed at Germany. But, as Grey himself observed only three days later, it was 'too much' to assert that Anglo-German relations were strained 'for we have asked nothing of Germany yet, nor she of us'. Of course, he added, relations 'might at any moment become strained', and Lloyd George ensured that they would. That is the historical significance of his Mansion House speech. If we wish to find a scapegoat (but that is never a very profitable game) we shall have to say that the Welsh wizard was the architect of the crisis. But he had, of course, plenty of aiders and abetters.

The new counter Lloyd George threw on the table was prestige, and everyone hurried to pick it up. Perhaps it was there already, in a minor way, in the French refusal even to consider bartering the Congo for Togo. The main, almost the only conceivable, attraction of the Congo was sentimental, particularly a sentimental attachment to the exploits of the great French explorer, Savorgnan de Brazza. How could France possibly hand over Brazzaville or Libreville to any other power? De Brazza's widow was even dug out of decent obscurity and brought into the fray to make tearful declarations. As for Libreville it was richer, as Grey sardonically observed, in historical memories than in practical commercial advantages. But it was Lloyd George who made prestige the name of the game (as the current jargon goes); and it was concern for prestige, the most hallucinatory of all mirages, and not for anything real, that brought the crisis to boiling-point. British prestige, Britain's place among the nations, were involved, Lloyd George loudly proclaimed; it would even, he broadly hinted, go to war if necessary to ensure that they were respected. But, Kiderlen replied, were not Germany's prestige and dignity equally involved? It was a childish game, but potentially a lethal one.

The results were seen immediately. Germany, Metternich was instructed to tell Grey, had no designs on Morocco; not a man had been landed, and there was no intention of landing any. Could he, Grey asked, announce this in Parliament and calm an over-agitated public? Metternich had to consult Kiderlen, and the answer was No. If Germany permitted a public announcement it would look as though it had bowed to Lloyd George's threats. 'The German government', Kiderlen told the British ambassador on 25 July, 'could not let the belief arise that, in consequence of the speech, they had made a declaration of intentions about Morocco.' After Lloyd George's speech, it was not 'consistent with our dignity to give explanations'. But 1911 is not the only year in history in which an international crisis has erupted from a house of cards, built of nothing more solid than dignity, prestige and national self-esteem.

The effect of Lloyd George's speech was also to toughen France's attitude to Germany and the German attitude to France. The French press immediately announced that the most that Germany would be offered was 2–3000 square kilometres of useless equatorial forest, and on 24 July Jules Cambon in Berlin was instructed – to his great discomfiture – to tell Kiderlen that his demands were exorbitant, and no French government would entertain them. The German answer was only too easy to foresee. When Metternich saw Grey on 25 July it was obvious that the fat was in the fire. It was a stormy interview. Not only did Metternich assert, not without reason, that Lloyd George's speech was provocative. He also stated that, if France repelled the hand proffered by Germany, 'German dignity as a great power would make it necessary to secure by all means, and if necessary alone, full respect by France for German treaty rights.' This was not far short of an ultimatum, and was interpreted by Grey in that sense. It looked as though war was in the offing.

Grey's reaction was predictable. The very same day he wrote to McKenna, First Lord of the Admiralty, alerting him of the possibility that 'the fleet might be attacked at any moment', and warning orders were immediately sent out. It was the first rumour of war. In fact, it was a scare rumour. There is not a scrap of evidence that the Germans had hostile action in mind; but Metternich's protests and Grey's reaction are the clearest evidence of the atmosphere of recrimination, suspicion, tension and crisis Lloyd George's speech had called forth.

*   *   *

There were at least two further occasions when war seemed on the cards, but on a longer-term view the rest of the story can only be called an anti-climax, for now two new factors impinged, both of which went far to shape the outcome.

The first was that Caillaux, seeing his longstanding schemes for a Franco-German *rapprochement* falling apart, decided to take a hand.

According to Lancken, the sinister back-room figure in the German embassy in Paris, he was under pressure from shady French financial circles, which seem to have had the means of twisting his arm; and this, from all we know of Caillaux, is likely enough. What part, if any, he had played between 7 and 25 July we do not know; but on that day, presumably alarmed by the fumbling of Selves and the Quai d'Orsay and their tough instructions to Jules Cambon in Berlin, he decided to open negotiations secretly behind their backs and sent his contact-man, Fondère, to get into touch with Lancken. His object, about which he made no secret, was to offer Kiderlen better terms than the Quai d'Orsay, its courage bolstered by Lloyd George's bluster, was ready to concede.

On the other side Kiderlen also was under pressure. The Kaiser arrived back from his summer cruise at the end of July, and Bethmann and Kiderlen went to see him at Swinemünde on 29 July. We do not know exactly what took place at the meeting, but there is no doubt about the change in Kiderlen's posture following it. Up to this point he had been blustering, intransigent and threatening. 'It seemed impossible to satisfy the Germans,' Selves told Bertie, and it looked as though negotiations had reached a dead-end. Selves once again played with the idea of sending French and British warships to Agadir. In that event, the Germans replied, they would mobilize two army corps in Alsace-Lorraine. The atmosphere in Berlin, Goschen told Grey on 27 July, was 'highly electrical'. But then came Kiderlen's interview with William II and an immediate change of tone. Kiderlen, Goschen now reported, was 'palpably ill at ease'; he was 'talking "big" to cover up his errors and miscalculations'. When Jules Cambon called on him on 1 August and notified him of 'what France could offer', his answer, to everyone's astonishment, was that 'the French proposals formed an acceptable basis for discussion'. Three days later he was even more explicit; he was ready now, he said, to throw over his demand for the whole of the Congo, and negotiate on the basis that only part would be ceded to Germany.

An important factor in bringing about this change of attitude was the arrival in Berlin, apparently on 28 July, of the news of Caillaux's secret feelers. The knowledge that Caillaux was intriguing behind his Foreign Minister's back and was determined to reach a settlement at almost any price undoubtedly convinced Kiderlen that he had only to be tough to get nine-tenths of what he wanted. Caillaux was the ace – or perhaps more correctly the knave – hidden up his sleeve. Unfortunately for Kiderlen his calculations went wrong. Almost immediately the correspondence detailing the secret talks with Lancken was deciphered by the French Foreign Office, Caillaux was compromised, and to save his own skin he had to take a stronger line than he had ever intended. That explains why the negotiations dragged on so long and ended so unsatisfactorily.

Nevertheless, Kiderlen's decision to negotiate evidently marked a decisive and irreversible retreat. In Germany it was greeted by the nationalist press with howls of indignation and wild talk of 'humiliation', 'unspeakable shame' and 'national ignominy'. If Kiderlen's idea had been to restore the tottering prestige of the government through a brilliant success in foreign policy, it was obvious from this moment that he had achieved the opposite. All that was now left was to haggle about frontiers, but whether Kiderlen got more or less did not really matter because whatever he got would not be enough.

In spite of the alarms which punctuated it, the rest of the story is, therefore, not very interesting. France, it was clear, was going to make concessions. At this distance of time, it is hard to be concerned whether or not it received the strip of territory in the northern Cameroons somewhat ludicrously called the Duck's Beak (the *Bec du Canard*) as some sort of compensation. People in Paris and Berlin fought over obscure areas of tropical Africa, about which they knew nothing and cared less, provided only that the maps French schoolchildren and German schoolchildren were forced to study were painted the right colour; and even Grey, the most insular of insular Britons, whose vision of the world scarcely extended beyond the trout streams at Falloden, sat in the Foreign Office when he might have been fishing, pondering whether Ubangi-Shari was, or was not, a vital British interest. Seventy years later the whole altercation seems ludicrous – and was ludicrous – until we realize that the same thing is going on in Foreign Offices and State Departments across the world today. That is why it is still worth while to cast our eyes back to the shadowy Edwardian figures – 'amiable incompetents', a contemporary called them who knew them well – who fumbled and bungled in 1911. They may look a little old-fashioned in their stiff, starched collars and frock-coats; but unfortunately their mental processes are not old-fashioned at all.

*   *   *

It would be absurd and tedious to follow the subsequent negotiations detail by detail and step by step from 1 August to 4 November, when the Franco-German convention was finally signed. Those who wish can trace the proposals and counter-proposals on the map, but even after locating the Sangha, Ubanghi, Ogowe, Logune and Alima and following their course, they are unlikely to be much wiser than before. Exact claims meant little in a region much of which was virtually unexplored and unknown. But they represented broader aims, and these, so far as they can be rationalized, can be summed up as follows: on the German side, to get as much of the coastline as possible and access to the River Congo; on the French side to prevent the Congo colony from being split into two, to retain access to the ocean, and to maintain communications between French West Africa and French Equatorial Africa. But it would be a mistake to think that either French or German calculations were governed by reason. The real issues were prestige and *amour propre*, so much so that, as late as 30 October, settlement was held up by the question whether the village of Djegando, on the borders of Togo and Dahomey, should be coloured French or German on the map. Unlikely though it seems, it was at this point that Selves, not otherwise the most adamant of men, decided to dig in his heels. No one, it hardly need be added, consulted the native inhabitants; and no one, apparently, thought it odd that peace or war in Europe should depend on the fate of Djegando.

No one seriously intended war, but there was plenty of provocation. From the start things went badly, and got worse rather than better, largely as a result of Selves' instructions to the French ambassador in Berlin on 4 August 'to negotiate with a view to restricting as much as possible the territory to be conceded to Germany'. He also sought to reopen the question of Togo, which he had rejected when Kiderlen had offered it in July. These manœuvres may have been natural; whether they were sensible is another question. Kiderlen had, after all, backed down; it might have been wiser to meet him half way, particularly as both Selves and Caillaux had already made up their minds to accept the two main German demands, namely, the coast north of Libreville and a band of territory connecting the Cameroons with the River Congo.

The situation was not helped, either, when Caillaux announced, almost as soon as negotiations had begun, that if they were not completed within a week, he would send a French warship to Agadir. This astonishing threat, probably explained by his discomfiture when his underhand intrigues with Lancken were detected, was received by Schoen with the contempt it deserved, but in Berlin it raised a hurricane. Kiderlen not surprisingly replied that he would not negotiate under threat, and Caillaux climbed down and pretended that he had been misunderstood. But the harm had been done. The French conjured up, without a scrap of evidence, the idea that the Germans were about to land troops at Agadir, and seem to have half persuaded Grey. If that happened they would do likewise, and that would mean war. In the middle of August Metternich, the German ambassador in London, told J.A. Spender, the well known editor of *The Westminster Gazette*, that he thought war was probable before the week was out. This also was probably bluff. But, rightly or wrongly, the threat was taken seriously in London and the Committee of Imperial Defence was called together on 23 August to decide what steps to take if Britain were drawn in. The military had already acted. A month earlier, the fire-eating Director of Military Operations, Sir Henry Wilson, had gone off to Paris on his own initiative and without authorization, and there had signed an agreement with the French for the deployment of a British expeditionary force in case of war. It was all very well for Grey to say that Wilson's action did not bind the government. Technically, it may even have been true; but for the military Agadir was a grand rehearsal of plans which were to take effect three years later.

* * *

By the end of August it looked like deadlock. When Schoen saw Selves and Caillaux on 25 August, and told them that Germany refused to modify its demands any further, they accused him of issuing an ultimatum. This was certainly an exaggeration, but it indicated how heated by now the atmosphere had become. Kiderlen complained repeatedly of French bad faith. They reduced offers they had previously made, he told Goschen, and at the same time asked for more in return. He had, in fact, good grounds for complaint, but the result was only to make him more obdurate. On 17 August he advised Schoen that, unless the French stuck to the terms Caillaux had offered through his secret emissary, a rupture of negotiations would be unavoidable. Then, tired and depressed, he set off for a vacation with Marina de Jonina in Switzerland, no doubt hoping that a few days in her company would give him new heart. Before he left he suggested to Jules Cambon, with heavy Swabian jocularity, that they should meet again at the beginning of September and 'decide whether it shall be peace or war'.

To begin with it looked like war. The September war scare was the most serious and at the same time the least explicable of all. The ostensible reason was that Kiderlen suddenly decided to reopen the Morocco question. Why he chose to do this at this time it is impossible to say; probably he simply wished to show that if the French could be difficult and obstructive so could he. It was a typical and not very clever manoeuvre. But behind it lay, in all probability, the prevailing war neurosis. Both in France and Germany, Sir Victor Corbett told Grey, war was being spoken of as a regrettable but unavoidable contingency. Grey himself certainly took the possibility seriously. So did President Taft who decided, on 11 September, that the time had come to offer his mediation. 'Before war comes (if it does come)', Grey wrote in a despatch to Bertie in Paris, and once again he warned the Admiralty on 17 September to be on the alert, and also asked the British ambassador in St Petersburg to ascertain what military preparations the Russians had made 'in the event of hostilities breaking out'. The Germans, he told Nicolson, 'may act very quickly – even suddenly'. There is no evidence that they had anything of the sort in mind. On the contrary, Kiderlen abandoned his Moroccan hare on 16 September as abruptly as he had started it. The Moroccan half of the conflict was quickly disposed of, and on 11 October Kiderlen and Cambon initialled a draft convention. But the Congo still remained. Was it worth a war?

At this stage Paris was fighting simply for some face-saving formula. It wanted somehow to make it appear that what was at issue was an exchange of territory, not a one-sided French surrender. Hence its insistence on some German *quid pro quo* in Togo. They did not, Selves told Schoen, expect any serious concession, just a petty frontier rectification to salve French *amour propre*. Kiderlen brusquely swept this pretension aside. At the same time there was mounting impatience with French intransigence. The Germans, Grey wrote, had conceded France 'a clean bargain in Morocco'. Why did Selves and Caillaux continue to haggle over the exact boundary between the French Congo and the German Cameroons? It was, he said, 'sheer unreason' to make 'the difference between peace and war depend upon the Wesso-Alima triangle'.

Grey's view was widely shared. From St Petersburg the Russians urged, more diplomatically, that France had more to gain than lose by approaching the final stage of negotiations in a conciliatory spirit. From Berlin Goschen wrote to Grey that he had always been a firm supporter of the Anglo-French entente, but he could not, for the life of him, see why British lives and money should be sacrificed 'in the interests of a few French financiers and people who are so shortsighted that they cannot see the handsome way in which their bread has been buttered in Morocco'. Even Jules Cambon lost all patience with his own government. It was, he told Goschen, 'idiotic to hesitate about making a really big sacrifice in the Congo' to get a free hand in Morocco, and begged him to urge Grey to put pressure on Caillaux and Selves to see reason.

But Caillaux and Selves remained unmoved. They may genuinely have believed that they had no chance of persuading the Chamber to accept further concessions; and they may have been right. By the beginning of October feeling in Paris was dangerously high, and Schoen warned Kiderlen that the government might fall and be succeeded by one far less conciliatory if he pressed too hard. But in the end it was Jules Cambon who broke the deadlock. He did so without instructions and on his own initiative after four days of apparently hopeless negotiations, during which (he said) he and Kiderlen stood nose to nose and there appeared to be no means of reconciling their views. Finally he took a pencil, sketched a few lines on the map and indicated how Germany could be given a strip of territory reaching to the Ubanghi and the Congo. It was scarcely more than a token concession, but it was the gesture Kiderlen had been waiting for. He immediately submitted the proposal to Bethmann-Hollweg, who gave his assent the same day, while Cambon telegraphed to Selves.

All this happened on 18 October, and by 20 October the decks were cleared. Both sides evidently wanted nothing more than to bring the confrontation to a close if it could be done without loss of face. Once Cambon discovered the right formula the rest was easy. By 22 October everything was settled except the question of the 'Duck's Beak', and that did not take long. On 4 November the Franco-German agreements on the Congo and Morocco were signed, and Caillaux turned his attention to the more congenial task of seeing what he could wring out of Spain.

*   *   *

The crisis was over; or was it just beginning? The disturbing thought for all who had been involved was that, far from satisfying their constituents, the solution that had been worked out left no one satisfied. This applied to Caillaux, to Kiderlen-Wächter, and even to Grey. In many ways, the aftermath of the Agadir crisis was more ominous than the crisis itself. But that is characteristic of any crisis on an international scale. You extricate yourself from one predicament by illusory, short-term solutions, only to get into another which is far more intractable.

Caillaux's problem we have already seen. What was the good for France of a Morocco shorn of its Mediterranean ports? Who wanted more desiccated Saharan desert, full of hostile Berber tribesmen? When, on top of this, it came out – as it did quite soon – that he had been intriguing secretly with the Germans behind the back of his Foreign Minister, Caillaux's fate was sealed. If he had brought off the major *coup* he had planned everyone except the socialists would have applauded. Instead, all he produced from his bag was half a duck's beak in exchange for two elephant tusks, as a Deputy mockingly observed. In the end the Franco-German treaty was passed by the Chamber – it had to all practical intents no alternative – but 141 Deputies showed their real opinion by abstaining from voting.

The position of Kiderlen-Wächter – though, unlike Caillaux, he weathered the storm – was in many respects even worse. The resignation of Lindequist, the Colonial Secretary, on 3 November was, in effect, a vote of no confidence, and was interpreted as such. It was not only that the territorial gains on the map – some 250,000 square kilometres of largely useless territory – were derisory by comparison with the prospects Kiderlen had held out; but who, with the Herrero and Nama risings fresh in their memories, could want any more tropical African territories? Not surprisingly, when the Franco-German agreement was debated in the Reichstag on 9 and 10 November there was far more criticism than applause. As the Kaiser observed a few months later, what could Germany expect to gain from an empire in central Africa 'with its population of Negroes so deprived of cultural and technical needs, and lacking the means to buy our industry's products?' Africans today, no doubt, would indignantly reject this racialist verdict, but William's point is clear: Kiderlen had not made a good bargain.

Grey's difficulties were different, but were scarcely less serious. There had always been a powerful element in the Liberal Party and in the Liberal Cabinet which questioned the Foreign Office's attachment to France and to the entente with France. They were not anti-French, but they were also unwilling to concede that an understanding with France precluded an understanding with Germany. They had already made their weight felt at the beginning of 1911, well before the Agadir crisis began, when they succeeded in getting a Cabinet Committee on Foreign Affairs set up to keep a watch over the Foreign Office. When they learnt of the secret negotiations between the British and French General Staffs and of the meeting of the Committee of Imperial Defence on 23 August, from which they were quite deliberately excluded, their indignation boiled over. Arthur Ponsonby and Noel Buxton launched a 'Grey Must Go' campaign, and the Foreign Office debate in the House of Commons, which took place on 27 November, was a stormy affair.

Grey and the Foreign Office, Liberals complained, had led the country to the verge of war in a cause in which no essential British interests were involved. Because he had won over Winston Churchill and Lloyd George, hitherto his most insistent critics, Grey rode out the storm. But here also was evidence, if evidence was needed, that the Agadir crisis had not abated with the signature of the Franco-German accords on 4 November. Far more important, however, were the storm clouds gathering on the international sky. When Italy invaded Tripoli on 29 September it was only too clear that the end of one chapter meant the beginning of another. The great mistake was to suppose that you can wipe the slate clean. In international politics there are no clean slates.

II

'The Policy of the Stiletto'

'This is not the time or occasion for a Quixotic crusade on our part on behalf of a conglomeration of noble bandits struggling to remain free.'
Sir Eyre Crowe, 29 May 1914

The Tripoli war belongs to the aftermath of Agadir rather than to Agadir itself, and as such we can treat it summarily. But the aftermath is too important to be ignored, because it started a chain reaction which could not be halted. The powers might congratulate themselves that they had wriggled out of the Agadir crisis without war and that the system of balance of power had proved its value once again. And it is true that Morocco ceased, after 1911, to be a bone of imperialist contention. But the repercussions of the crisis remained; like a stone hurled into a pond, it sent ripples through the international system which, whipped up by winds from outside, gathered strength until in 1914 they swept the old order aside.

According to the rules of the imperial game Italy had every reason to act. It had come out the loser in the contest with France over Tunis, and the fact was not forgotten. If France was now going to swallow Morocco as well it could not stand idly by. England had been compensated and Germany was being compensated in the Congo. Italy also must have compensation, and since the only part of North Africa not controlled by England and France was Libya, compensation could only be found there. In spite of much rhetoric by Corradini and his like about Italy's civilizing mission and the heritage of Rome, the Italian calculation was as simple as that. 'Our prestige and national dignity were in danger,' the Italian prime minister declared. This was the authentic language of imperialism.

The Italian attack on Tripoli was a direct sequel to the French march on Fez; the one called forth the other. Italy's Libyan ambitions were, of course, no secret. As we have seen, it had cleared the deck many years earlier with France in 1900, and with England two years later. Germany and Austria were committed to support by the terms of the Triple Alliance, and a similar deal had been made with Russia in 1909. But the problem, as always, was timing, the knack of finding the right moment to cash the post-dated cheques. This was where the Agadir crisis was decisive. First, it convinced the Italian Prime Minister, Giolitti, and the Foreign Minister, San Giuliano, that they had no time to lose if they wanted to get into the game before the fate of North Africa was decided; it was now or – probably – never. Secondly, it provided the golden opportunity for which Italy had been waiting. If Italy acted while the other powers were preoccupied with Morocco and the possibility of war between France and Germany, it had a good chance of getting away with murder (which it was) without interference. He did not think there would be difficulties with the French as long as the Moroccan trouble lasted, San Giuliano said, but afterwards they might not 'care to see Italy established near to the French colonies in northern Africa'. Hence the need for speed.

San Giuliano was a Sicilian, and he and Giolitti, like true Sicilians, wasted no time in drawing their stilettos. 'The diplomatic situation', Giolitti explained, 'counselled us to hurry matters on.' On 26 September an ultimatum was despatched to Turkey. Taking a leaf out of the French book, it urged the necessity of putting an end to 'the state of disorder and abandonment into which Tripoli and Cyrenaica had sunk'. Taking a leaf out of the German book, it complained of the 'imminent peril' of Italian citizens. These were the stock excuses of imperialism and they led to the stock conclusion. 'To safeguard the country's dignity and interests', Italy had decided to occupy Tripoli and Cyrenaica by military force, 'since there was no choice of action left.' Three days later war began, and on 4 November Italian sovereignty over Libya was proclaimed. Since the conquest of Libya and Cyrenaica was not completed until the days of Mussolini this was a blatant fiction. But it was necessary, Giolitti asserted, 'for fear of an intervention of the allied and friendly powers'; they must be brought 'face to face with a *fait accompli*'.

*   *   *

It would be pointless to follow this sordid story in all its detail. It was an act of flagrant aggression. The phrase 'the policy of the stiletto' was coined by a Polish journalist, but everywhere the Italian action was denounced as unprincipled and immoral, and the protests grew in volume when the Italians, halted by stubborn Turkish and Arab resistance, began a policy of indiscriminate terrorism. In Germany speakers in the Reichstag described the Italian attack as 'an act of piracy', forcing Kiderlen-Wächter to protest against the use of such language about an allied government. At Westminster also the outcry was loud, and Grey had to appeal for what, characteristically, he called 'a decent neutrality'.

There is no doubt, nevertheless, that even statesmen were alienated, one and all, by the Italian action. From the point of view of morality it was not, perhaps, much worse than the French attack on the independence of Morocco. But there was one fundamental difference: Morocco was an independent state, whereas Libya and Cyrenaica were integral parts of the Ottoman Empire. The danger, which everyone foresaw, was that an attack on the integrity of the Ottoman Empire in one place would lead to an attack on its integrity in another, in Europe as well as in Africa, and that the whole ramshackle structure would come toppling down with consequences no one could foretell. And precisely that was what happened. As Italy fought its not very successful campaign in Tripoli, all the discontented minorities in the Turkish dominions in Europe sharpened their swords, preparing to take advantage of the moment, now visibly approaching, when they could shake free from Ottoman rule. From the point of view of the public, what rankled was the brutality and immorality of the Italian aggression; from the point of view of governments, not greatly concerned about questions of morality, it was the fact that the Italians had opened up a hornets' nest and they might all get stung. As Grey put it, in a characteristic understatement, the Italian action was 'very embarrassing'; they had, he said, been 'very foolish in putting out their foot so far in this Tripoli business'.

Grey's irritation and misgivings were widely shared. After the war scares of August and September there was a general disposition to draw back from the brink. The British Cabinet, appalled at the impasse into which the Foreign Office had so nearly landed it, was pressing for an Anglo-German *rapprochement*, and Grey himself seems to have been genuinely willing to go along. Bethmann also, if only for domestic reasons, was in a conciliatory mood. The dogs of war, it seemed, were settling down again and going to sleep, and no one wanted to disturb them. That was why the Italian action, with its unpredictable consequences, was everywhere regarded as unwelcome and inopportune. When the news of the Italian ultimatum reached the Kaiser, peacefully enjoying a late summer holiday in his hunting-lodge at Rominten, the result was consternation and a fateful prediction: 'Fall of the Turkish ministry, revolution in Constantinople, massacre of foreigners, unrest in Albania, Bulgarians, Serbs, Greeks and Cretans taking advantage of Turkey's misfortune, the Dardanelles question reopened, a British occupation of Arabia, the lighting of a world conflagration with all its horrors.'

William II's imagination was always vivid, but on this occasion events were to prove that he was not far wrong, down to and including the British occupation of Arabia, which occurred in fact, if not in name, in 1919. Other reactions were less excited, but distinctly cool. Aehrenthal in Vienna and Kiderlen-Wächter in Berlin warned the Italians of the 'grave responsibility' they were incurring. All pointed out the risk of the conflagration spreading. Isvolsky, the former Russian Foreign Minister, knew at first hand the danger. 'Be careful', he told the Italian ambassador in Paris, 'not to find yourself suddenly faced with the break up of Turkey and the necessity of a European intervention in the Balkans.' Only the French, happy to find another bandit joining them in the robber-band, were 'cordial'; but even they soon changed their tune.

There is little doubt that the powers, if their hands had been free, would have intervened to bring the Italians to a halt; and in fact, in late October, when the Italian expeditionary force seemed hopelessly bogged down in Tripoli, a feeble effort was made to end the war by collective action. The trouble was that the powers' hands were not free. They were tied not so much by their commitments to Italy, which they could perfectly well ignore if it suited their purposes, as by calculations of self-interest. True, there were voices in all countries – Kitchener in Britain, for example, and Marschall von Bieberstein in Germany – arguing that more was to be gained by supporting Turkey; but, though Italy was only a minor piece on the international chessboard, no one wished to lose it. This was a fact of which Giolitti was well aware, and he was not slow to use it, blackmailing Germany with threats of deserting the Triple Alliance, and Britain with a warning that any country which opposed him 'would inevitably forfeit the friendship of the Italian people'. Objectively these threats had little substance, and the sensible course would have been to call the 'sturdy beggars'' bluff. But surprisingly they worked. The Austrians, who correctly suspected Italian ambitions at their expense in the Adriatic, were brought to heel by Berlin. In London, Grey, still obsessed with the supposed German threat, laid down on 19 September that it was 'most important that neither we nor France should side against Italy now'. Though the war, as usual with Italy, had no shadow of excuse, no government protested against it, and none, certainly, showed the least sympathy for the unfortunate Tripolitanians. This was no time, as Crowe subsequently observed, to worry about the fate of 'noble bandits struggling to remain free'.

The calculation, spelled out particularly clearly by Grey but operative also in the other capitals, was that the best way to get the unhappy incident over was to do nothing. Any sign of sympathy for the Turks might encourage them to fight, and so lengthen the war. Hence Grey's policy of neutrality and non-intervention, which, as usual, favoured (and was meant to favour) the aggressor. When the Turks appealed to Britain Grey referred them to Germany and Austria; when they appealed to Germany, Kiderlen referred them to Great Britain and France; and Selves in Paris contributed his mite by vetoing the flotation of a Turkish loan. If only the Turks could be made to see sense and wash their hands of North Africa all might still be well. So long as the war was confined to Africa it might be possible to avoid the European complications which had made Agadir so dangerous.

Unfortunately, the powers calculated without the bungling incompetence of the Italian generals, to say nothing of the reluctance of the Italian peasant conscripts to lay down their lives for a cause which, whatever Giolitti might say to the contrary, was anything but popular with the Italian working class. When a brilliant agitator named Benito Mussolini organized a general strike in Forli as a protest against the war towards the end of 1911, Giolitti decided that the time had come for more decisive action. Things were not going well in Africa. Operations must be stepped up and extended. The Turks were still shipping arms and ammunition to Libya; and since it was impossible to patrol the whole coast they must be stopped at source. On 24 February 1912 – setting a precedent for Israel seventy years later – Italian battleships bombarded Beirut. In April operations were extended to the Aegean, and in May Italy occupied the Dodecanese, both moves preparatory to an attack on the Dardanelles, and the Turks in reply closed the Straits, until forced by Russian threats to reopen them. When even these measures failed to intimidate the Turks, Giolitti went further, threatening in August to carry the war into Arabia, Asia Minor and Albania, where the Ottoman government was already faced by a serious insurrection and demands for autonomy. Shortly afterwards he instructed San Giuliano to inform the powers that Italy intended to extend the war to 'the most vital parts of the Ottoman empire' and preparations were actually made for an attack on European Turkey.

By now the fat was in the fire. Italy, Giolitti wrote, 'had been obliged for inevitable reasons to disturb the peace of Europe.' We may wonder about the inevitability, but for once he was speaking something near the truth. The idea, which all the powers had entertained in the closing months of 1911, that the Italian war could be rendered harmless by being confined to Africa was always illusory, a product of desperation rather than reason. Instead, it was the first act of a new drama which was to be played out in the Balkans.

As early as October 1911, within days of the Italian aggression, negotiations were under way for a Serbian-Bulgarian alliance, and though ostensibly it was defensive, everyone knew that in reality it was directed against Turkey. The agreement was signed on 13 March 1912; Greece joined the alliance in May, and Montenegro in September. The wolves were gathering for the kill. By now any pretence had been dropped; the pact with Montenegro required it to begin hostilities against Turkey not later than 20 September. As usual it was not ready, but on 8 October, the very day on which the powers, by now thoroughly alarmed, presented a joint note warning the Balkan states that no change in the *status quo* would be permitted, Montenegro declared war. Within ten days it was joined by Serbia, Bulgaria and Greece, and by November every Turkish army in Europe had been defeated. A by-product was the decision of the Ottoman government to conclude peace with Italy, which it did on 15 October; but this, an incidental consequence of the Balkan war, was no longer important. By now all eyes were on Europe. Apart from Constantinople and a narrow strip of territory along the Straits – and even this looked for a moment as though it might fall to the Bulgarians – the Turkish position in Europe had been destroyed beyond repair. This, not Libya, was what mattered. After 1912 the demise of Turkey in Europe was the dominant fact in the international scene.

*　　*　　*

In retrospect there is something almost pathetic about the endeavours of the powers to cope with the consequences of the Italian action. No one wanted war. Not even the Russians, supposed traditionally to be lying in wait, ready to pounce and lay hands on Constantinople, sought to profit from the Turkish misfortune. It is sometimes said that the consequence of Agadir was a new belligerency. The government of Poincaré, which succeeded Caillaux's bankrupt and discredited administration in France in January 1912, has often been described as the beginning of the much celebrated *réveil national*. That may be true, but the evidence is not very convincing. No doubt, there was everywhere, in France as well as in Italy and Germany, a vociferous nationalist fringe of intellectuals and semi-intellectuals, whom historians looking back can, if they so wish, portray as the precursors of post-war Fascism. But it would be a mistake to identify Daudet and Maurras with France, or Corradini and d'Annunzio with Italy. In Italy, where Mussolini rose to prominence as the anti-war leader, railway lines were obstructed and stations attacked to prevent the passage of troop-trains. In France, as Isvolsky reported to his government in December 1912, the pacifism of the provincial bourgeoisie, the very backbone of the Republic, was still a powerful factor, and nothing is more remarkable than the return to favour of the arch-collaborator, Caillaux, with his programme of Franco-German collaboration still intact. At the beginning of 1912 Caillaux's name was mud: a year later his star was rising again, the premiership apparently within his grasp, and it was probably only the scandal caused by his wife's assassination of the editor of *Figaro* that prevented his comeback. Even so, the basic pacifism of the country was demonstrated by the resounding left-wing victory in the elections of April 1914. Ironically, it was the most pacific Chamber the country had ever known that led France into war in 1914.

The strong pacifist current in Europe following the Agadir crisis is shown also by the great Social Democrat victory in the German elections in January 1912, and by the lively Radical attacks on Grey's conduct of foreign affairs in England. How far they affected the policies of statesmen and chancelleries, it is difficult to say. Nevertheless, there is no doubt, whatever the reason may have been, that they approached the new situation with dismay and alarm. There were, of course, everywhere hotheads for whom the Italian war and the Balkan complications were an opportunity to pursue supposed national interests. Isvolsky, the Russian ambassador in Paris, and Tcharykov, the ambassador in Constantinople, hatched wild schemes to bring the Straits under Russian control. They were promptly sat upon by the Foreign Minister, Sazonov, whose sole wish was to preserve the *status quo*. In Vienna, the irrepressible Chief of Staff, Conrad von Hötzendorf, urged a preventive war against Italy while its troops were bogged down in Tripoli. He was promptly dismissed, but unfortunately restored to office in December 1912 with disastrous consequences in 1914. But Conrad and his like were the odd men out in 1911 and 1912. A quarter of a century earlier everyone had been talking about the dissolution of the Ottoman Empire. Now, paradoxically, it had become the lynchpin of European peace, and no one was ready to pull the lynchpin out. No doubt, if any country had felt sure of profiting from the consequent confusion it might have acted, but the Balkan conflagration had caught them unprepared. Earlier crises had been provoked and manipulated by one or other of the powers. This was a spontaneous outburst and the only thing they could think of was to organize a voluntary fire brigade and damp down the flames.

The result was a last, tardy recrudescence of the old idea of a Concert of the great powers, working together to impose peace on the lesser fry of Europe. 'Do not let us fall into two groups over these Balkan questions,' Grey entreated Bethmann-Hollweg in the spring of 1912. 'Let us keep in close touch with one another.' Surprisingly, it worked. Once it became clear that there was no hope of putting Humpty-Dumpty together again, which was what all powers would have preferred, all they could do was to try to regulate the new situation and prevent it from getting out of hand. By the beginning of December 1912, when the Balkan states and Turkey signed an armistice, it was obvious that the territorial *status quo* had been permanently shattered. The only question now was how far the belligerents should be allowed to settle their own affairs. The answer was: wherever the overriding interests of the great powers were not involved. They could not undo the results of the Balkan war, but they could at least ensure that they did not lead to complications between the powers, particularly between Austria and Russia, the two powers most directly involved in Balkan politics. With this in view Great Britain and Germany took the initiative in summoning a conference of the six leading powers to meet in London. The opening session took place on 17 December 1912, and the meetings – more than sixty in all – continued until August 1913.

This is not the place to follow in detail the history of the Balkan complications of 1912 and 1913, or even the various measures of the powers to cope with the situation. Suffice it to say that the London conference was remarkably successful in its immediate objectives. There had been genuine fear that the Balkan explosion would lead to a conflict between the great powers. Instead it passed off with a minimum of friction. Particularly encouraging was the co-operation of Britain and Germany, which seemed to herald a new era in Anglo-German relations and a relaxation of tension between the Triple Entente and the Triple Alliance. The main problem was the ambition of Serbia for an outlet on the Adriatic, anathema both to Austria and to Italy, the main fear that Russia might feel compelled to support the Serbs. Both Austria and Russia were held back by their allies. 'I shall not march against Paris and Moscow for the sake of Albania and Durazzo,' William II told the Austrians; and the question was settled by the creation of an independent Albania. Once again, it seemed, the international system had been vindicated; it had nipped the crisis in the bud. But the reality was more mundane. It was not the pressure of their allies, still less the labours of the London conference, that held Austria and Russia back, but the tacit agreement of both that Durazzo was not worth a war. The London conference was useful for working out the detail of the settlement and drawing lines on the map; but the vital decisions were taken elsewhere. More seriously, it could not impose its mandate on the Balkan states. When, in the middle of its labours, the thieves quarrelled among themselves about the spoils and the second Balkan war broke out, with Bulgaria on one side and Serbia, Greece and Romania on the other, it sat helplessly by, a mere onlooker waiting for the fighting to end. When it did end the Balkan states settled their affairs among themselves. This is perhaps the most significant fact of all. The Treaty of Bucarest, signed on 10 August 1913, was not submitted to the great powers for approval, still less, as the Austrians demanded, for revision. It was a clear intimation that their tutelage of the Balkans was at an end.

* * *

Giolitti always protested against critics of his policy who maintained that the Italian attack on Tripoli was the first link in the chain of events leading to the First World War. At first sight the success of the London conference in coping with the Balkan upheaval and preventing it from spreading seems to prove him right. Even granting that the Italian action had sparked off the Balkan conflagration, was it not a fact that the fire had been contained before it burned down the whole building? But this argument is more plausible than convincing. There was, indeed, no war between the great powers in 1913. But the London conference had not brought peace to the Balkans, only postponed the problems. It may be true that Turkish rule in Europe would not have survived for long in any event. The signal for its collapse had perhaps already been given when Austria annexed Bosnia and Herzegovina in 1908. But it was Giolitti who set the time-bomb going, and to that extent he was responsible for starting a chain reaction which in the end passed out of control.

The first evidence that the situation was out of control was the second Balkan war, beginning on 29 June 1913, which took place under the noses of the powers who were totally unable to prevent or even to halt it. Its most significant result was the further aggrandisement of Serbia, which emerged from the conflict with its territory increased from 18 to 33 thousand square miles and its population from 3 to $4\frac{1}{2}$ million. From the point of view of Austria-Hungary the outcome was an unmitigated disaster, and Austrian statesmen cast about desperately for some way out. They had reluctantly accepted the results of the first Balkan war, at the same time insisting that they would allow no new Serbian aggrandisement. Now that it had happened, what should they do? Launch a preventive war, or come to terms with the new situation and seek some form of peaceful co-operation with Serbia, as the Germans urged? But could the ramshackle Habsburg Empire, with its shaky finances, stand a war, even a successful war? And was the alternative really practicable? For one thing the Serbs, though they had been forced to back down in 1909, regarded Bosnia-Herzegovina as their rightful heritage, and refused to accept the Austrian annexation as final. In their eyes, it was the Alsace-Lorraine of the Balkans. Secondly, there was the problem of the Slav peoples within the Habsburg dominions who looked increasingly to Belgrade to free them from the German and Magyar yoke. By the time of the Balkan wars sedition was rife in all the Slavonic parts of the Austro-Hungarian Empire.

'The year 1913', a well-informed observer wrote at the time, 'was the year of revolutionary organization in Bosnia.' Actually, organization had begun two years earlier when the amorphous and not very effective nationalist movement 'Young Bosnia' was displaced by a new secret revolutionary organization, 'Union or Death' – the organization better known as 'The Black Hand' which planned and executed the assassination of Franz Ferdinand at Sarajevo in 1914. This was in 1911 – in this way as in others a year of fateful decisions – but there is no doubt that the Serbian victory in the Balkan wars gave added impetus to the revolutionary activity in Bosnia and Croatia. It also spread to other parts of the Habsburg dominions. Movements for autonomy were already on foot in Bohemia and Galicia, and in Bucarest an agitation was started for the liberation of the Romanians in Hungary from Magyar domination. By 1913 most people were convinced that the collapse of Austria-Hungary was near at hand, and in Germany they had even begun to wonder 'whether it really pays us to bind ourselves so tightly to this phantasm of a state which is cracking in every direction'.

These facts alone are enough to show how illusory it was to suppose that the crisis unleashed by the Italian attack on the Ottoman Empire had been overcome. They are not the only ones. Most ominous of all was the arms race which now began in earnest. In 1911 Tirpitz had used the Agadir crisis to press for a larger fleet, and on 22 March 1912 the new Navy Law was promulgated. It was his last triumph. Once the assault on the Ottoman Empire was launched, with its threat of a continental war, the emphasis of German military planning switched from the navy to the army. In March 1913 a new Army Bill was introduced, financed by a capital levy of over £50 million to meet the 'non-recurring expenditure required by this scheme'. Its alleged cause was the 'extraordinary vitality' shown by the Balkan states in their war with Turkey, and it added 20 per cent to the peace strength of the German army and a fighting strength in the event of war of 5 million men under arms. Inevitably it was followed by parallel increases. The French, who had no extra manpower to draw on, raised the period of military service from two to three years, the Russians from three to three and a half, and even Austria-Hungary, in spite of the strain on its resources, added another 30,000 men to its peace strength in October 1913. In this way, step by step, the balance of military power was unbalanced, rebalanced and unbalanced again, and military circles, aware that the effort could not be repeated for ever, began feverishly calculating the exact moment at which they would enjoy a comparative advantage.

It was not only the military who thought that war was inevitable. In London, the Foreign Office based all its calculations on the assumption of a coming Franco-German conflict, and King George v, talking to the Austrian ambassador at the very moment when Giolitti launched his attack on Tripoli, said that the situation would inevitably lead to war between the Triple Alliance and the Triple Entente, unless the present grouping of the powers were changed. Much has been made of the atmosphere of peace and tranquillity at the end of 1913 and the beginning of 1914. At no time since he had been at the Foreign Office, Sir Arthur Nicolson said, had he seen 'such calm waters'. But the calm was illusory. After the Balkan pot had been brought to the boil the waters continued to sizzle and bubble. Within months of the signature of the Treaty of Bucarest, Turkey and Bulgaria, the victims of the Balkan wars, concluded a military alliance to reverse their verdict. With the relaxation of naval rivalry, relations between Germany and Britain showed a marked improvement, and Grey began to think of reconciliation and agreement on the basis of colonial concessions in Africa and Persia. But this also was an illusion. Once the Italian action had shifted the focus to Europe, colonies took a back seat. Germany did not refuse to talk – why should it? – but its attention was concentrated on the Balkans, Austria and Russia. Colonial adventures were all very well in 1911; by 1914 they had become a diversion with scant bearing on the central issue.

*　　*　　*

From Morocco to the Balkans and the murder of Franz Ferdinand at Sarajevo may seem a long journey; and so it was. But the path, even if indirect, was unmistakably marked out. Adagir, we are sometimes told, was not the prelude to the First World War, except in the purely formal sense that it preceded it chronologically. To some extent this may be true. But the consequences of the events of 1911 cannot be shrugged off as though nothing had happened. The one that is always emphasized is the strengthening of the ties between France and England and therefore the hardening of the division between the rival alliances. The crisis is also said to have produced a stiffening of public opinion and a demand for a tougher policy in all the countries involved. But the really important consequence was the incentive the Morocco crisis gave to Italy. Public opinion was not by any means as bellicose as is sometimes alleged. Britain still retained its freedom of action, and was careful to the very end to steer clear of a binding alliance with France. But Italy, when it invaded Tripoli, lit a fuse which could not be put out and which ignited the inflammatory material already piled up in the Balkans. After 29 September 1911 there was no hope of closing the Agadir ledger.

The Italian action may have been unwelcome, but it should have been no surprise to the ministers and diplomats who spent their lives following the operation of the international system. Nothing was more unlikely than that the Italians would allow themselves to be by-passed in the African scramble. The sequence from Fez to Tripoli was not accidental, and neither thereafter was the sequence from Tripoli to the Aegean and the Balkans. The powers, had they been so minded, could easily have broken the sequence and brought the Italian aggression to a halt. What prevented them from doing so was the grinding logic of the alliance system, and once it was in operation there was no stopping it. Though they were all painfully aware of the dangers, neither Britain, Germany nor France would interfere for fear of losing Italian friendship; and later it was the same with Serbia and Bulgaria and Romania. 'What then is to be done?', asked Grey as he looked round at a Europe arming to the hilt. And his despairing answer was: 'I can see very little to be done.' Within the parameters of the system he was right.

In the colonial world there was still scope for manoeuvre, particularly when bargains and compromises could be struck at the expense of luckless Asians or Africans. That was why the Agadir crisis passed without war except between France and Morocco. Colonial conflicts could be localized, and the day of reckoning postponed. But when the scene of conflict moved to Europe, as it did after the Italian intervention, it was different. Even here, some sort of attempt was made at the London conference to localize the conflict; but given the way the international system was organized, with its intricate network of clients and hangers-on, localization was impossible. That is the difference between 1911 and 1914. But the difference should not be allowed to obscure the connection between the two. If France had not gone to Fez, would Italy have gone to Tripoli? And if Italy had not gone to Tripoli, would the Balkan League have fallen on Turkey? No doubt the disintegrating process which brought the calamity of 1914 can be traced further back, even perhaps as far back as the previous century; but if we wish to pinpoint the opening of the decisive phase, no date stands out more clearly than 1911. After that only a miracle could have staved off the catastrophe; and diplomacy does not deal in miracles. Not in 1911, and not in 1981 either. That is why, after seventy years and much which has impressed itself more dramatically on our memories, Agadir is not dead history.

12

'Pushing Things to a Head'

'The Moors have lost their independence and their country. But, if it be any satisfaction to them, they have their revenge. For the legacy of international ill-will to which their treatment gave rise, must count as one of the most powerful of the originating causes of a war which finds Britain and Germany at one another's throats.'

E.D. Morel, *Morocco and Armageddon* (1915)

When Agadir, Morocco and the whole course of events during the previous summer were debated in the German Reichstag on 9 November 1911, the veteran Social Democrat, August Bebel, warned the German ruling class that it was 'pushing things to a head'. With every repetition of the policy of bluff and bluster catastrophe came closer; sooner or later one side or the other would call a halt, and then the tocsin would sound in Europe. Sixteen to eighteen million men, the flower of the nations, would march against each other into battle. 'It will come', he warned, 'it has only been postponed. It is not our fault that it will come, it is your fault – you are pushing things to a head.'

This was Bebel's last major speech on foreign policy – he died in 1913, and was spared the unhappy experience of seeing how right he was. But it was not only the German ruling class and its vociferous supporters who were pushing things to a head. If the story we have followed has any lesson, it is that the ruling classes everywhere – the new Machiavellians in the seats of power – were all implicated. 'You are all guilty – everyone!' the angry British Radical, E.D. Morel, declared after the carnage of 1914 had begun. Kiderlen-Wächter may have been a little cruder, a little more blatant; but Nicolson and Crowe, even Sir Edward Grey, were not innocent either, still less Giolitti, or Monis and Cruppi, the French ministers who seem to have fathered the Moroccan adventure. They were all playing the same game, oblivious apparently of the fact that politics is not a game and that human beings, black, white or brown, are not pawns to be pushed around on an international chessboard. But at the end of the account the important fact for us is that the same game is being played today, according to the same rules and with every prospect of ending in the same disastrous way. To that aspect we must now turn. It is what gives the story of Agadir its peculiar relevance.

*   *   *

Historical analogies, we are told, are dangerous and often deceptive. They are also necessary if we are going to learn anything from the past before it is too late. But they must be drawn with care. It would be absurd to expect an exact repetition, event by event, year by year, person by person. Because the First World War occurred three years after Agadir, it did not follow that the Third World War would follow three years after the upheaval of 1979 in Iran. It might be amusing to look around the contemporary scene for a modern Kiderlen-Wächter, and it would not be too difficult to find one; but it would tell us little worth knowing. If we wish to establish any useful parallel, we must look deeper – not at the surface, but below the surface. The real comparison is between two systems in the throes of incipient crisis, and the story is the story of their increasingly desperate efforts to find a way out.

This was the German dilemma when Bethmann-Hollweg was brought in as Chancellor in 1909 and when Bethmann summoned Kiderlen-Wächter back from Bucarest as Foreign Secretary in 1910. Anything was better than drift and stagnation. The election of President Reagan in 1980 was a similar response to a similar predicament. In the German case, as we know, the switch from Bülow to Bethmann was no panacea. Is there any reason to think that the switch from Carter to Reagan will fare better? Bethmann-Hollweg was genuinely anxious to clean up the mess left behind by Bülow. But what can any statesman do when the world he is pledged to uphold is falling apart around his ears?

Different men meet a crisis in different ways. After a period of bluster under Bülow, Bethmann hoped to do better with a policy of moderation and conciliation. After a period of wavering and hesitancy, Reagan evidently decided that the time has come for a policy of forcefulness. These are differences of style and method. They do not alter the fact that Bülow and Bethmann, and Carter and Reagan also, were operating within the iron framework of a social system whose constraints they could not, and did not want to escape. It left a small margin of freedom to press in one direction or another; but in the end it was the system – that is to say, the closely-woven network of prevailing interests – that shaped their actions.

That is why, in a time of crisis, it is always a useful exercise to look back at earlier crises of a similar dimension, and examine their similarities and differences. When we look back to 1911, what do we see? First of all, the similarities between the situation then and the situation now are unmistakable. No doubt, we should take care not to press them too far; but we cannot afford to ignore them. Naturally, the protagon-ists have changed. Then they were Great Britain and Germany; now they are the United States and the Soviet Union. The scene of conflict also has shifted. Then it was North Africa; now it is the Persian Gulf (though Persia was also a major bone of imperialist contention in 1911). But these are the sorts of mutation we should expect. They do not alter the fact that the underlying pattern is strikingly similar. The system which operated in 1911 is still intact in all essentials. The game of politics is played according to the same rules. Imperialism, though it may have changed it colours, has lost none of its force. And western society is suffering today from tensions and discontents even more severe than those European society was experiencing in 1911. These are the essential similarities; and it is on them, rather than the inci-dental differences, that we should concentrate. They are what is going to matter in the next few years.

$$* \quad * \quad *$$

Let us look first at some of the more obvious points of comparison, beginning with the immediate origins of the crisis. Its most obvious feature, then and now, is that it is an imperialist crisis, its parameters defined by imperialist assumptions and attitudes. It began, in the spring of 1911 and in the latter half of 1978, with the revolt of a sorely tried people against the extortion and oppression of a ruler who, in their eyes at least, was little better than the agent of an alien imperial-ism. What turned it into an international crisis was outside interven-tion. The despatch of the *Panther* to Agadir was a prime example of 'gunboat diplomacy'. When the United States moved a carrier task force of the Seventh Fleet from the Philippines to the Indian Ocean and the Persian Gulf in the last week of 1978, commentators every-where immediately described it as a revival of gunboat diplomacy, with all the ominous possibilities that implied; and the revival of gunboat diplomacy – greatly intensified twelve months later – drove home the analogy with 1911. It also meant, in both cases, that the conflict could not be localized.

The parallels, it is true, are not exact. In the first place, the positions of Mulay Hafid in Morocco and of Mohammed Riza Pahlevi in Persia are not identical. The former, as we have seen, had come to power in 1907 as leader of the Moroccan nationalist opposition to France, and had fought hard for independence before he was broken to the French yoke. The Shah, on the other hand, had been driven out by the

Persian nationalists in 1953 and only recovered his throne with American assistance. For the next quarter of a century he ruled as an American puppet, the 'policeman' (it has been said) of American interests in the Persian Gulf. In 1911, the French were still piecing together their empire; in 1979 the United States was defending an empire which had been in existence for thirty years. And finally the analogy between the despatch of the *Panther* to Agadir and the despatch of the Seventh Fleet to the Persian Gulf should not be pressed too far. Both Germany and the United States were, indeed, serving notice that their interests could not be ignored; but the motives and calculations behind their actions were very different. Kiderlen-Wächter was fishing in troubled waters, deliberately stirring up trouble, in the hope of getting something for Germany out of it. The aim of Carter's National Security Adviser, Brzezinski, was to calm the troubled waters, fearing that they might start a flood which would overrun the American foothold in the Middle East and wash it away.

But if the motives and calculations behind German policy in 1911 and American policy in 1979 were different, the consequences were strikingly similar. In the long run, this is the important fact. Neither the Agadir incident nor the despatch of an American armada to Persian waters led to war; but they certainly caused a sudden heightening of international tension. Rumours of war were rife in the late summer and autumn of 1911; they were rife also in the early months of 1979. And they were accompanied in both cases by financial panic, the traditional concomitant of war scares: the run on the banks in Germany in September 1911 and the flight to gold in February 1979, when it shot up almost overnight to the (then) giddy height of $254 an ounce. (A year later, when the second act of the drama unfolded, it shot up to the even giddier height of $850 an ounce, amid predictions that the price would soon top the $1000 mark.) At the same time, as markets were 'gripped by a war psychosis', the whole currency sector was 'in disarray'.

More significant, in the long run, is the fact that talk of war did not die down even after the immediate crisis had passed. It might have been thought, in 1911, that tension would have relaxed after the signature of the Franco-German agreement over Morocco and the Congo on 4 November. On the contrary, it was then that talk of war, and of the inevitability of war, became endemic. In December 1911 Isvolsky, the former Russian Foreign Minister, who, after the fiasco of his Balkan policy in 1908 and 1909, had wisely retired to the less demanding sanctuary of the Russian embassy in Paris, sent a long report on the Agadir crisis to the Foreign Ministry in St Petersburg. The crisis, he said, had indeed blown over, but he was not 'optimistic'. It had left the international situation worse than before, and it would only need another incident to cause a general conflagration; even with God's help, the best that could be hoped for was that the inevitable conflict might be postponed. Meanwhile in London, Winston Churchill, now First Lord of the Admiralty, was speaking uninhibitedly of 'the coming European war'. So, as we know, were his opposite numbers in Berlin. It is probably no different in Washington and Moscow today.

Whether he realized it or not, Isvolsky was proclaiming the bankruptcy of the existing system. A system that can only survive with God's unpredictable help, is no system at all. But, committed to the world in which he had been brought up, he had nothing to put in its place; and none of his contemporaries had either. All that was left to them was to stumble into the abyss, which dimly but helplessly they saw opening before their feet. In the Foreign Office in London Crowe and his colleagues had smelt German intrigues and manoeuvres everywhere during the summer of 1911, and had bent all their efforts to thwarting them. It was not unlike the sudden discovery by Reagan and Secretary of State Haig at the beginning of 1981 that the Russians were fomenting civil war in El Salvador, and anywhere else within their reach. It does not appear to have crossed their minds, in either case, that a policy postulated, as theirs was, on mutual suspicion was bound to result in an explosion. Instead all they could think of was the need to prepare for it, not how it could be avoided.

Isvolsky ended his report to St Petersburg with an exhortation to re-arm. In Britain, Churchill told his audience that the only threat to peace was having too few armaments, not too many. 'If you want peace, prepare for war:' two thousand years of history had disproved the old Roman axiom, but for those in the seats of power in 1911 it was the quintessence of political wisdom. Seventy years later it still is. Between 1910 and 1914 military expenditure rose by approximately 30 per cent in Great Britain, 50 per cent in Russia, 70 per cent in Germany and 85 per cent in France. In the United States it already accounted for one-quarter of the federal budget in 1981. If President Reagan's proposals to increase it from $162 billion to $250 billion by 1984 are implemented it will account for almost one-third. But that is only a start. By 1986, if Reagan is re-elected, the bill will be a cool $343 billion. This, as Lester Thurow has pointed out, implies a build-up three times as large as that which occurred during the Vietnam war, but now in a time of so-called peace.

The arms build-up after Agadir reflected a growing fatalism about the prospects. Granted the inherited attitudes and presuppositions of the ruling classes it is easy to understand. By then the French march on Fez had already been followed by the Italian invasion of Tripoli. What would be next in the chain reaction? In 1979 the sequel was slower to come; but it came nevertheless. The reasons for the Soviet invasion of Afghanistan at the end of 1979 are still a matter of dispute; there is no Russian Giolitti to tell us the brutal truth, but it is safe to say that the American presence in the Persian Gulf, the possibility that the United States would intervene in Iran, and the ferment stirred in the Moslem world by the Iranian revolution, were important factors behind the Russian move. This was in the hallowed tradition of imperialism where, if one party advances a pawn in one direction, the other party counters by advancing a pawn on an adjoining square. The Soviet Union evidently is as versed in the rules of the imperialist game as the capitalist powers. Like the United States, it was defending its sphere of interests, just as Italy was doing, or claimed to be doing, in 1911.

What was also obvious in 1979 was that the dislocation of the *status quo* would produce exactly the sorts of complication that were seen in 1912 and 1913. As long as Iran had the United States behind it, it could assert a sort of hegemonial position in the Middle East. When the 1979 revolution changed all this, the Iranian position crumbled. The United States, unable or unwilling to learn from its experience in Iran, switched its support to Saudi Arabia, the last (but decidedly precarious) bastion of Arab reaction. Iraq, the primary victim of the American-Iranian alliance, picked up its courage and decided that the opportunity had come to recover the territories it had surrendered to Iran in 1975. Once again there is perhaps no exact parallel with the Serbian-Bulgarian attack on the Ottoman Empire in 1912; but the analogy is close enough to be significant. It is often said that the Middle East will be the Balkans of the 1980s. The suggestion is not farfetched. Once the artificial balance created by the imperialists crumbles – and it is obviously crumbling – we are confronted there by a region every bit as turbulent and uncontrollable as the Balkans proved to be in 1912 and 1913.

The Iraqi-Iranian war seemed to have brought things to a head. With American and Soviet warships and aircraft-carriers massed in the narrow waters of the Persian Gulf and the Strait of Hormuz, it looked in September 1980 as though the Third World War was near. In fact, it was a false alarm. Both Carter and Brezhnev drew back from the brink, deciding that intervention in the conflict was too great a risk. But it would be a mistake to draw comfort from that.. It was exactly what Russia and Austria-Hungary had done in 1912 and 1913, but it did not prevent the escalation of the Balkan conflagration in 1914. The political leadership could still impose caution, but it could not prevent the eruption of a bellicose, jingoistic nationalism. The immediate reaction in the United States to the revolution in Iran was the notorious Easton meeting of the Republican Party leaders in February 1979 with its strident nationalist appeal. It was the same in 1911 in Germany and in France. Carter resisted it at first, much as Bethmann-Hollweg resisted it in Germany. But in 1980, an election year, he gave way to what was clearly the popular mood. It did him no good, because he could always be overtrumped by more strident rivals. Reagan's election in 1980 parallels closely the election of the conservative, right-wing nationalist, Raymond Poincaré, as First Minister of France in 1912, and then as President in 1913. It was the beginning of a *réveil national*, in the American case of a deliberate rejection of the post-Vietnam mentality, and with it, more ominous still, a resurgence of the arms race. 'Cannons, not butter', proclaimed *Business Week*, and *Newsweek* came out with a headline: 'An End to the Slogan "No More Vietnams"!' It was uncomfortably reminiscent of the language of the Pan-Germans at the end of 1911.

There were people everywhere, in 1912 and 1913, just as there were in 1981, who urged that lack of weapons, not weapons, was the only threat to peace, early exponents of the theory of the balance of terror. As we have seen, Winston Churchill was among them. There were also, as there are today, exponents of the 'pre-emptive bid', or, as *The New York Times* more circumspectly phrased it in 1980, the 'strategy of getting there first'. That, as we all know, was the strategy of the German Chief of Staff, General Helmuth von Moltke, in 1914. Today, on a comparative timescale, we have not reached our 1914, and maybe the exponents of the theory of the balance of terror may prove right this time. But what, in the era of the neutron bomb which is looming up, if they do not? No one looking back to 1911 could say that the precedents are encouraging; which is the reason why it is worthwhile to take another final look at the Agadir crisis and sum it up, not for what it signified for people then, but for what it signifies for us now.

* * *

The first thing to say is that the outcome was not inevitable then, and it is not inevitable now. There was no intrinsic reason why a colonial dispute in and over Morocco should have led to a murderous internecine struggle in which Europe devoured and destroyed itself. The chain of events could have been broken. The important fact is that it wasn't. And the important question is: why wasn't it? Because this is also the question we are facing today.

There were plenty of people in 1911 who foresaw only too clearly the direction in which things were moving. They included Bebel and the German socialists, and Jaurès and the French socialists. Because Europe was full of explosive tensions, Jaurès warned, any local conflict would mushroom into 'the most terrible holocaust since the Thirty Years' War'. But it was not only the socialists, easily dismissed (as they are today) as doctrinaire outsiders, who uttered warnings. There was also a growing phalanx of Radical dissidents – the people whom Eyre Crowe and his like called 'faddists', 'pacifists' and 'meddlesome busybodies' – and they were probably as numerous and certainly as vociferous in their denunciations of secret diplomacy, the balance of power, international finance, armament manufacturers, imperialism, the arms race, and the exploitation of backward peoples as their counterparts today. In England they included E. D. Morel, famous for his campaign against atrocities in the Belgian Congo, Wilfred Scawen Blunt, the inveterate opponent of British policy in Egypt, C. P. Scott of *The Manchester Guardian*, and H. W. Massingham of *The Nation*, and they had their counterparts and correspondents spread out over the length and breadth of Europe.

Agadir was the catalyst that stung them into action. Morel's pamphlet, *Morocco in Diplomacy*, published early in 1912, traced step by step the whole sordid imperialist entanglement, and its success is a clear indication of the extent of public concern. It is worth remembering that 1911 was not only the year of Agadir; it was also the year of the First Universal Races Congress and of the first (rather muted) Conference on Disarmament. Pacificism and anti-militarism were strong among the working classes in all the major European countries; military budgets, which workers knew very well cut into their standard of living, were under fire everywhere. The jingoism which surged up in the wake of Agadir was essentially a middle-class phenomenon. That is one contrast with today, and not an encouraging one. Today blue-collar workers are probably the most strident nationalists; and President Reagan and Prime Minister Thatcher, who quickly perceived the swing away from détente, are busy cashing in on it with their abrasive anti-Soviet rhetoric. It does not seem to have crossed their minds that they may be playing with fire.

It was different in 1911. Bethmann-Hollweg was genuinely alarmed by the upsurge in Pan-German agitation. The British and the Russians, allies of France, were anything but happy when they realized that the French had decided to embark on the conquest of Morocco. But more important is the evidence of their growing disenchantment with the system of checks and balances as a whole. Of this Isvolsky is the crown witness. According to the rules which diplomats and politicians had picked up at the university from a desultory reading of Talleyrand's *Memoirs*, the balance of power was supposed to ensure equilibrium and therefore peace. This was the essence of 'the game of politics' they were playing – a phrase, incidentally, which betrays only too cruelly their adolescent mentality – but by the end of 1911, it was evident that the game was not obeying the rules. A sort of equilibrium had been achieved; but peace, as Isvolsky observed, was farther away, dependent now on any chance incident. This, perhaps, was the most significant point. When those who operate a system no longer believe in its efficacy, when they realize that checks and balances and compensations are no assurance of peace and stability, the end is near. The wonder, looking back to 1911, is that it was postponed until 1914.

It is sometimes said that a major difference between the situation in 1911 and the situation today is the change in our attitude to war. Not simply that before 1914 war was regarded as a legitimate instrument of policy, for who in his right mind would maintain that the same is not true today? Rather that we, living precariously under the shadow of the A-bomb, the H-bomb, and now the neutron bomb, are acutely aware of the consequences and they were not. We expect a universal Hiroshima; misled by the analogies of 1866 and 1870, they expected a short and 'happy' war, a war which would make things better, not worse. In reality, nothing could be further from the truth. It may have been the mood in the immediate excitement of August 1914, when a chance photograph has caught a picture of Hitler happy and cheering in the gesticulating crowd on the Odeonsplatz in Munich. But before the guns went off (and afterwards in the case of Bethmann-Hollweg), the mood of statesmen was sombre and disillusioned. Anyone who thinks they went into war in a mood of happy confidence is wide of the mark. Necessity might leave them no alternative. But is that not exactly the plea we heard from Carter in 1980 and are hearing from Reagan today?

No responsible statesman, in the first place, expected a short war. That, unfortunately, is not the case today. The doctrine of nuclear deterrence which ruled from the mid-1950s to the mid-1970s – the doctrine that nuclear weapons exist not to be used but, rather like Tirpitz's fleet, to make it too risky for the other party to attack – is out of fashion. In 1913 the argument was that Germany needed stronger armaments 'to secure peace and the benefits of peace'. By 1914, even before the Sarajevo crisis, a German journalist reported, 'no one any longer took so negative an attitude'. War, a Foreign Office spokesman told him, was no longer 'unthinkable'. The assumption behind military thinking today, as set out in Carter's Presidential Directive 59 in July 1980 and re-affirmed by President Reagan, is much the same. Weapons exist to be used, and, given technological superiority, a nuclear war, which will necessarily be a short war, is a 'winnable' war.

This is a return to the position of Helmuth von Moltke, who said, in August 1911 at the height of the Agadir crisis, that if Germany did not fight, he would resign and 'move to abolish the army and place ourselves under a Japanese protectorate'. Moltke did not get his way in 1911, and did not resign either. But within three years the position had changed, the political leadership had capitulated, and Moltke prevailed. The Schlieffen Plan went into effect; German troops were hurled against Luxemburg and Belgium in a pre-emptive bid to encircle France; and the First World War had begun.

*　　*　　*

This evolution occurred in a span of three years despite the fact that none of the leading statesmen thought that the consequences would be less than disastrous for the world they held so dear. Bethmann echoed Jaurès' analogy with the Thirty Years' War, and declared that war 'would strengthen Social Democracy immeasurably' and 'cause the overthrow of many a throne'. In St Petersburg, Sazonov gloomily foresaw the collapse of 'the established religious, moral and social order'. And in London the position of Grey was no different. 'The industrial workers would rebel,' said Grey; 'the monarchic principle would be swept away'; and war would generate 'revolutionary movements like those of the year 1848'.

And yet war came. The voices against it were powerful and permeated every rank of society. Why, in the end, were they so ineffective?

We may dismiss, first of all, the socialist challenge. Precisely because it came from the socialist camp, it was not listened to by those in authority. But why did the dissident Radicals, who had access to the seats of power (in Britain not a few were Members of Parliament), make so little impact? One reason, without doubt, is that their targets were not popular. Anti-imperialism was never a popular cause. At a time when the workers' standard of living was under attack people were far more concerned with the situation at home. But it was also due to the failure of the Radicals to go to the root of the problem; and here it is impossible to overlook the parallel with today. The British Radicals, including Morel, attacked secret diplomacy, as though open diplomacy would solve all the problems. Others placed the blame on Grey and his supposed subordination to the influence of the permanent staff of the Foreign Office, suggesting that someone else would have produced a more acceptable alternative policy, not unlike those who voted for Reagan in place of Carter in the expectation of a quick and decisive change. Their remedies, as the great French historian Elie Halévy said, were little better than pills to cure an earthquake.

When we look back on the Radical opposition and its quick collapse, the most striking fact – and presumably the explanation – is the confusion between symptoms and causes. For Morel the source of all the trouble was the Anglo-French agreement of 1904, the 'secret bargain' by which Britain sought to consolidate its hold over Egypt by handing over Morocco to France. 'From 1904', Morel later wrote, 'European policy hatched war as a hen hatches chickens.' But why stop in 1904? For Blunt, the decisive date was 1882, the year of the British intervention in Egypt. But 1882 also is an arbitrary date, one episode, though admittedly an important one, in the history of imperialism; and imperialism – not this episode or that episode in the history of imperialism, Egypt, Morocco, Tripoli, or Persia and China, which also loomed large in 1911 – was the enemy. It still is.

The problem for the statesmen, politicians and diplomats was different. In 1912, Blunt – by now an old man, 'weary' (he said) 'of the useless struggle' – told Winston Churchill that the British government could easily have halted the Italian attack on Tripoli if it had wanted to by ordering the fleet to the Mediterranean. True, replied Churchill; 'but we could not afford to make for ourselves yet another enemy in Italy'. Whether this assertion of naked self-interest really paid off, when the chain reaction started by the Italian assault on the Ottoman Empire resulted – as it surely did – in the European war of 1914, is a question Churchill never seems to have addressed. He was simply following the rules of the game as he understood them. According to Crowe, who had set himself up as an authority on the subject many years earlier, the balance of power, and the system of alliances that went with it, was an immutable 'law of nature'. It was nothing of the sort, but it was certainly an irremovable obsession in the minds of diplomats and foreign offices, the measure by which they judged any happening in any part of the world, no matter how remote and inconsequential, and distorted it out of all proportion. To protect its interests in India, England was, or claimed to be, compelled to intervene in Uganda; in the end it was even arguing, unbelievably, that the same imperative required it to exercise control of the Caucasus. We have only to look around the world today, to El Salvador, Afghanistan or Zaïre, to see that the argument has not changed – nor the distortion either.

Tripoli was only one example of the way the shibboleth of balance of power worked, and still works. It was the same in Persia and in Morocco. Persia, *The Nation* proclaimed, had been sacrificed to 'that foul idol, the Balance of Power'; its partition was the price paid to the Russians to keep them loyal to the Triple Entente. As for Morocco, the Irish nationalist, Dillon, denounced British acquiescence in the march on Fez as 'the dirtiest bit of business an English government has ever been guilty of'. The trouble was that Grey and the Foreign Office, for all their misgivings, dared not give vent to them for fear of destroying the entente with France; they were locked into the system. The Russians were in the same boat. Isvolsky, to his credit, more than once hinted to the French Foreign Minister, Cruppi, that he was stirring up a sea of trouble; but, ensnared in the alliance system, he could only drop hints which were not taken. It is uncomfortably reminiscent of the German Chancellor Helmut Schmidt and Carter in 1980, or, indeed, of Schmidt and Reagan in 1981 and 1982. The Federal Republic and other European countries (except, apparently, for the Thatcher government in the United Kingdom) are as uneasy about American policy and its consequences as Great Britain and Russia were about French policy in 1911; but, constrained by the false logic of the balance of power, they can do nothing about it. That, needless to say, is the way conflict is generated.

It will be said – indeed, it has often been said, and is still being said – that the stakes today are of a quite different dimension from the stakes in 1911. Imperialism then was, in Schumpeter's much quoted phrase, 'the objectless disposition to unlimited forcible expansion'. No overriding economic need drove France to intervene in Morocco, or Italy in Tripoli. Today it is different. Oil is a life-and-death question for the West. Any country, the Soviet Union or a revolutionary Arab state, which is in a position to cut off supplies will have a stranglehold over the industrial world. This was the argument of Carter and Brzezinski for creating a Rapid Deployment Force, now estimated at

200,000 men, and for building up the American presence in the Middle East in October 1980; it is still the argument of Reagan and Haig. But though the circumstances may be different, the argument is not new. In 1911, when industry was powered by coal, it was not a question of oil; but competition for the raw materials without which industry cannot function, and determination to secure them – if necessary by military action – was just as powerful a motive for imperialist expansion.

This was the underlying theme of the pamphlet *Westmarokko deutsch!*, which the Pan-German leader Heinrich Class published in 1911 – a pamphlet which found an avid readership among the German middle-class public. According to Class, German heavy industry – the industry upon which Germany's whole future depended – was threatened with strangulation owing to the drying-up of its supplies of iron ore. In 1871, its own production had been sufficient for its needs; by 1890 one-quarter had to be met by imports; and in 1911 its import requirements were approximately half. Morocco was essential to provide an alternative source of supply, particularly as Germany was falling into dangerous dependence on French supplies. It was the same sort of fantasy as Reagan's fears of the threat to the western alliance if western Europe becomes dependent on Russian supplies of natural gas.

These are the stock arguments of imperialism at all times. The only difference is that they are more strident today. In advancing them, it never entered Class's mind to consider the wishes and interests of the Moroccan people. The overriding imperative was the needs, or alleged needs, of the industrial world, just as today the interests of European and American industry – to say nothing of those of Aramco, Gulf Oil and British Petroleum (the former Anglo-Persian Oil Company) – take precedence over those of Saudi Arabians, Kuwaitis and Iranians. In this respect Class was speaking for his generation, just as Reagan is speaking for his. Economic exigencies overrode national boundaries, particularly the boundaries of poor and weak peoples. By 1911 even Hobson, whose blistering attack on imperialism in 1902 provided ammunition for Lenin's famous anti-imperialist tract of 1916, was arguing that no people had a vested right in the world's wealth. It was 'the inheritance of all men', and if they couldn't or wouldn't develop it, 'those who can best use it' were entitled to do so.

It was a plausible argument, and it has lost none of its force from that day to this. American imperialism went into eclipse after Vietnam, just as British imperialism went into eclipse after the Boer War of 1899–1902. But it did not take long, in either case, to come out again into the full light of day. What German industrialists were saying about iron ore in 1911, American and European industrialists were saying about oil after the Arab oil embargo of 1973. America's need, like Europe's need two generations earlier, was too pressing, its appetite too voracious, to stand on niceties. As early as 1975 Kissinger was threatening the Arab oil-producing countries with the use of 'military force'. In 1979 and 1980 the Carter administration repeated the threat. 'If the flow of the vital source of energy to the economies of Western Europe and the Far East is interrupted or placed under the control of an adversary power', Brzezinski announced on 20 September 1980, 'there will have taken place a fundamental tipping of the balance of global power.' The implication was that the United States would go to war, if necessary, to prevent this from happening.

*   *   *

The risk of a world conflagration arises not so much when a state deliberately provokes a general war – that is hardly ever the case – as when the great powers' willingness to compromise and find peaceful solutions has been eroded by a growing sense of crisis and the sudden emergence of problems to which the traditional solutions provide no answer. That is the situation today. What we are witnessing, as people were witnessing in 1911, is the crumbling of a system, the crisis of a society in the throes of irresistible change.

French commentators in 1911 said that Germany, for all its astonishing economic growth, was a giant with feet of clay. The same is often said of the Soviet Union today, and could be said, without much exaggeration, of the United States. Western commentators have consistently exaggerated the strains in the Soviet system; but as the Brezhnev era draws to its close, the evidence of growing tensions is unmistakable. Smouldering discontent in Poland has not been quelled by General Jaruzelski's imposition of martial law; here total breakdown is certainly not impossible, confronting the Kremlin with cruel and unpalatable alternatives. Equally serious in another sphere is the stagnation of the Soviet economy, the urgent need for a thorough overhaul of the whole structure of industry and agriculture. The need for a similar overhaul is becoming increasingly apparent in the United States. Americans for long took pride in being Number 1 in the GNP *per capita* league. By the end of 1981, after four years of negative growth, the United States had fallen to tenth place, and showed every sign of falling further. The American economy was in deep recession, pulling down with it the economies of its allies and associates in western Europe; even Japan finished 1981 with a stagnant economy and a declining gross national product. In 1982 the position was even worse.

The links between dislocation and instability at home, and adventurism and opportunism abroad are never clear cut. They do not fall into a neat pattern of cause and effect, but no one supposes that they do not exist. When the French government sent its troops to Fez in April 1911, the German ambassador in Paris immediately concluded that it had embarked on a 'prestige policy' to cover up its economic failures at home. The danger is that the same thing could happen today. Needless to say, it was not necessary then, and is not necessary now. France could have put its house in order if it had concentrated on remedying internal discontents; instead the government hoped that a successful adventure abroad would enable it to by-pass them. The situation is not much different today. A thorough overhaul of the Soviet economy would require measures so drastic that they might unseat the government, perhaps even the regime; a thorough overhaul of the lagging American economy would be a deadly blow to powerful business interests which Reagan cannot afford to offend. The risk that they also, like the Monis government in France in 1911, will turn to foreign adventure as a way out is only too obvious.

The difference between 1911 and now is that conditions today are even less manageable, and the temptation to deflect the consequences against the enemy without the gate is correspondingly greater. In 1911 Crowe and Nicolson in London blamed the crisis on Kiderlen-Wächter. In 1980 and 1981 Carter and Reagan blamed it even more emphatically on Brezhnev, and Brezhnev predictably blamed it on the United States. 'Whose aircraft carriers', he dramatically asked, 'are permanently hanging like the sword of Damocles over the independent states of the Persian Gulf?' After the Soviet invasion of Afghanistan it sounded to the innocent bystander a little too much like the pot calling the kettle black. Nevertheless, the alacrity with which Carter, in an election year, attacked the Soviet invasion of Afghanistan, although two years earlier, when Tarraki's pro-Soviet regime took over, the United States had scarcely reacted at all, is significant enough. As an American commentator observed at the time, Soviet intervention was a 'campaign blessing'.

And yet, as *The Times* soberly commented, there was 'no particular American interest at stake' in Afghanistan; in fact, the State

Department had hitherto tacitly recognized that it lay within the Soviet 'sphere of interest'. But it was an opportunity to divert attention from the dismal state of the American economy, perhaps to bolster Carter's image. Might it not even be possible to convince the American public that its problems were due, in one way or another, to the men in the Kremlin? Hence also Carter's attempt, in August and September 1979, to whip up a scare over Cuba and its alleged anti-US machinations. It was so inept and implausible that it boomeranged. But that did not prevent Reagan from returning to the same charge in 1981, from announcing as a fact that the Soviet Union was using Cuba and Nicaragua to spread disaffection throughout central America, and from sending 'advisers' and 'instructors' to El Salvador, and issuing scarcely veiled threats of military intervention.

We do not know whether Reagan and Haig believed their anti-Soviet propaganda, any more than we know whether Brezhnev believes his denunciations of the United States. What we do know is that their reactions are overwrought, just as Crowe's reaction in 1911 to Kiderlen-Wächter's supposed machinations was overwrought, and that the reality is less melodramatic. Modern conflicts begin, not because perverse or ambitious individuals foment them, but because economic and political conditions generate the basis for conflict. No one in his right mind supposes that unrest in the Third World is fabricated in Moscow, though the Russians might cautiously (but so far not very successfully) seek to profit from it. The neurotic fear of the Soviet Union and of Communist subversion which appeared to inspire American policy under Reagan and Haig, the belief, real or pretended, that it has a finger in every pie, stirring up disaffection in Africa, Latin America and the Middle East, corresponds less to political reality than to a gathering sense of frustration, as the United States watches a world built in the American image falling apart about its ears. It is no less dangerous because of that. In 1911 Grey and his advisers in the Foreign Office in London feared that the Triple Entente upon which, they believed, their whole security depended, was threatened with collapse. Seventy years later Washington and Moscow were assailed by similar fears about the stability of the security systems they had built up, and which, like Grey, Nicolson and Crowe, they were determined to maintain at all costs. The difference today is that the cost could be prohibitive.

The fear of disruption of the existing, precarious balance is nevertheless as operative today as it was in 1911. As the defensive belt of client-states built up by the United States begins to crumble, the stakes get higher, the risks greater, and the room for manoeuvre narrower. The same, almost certainly, is true of the Soviet Union. In Moscow, events in Poland clearly conjure up the spectre of a Soviet bloc in disarray. Reactions in Europe to American pressures to mount a new, more lethal generation of nuclear weapons conjure up an equally unwelcome spectre in Washington. So do the conflicts between Europe and the United States over steel and other exports, harbingers of an incipient trade war. Meanwhile, there is the disturbing reluctance of Middle East governments, hitherto docile clients, to follow the American and Soviet lead. When Saudi Arabia announced point-blank that the source of trouble in the Middle East was not the Soviet Union but Israel, and when President Zia of Pakistan blamed the 'unstable conditions' on the 'pressures and counter-pressures of super-power rivalry', they were announcing, however discreetly, their determination to follow an independent line. During the long drawn out Iraqi-Iranian war the United States and the Soviet Union stood helplessly on the sideline, unable to contain the fighting. It was not unlike 1913, when the Balkan countries shook free from great power tutelage and decided their problems among themselves. But 1913, as we all know, was followed by the holocaust of 1914.

In retrospect, we can see that it would have been better if the great powers had left the Balkan states, after 1913, to fight out their quarrels among themselves. Unfortunately, they couldn't and didn't. It is the same today. So long as the Shah of Persia was functioning effectively as the United States' watch-dog in the Middle East, American interest in Afghanistan was minimal. When the Shah's regime collapsed in 1979, leaving a vacuum behind it, Afghanistan suddenly acquired a new – but quite undeserved – significance. At the same time, Washington quickly moved to fill the gap by reactivating its interest in Saudi Arabia, Pakistan and Egypt. These were to be the new pillars of the crumbling American empire. It was all too like the involvement of Czarist Russia with Serbia before 1914. Instead of learning from its Iranian involvement and its unhappy outcome – as Russia might have learnt, but didn't, from its Bosnian experience in 1908 – the United States got deeper into the quagmire. Under Reagan, it is busy getting deeper still. The question is how, when the crunch comes, one can draw back. Russia did not in 1914, nor did Germany. Few Germans in 1914 had much faith in Austria; but they were involved up to the hilt.

The course of events in 1914 showed as plainly as possible the danger of a great power getting involved in the internal politics of an inherently unstable area. And yet that is precisely what the United

States is doing in central America and the Middle East. Not even the most hardened gambler would lay odds on the stability of Saudi Arabia, Egypt or Pakistan, to say nothing of the military junta in El Salvador or in Argentina. Long before the Soviet takeover of Afghanistan, Pakistan was threatened by disruption and the secession (fomented, incidentally, by Afghanistan) of Baluchistan and Sind. At the beginning of 1979 it was widely reported that Saudi Arabia and Egypt were ripe for a fundamentalist Islamic uprising, a prediction proved correct almost immediately in the former case by the seizure in November 1979 of the Grand Mosque at Mecca by a group of Wahhabist extremists, and in the case of Egypt by the assassination in 1981 of the President, Anwar Sadat. Neither, it is true, succeeded, but neither did the early actions of Bosnian terrorists.

The lesson, if there is a lesson, is that no one in his right mind would put his head into a hornets' nest of this sort. The reply is familiar enough. Czarist Russia had to support Serbia, since otherwise Austria–Hungary would assert control. The United States must support President Zia, for fear lest the Soviet Union; having devoured (but not digested) Afghanistan, proceeds next to eat up Pakistan. Need it be said that there is scarcely a word of truth in this argument? We know today that the shaky Austro-Hungarian Empire, torn by internal dissension, was in no state in 1914, even if it had so wished (which on the whole, it did not), to absorb the Balkans. As for the Soviet Union today, its situation is not a great deal better. Whatever view one takes of the Soviet invasion of Afghanistan, there is no tangible evidence that it has designs on Pakistan, and only the sterile minds of diplomats could interpret Moscow's decision to consolidate its hold over a country generally recognized as lying within its sphere of interests, as a threat to the balance of power. Soviet intervention in Afghanistan was brutal enough but it is not easy, on any rational calculation, to understand why the substitution of one pro-Soviet regime for another, even if the latter had to be installed by 80,000 Russian bayonets, should have necessitated the dispatch of American warships and the setting up of a rapid deployment force. The answer, of course, is that it didn't.

The parallel with 1911 is not farfetched. Then, also, Nicolson and Crowe professed to see in the alleged German claim to west Morocco a threat to the balance of power. In fact, it would have made no appreciable difference to the balance of power if Germany had occupied west Morocco, or even if it had taken over the whole of the French Congo. The crisis was a product of diplomatic imagination.

Nevertheless, the British fleet was put on a war footing. Even three years later, when Austria issued its notorious ultimatum to Serbia, thereby unleashing the First World War, the crisis was more imaginary than real. If Serbia had accepted the Austrian demands *in toto*, it would, no doubt, have been an affront to Serbian national pride; but neither Russia's safety nor France's safety would have been imperilled. The idea that Russia, for its own security, had to stand by Serbia, and that Germany had to stand by Austria, was a myth. But it was this myth, the supposed imperatives of the balance of power, which require a state to stand by its clients, no matter what the rights and wrongs, that led Europe to the brink of war in 1911 and over the precipice in 1914. It could be the same today.

We know that Bethmann-Hollweg and Kiderlen-Wächter were bluffing in 1911. They did not seriously intend to go to war. It is possible, perhaps even likely, that Carter and Brzezinski were bluffing in 1980, and that Reagan and Haig were bluffing in 1981. They hoped by a show of force to get their way. Carter's despatch of American forces to the Persian Gulf in 1980, it was said at the time, was 'a small calculated risk'. This was exactly what Kiderlen-Wächter had said about the despatch of the *Panther* to Agadir in July 1911. But the 'risk policy', once embarked on, gathers its own momentum. No one, perhaps, deliberately chose war in 1914, certainly neither Bethmann nor Grey, both of whom had a shrewd idea of what it would entail. But war came, nevertheless, because they were prisoners of a system in which war was implicit. It did not look very different as 1980 turned into 1981, and 1981 into 1982.

* * *

Let us at this point leave the parallels between 1911 and 1981. The important question is not whether they are true or false, rather it is why statesmen then and now felt impelled to embark on a policy of bluff and 'calculated risk'. It was not, and is not, the only possible reaction to the challenge of a world in turmoil. But it is certainly an easier way out than grappling with the insistent economic and social problems which beset all governments in 1911 and which beset them to a far greater degree today. The temptation for heavily armed states with apparently insoluble internal problems to break through the stalemate by military action, or by bluff and bluster with the threat of military action in the background, can become irresistible, particularly if economic difficulties reach a point of no return.

In 1911 the overriding issue for all governments – for Bethmann-Hollweg in Germany, for Asquith in Britain, for the shadowy governments of the France of President Fallières – was the rising tide of democracy. Unchecked, they believed, it would sweep away the existing order. In retrospect, we can see that their apprehensions were exaggerated. Most of the things the workers were demanding in 1911 came to pass, and the old order weathered the storm pretty well. But that was not how it looked at the time. When the British miners demanded a minimum wage, even the Irish nationalist Dillon denounced it as 'an extreme form of Socialism' which must be resisted to the hilt. Otherwise it would 'open the door to a system of minimum wages for every class of labour' and the whole economy would be undermined. Today we have a system of minimum wages, but the arguments have lost none of their force. We cannot afford, Reagan and Thatcher tell us, to look after the poor and needy, the victims and derelicts of our economic system; we must retrench on the social services, though at the same time we must boost military spending and subsidize the sale of lethal weapons to irresponsible and unreliable clients abroad.

It is an argument with an obvious appeal to people who see their standard of living being eroded by taxation and inflation. It was no less effective in 1911. The upper classes, Blunt noted in his diary, were having to give up their London houses and 'live within their means'. Characteristically, this made them less, not more, sensitive to the plight of the poor, and almost neurotically obsessed with the fear of revolution. When the English miners went on strike early in 1912, Blunt, more fervent for revolution in Egypt and India than at home, decamped from London to his country estate in Sussex 'where we can better stand a siege'. Already, he says, people were talking of the day when revolution would be followed by counter-revolution, and were looking forward to the time when Kitchener, the British general who had been sent out in 1911 to rule Egypt, would be brought home 'to play the part of military dictator'.

In Germany, at the same time, there were plenty of voices denouncing 'Reichstag parliamentarism' and advocating a *coup d'état* and a military dictatorship as the only means of halting the advance of Social Democracy. They have their counterparts today, bemoaning the so-called 'crisis of democracy' and looking forward hopefully to its replacement by some form of 'capitalistic fascism'.

No one doubts that fear of revolution played a major role in German policy in 1911 and after. So far as Germany was concerned, Golo

Mann concluded, the war of 1914 'resulted from the distorted, tense class situation'. But it is also argued that Germany, with its antiquated social structure, was exceptional. That may be true; but it is also true that everywhere, even in republican France, the franchise was heavily weighted against the urban, industrial working class. Admittedly, the Prussian three-class electoral system was an anomaly; but similar results could be obtained by different means. In Britain, where one-quarter of the adult male population was still without the vote in 1918, one means was the system of plural voting. Right down to the time of the Second World War, my father and I each had two votes – he as a businessman, I as a university graduate. Blunt in 1910 had no fewer than five! This, in the end, was the privileged position the governing classes were fighting to preserve. Today, with a virtually universal suffrage everywhere, the methods are necessarily different, but the objects remain the same.

The difference today is that the problems are worse, the scope for manoeuvre more limited. In 1911 people were worried about the obvious signs of coming depression. Today we are in the midst of a depression which has been with us, on and off, since 1973, if not earlier. In 1911 inflation, and the consequent erosion of living standards, had reached the then startling height (on a rough average) of 10 per cent over ten years, or 1 per cent per annum. Today any governments that can hold it down to 10 per cent a year – and some governments, for example Argentina and Israel, that can hold it below 100 per cent a year – take credit for themselves as miracle workers. This is where the fears of the middle class, worried about prices and their effect on its living standards, are centred. But it is also where the fears of the working class are centred, because workers are fully aware that the only answer governments are likely to come up with is a deflationary policy which will throw them out of work and leave them to fend for themselves as best they can. And it is also where the fears of governments are centred, for they know, with over 30 million unemployed in the advanced industrial countries, and some 10 million in the United States alone – quite apart from the unregistered millions who have given up the struggle in despair – that they will not survive unless they can find some way out.

This is the sort of situation which impels governments to take risks they would otherwise not have taken. A world of great powers which sense themselves in decline, and at the same time increase their military power to offset the decline, is combustible material, particularly when it can be argued, plausibly though incorrectly, that economic problems stem from the international situation – in this case the stranglehold of the oil-producing countries over the price and supply of energy – and that the only way out of the impasse is direct action. This, ironically, was the position Germany saw itself in in 1911. More ironically still, it is the position the United States sees itself in seventy years later. In neither case is the diagnosis borne out by any objective review of the evidence. Imperial Germany in 1911 was at the height of its power, its economy immensely strong, its economic problems, though real, greatly exaggerated. Furthermore, there is not a scrap of evidence that any country anywhere was planning to attack it. But it saw itself as being hemmed in and encircled, and the German General Staff calculated anxiously that before long it would be overtaken militarily by a rejuvenated Russia. Seventy years later, the United States was busy making the same calculations about Soviet nuclear power. In addition, it was beset by the same irrational fears of decline. In reality, the immense resources of the United States were intact. But Vietnam had eroded the old confident belief in America's mission. It had moved back from being indisputably the world's leading power to being one power among many in a confused, multipolar international system, and it had failed, as Dean Acheson twenty years earlier had accused Great Britain of failing to do, to find a new role in a new world.

Even in 1969 it was possible to see that American withdrawal from Vietnam meant less an abandonment of imperialism than a reassessment of America's imperial role. What was not so clear was how powerful the reaction would be when it came eleven years later. Now we have a United States as thrusting as the Germany of Kiderlen-Wächter, and perhaps – one hopes not, but the uneasy fear persists – as dangerous to the world's peace. But it would be wrong to attach responsibility onesidedly to the United States, just as it would be wrong to attach responsibility onesidedly to Imperial Germany for the outbreak of the First World War in 1914. Unfortunately, the reality is more complicated than that. In international politics there are no innocents. France, Germany, England and Russia are all contributing in different ways to the growing international anarchy, just as they did in 1911. In the end, it is the system that is at fault – the system to which they all (it seems) are bound by hoops of iron – and after seventy years of bitter experience there is no reason to think that it has changed or is likely to change. That is our tragedy.

13

'Suicide for Fear of Death'

'Any imperial system, by whatever high-sounding name it may be called, must be the enemy of any true international order.'
Jawaharlal Nehru, *An Autobiography* (1936)

'Shall we perish in the dark, slain by our own hand, or in the light, killed by our enemies?' asked the Earl of Selborne speaking in the House of Lords on 10 August 1911. He was talking, incongruously, about the right of the Upper House to veto legislation initiated by the House of Commons – hardly a stirring issue, except for a handful of diehard peers, at a moment when Europe seemed to be stumbling on the edge of war. But Selborne's words could also serve as an epitaph on his age and generation. And they could easily serve as an epitaph on our own, if we handle our crisis no better than they did theirs.

1911 was on all counts a critical year. This book has attempted to analyse the character of the crisis and to depict its anatomy. If it has concentrated on foreign policy, imperialism and the balance of power, it is because these were the issues that the Agadir crisis brought into prominence. But in the end they were only the external projection of a crisis which cut much deeper. What we have been examining, in reality, is the crisis of a whole society; and imperialism – the struggle for markets and raw materials, for wealth and power, for exclusive rights and leverage in Asia and Africa and Latin America – was a direct reflection of that crisis.

It also carried with it its own nemesis. Neither France, Spain nor Italy was left in peace to enjoy its spoils after 1911. As early as May 1912 the fierce tribesmen of southern Morocco rose in revolt against the French, proclaimed a new Sultan in place of Mulay Hafid, and began a struggle which was not to end until Morocco secured its independence in 1956. Spain's reverses in the Rif, particularly the disastrous defeats inflicted by Abd el-Krim, led directly to the dicta-torship of Primo de Rivera in 1923, and ultimately to the fall of the monarchy. Italy struggled unsuccessfully for years against the Senussi of Cyrenaica, until finally the country was pacified, with enormous bloodshed, by the Fascist general Graziani in 1932.

In retrospect, it is not difficult to see in 1911 the stirring of the revolt against the West which has become a dominant theme of our time. No doubt, it was still inchoate and incipient. In 1911, Moroccans and Libyans – and Persians also – stood on their own and were hopelessly outmatched. Today the developing countries have organs of mutual support, OPEC, the Arab League, the 'Group of 77'. Even so, it was possible in 1911 to perceive the way things were moving. When the Chinese revolution broke out in October, Blunt recorded in his diary that it was 'the most important news of the last few days', a far more important event in world history than Agadir or the Italian invasion of Tripoli. He might have added the Mexican revolution as well; even so, it was a remarkably percipient observation. Something was stirring which finally took shape in 1974 with the demand for a New International Economic Order. The peoples of Asia and Africa had been treated for years as pawns on the diplomatic chessboard, handed from one imperial power to another without consideration for their wishes. In the end they were bound to revolt.

Another who saw clearly the way things were going was Rosa Luxemburg, the great Polish socialist intellectual who was brutally murdered by German reactionaries in 1919. In the most challenging of all her writings, published in 1913, Luxemburg analysed the basic contradictions which, she argued, lay at the heart of imperialism. By lunging out into the underdeveloped world the industrial nations were prolonging the existence of capitalist society. At the same time, without knowing it, they were cutting the ground from under their feet. So long as they could secure new outlets their position was secure; once the outlets dried up, once the whole world had been ransacked, the system would stagnate and collapse. Not, Luxemburg added, that the capitalist powers would actually wait for this to happen. Far more likely was a desperate struggle for a redivision of the spoils – force, fraud, violence, oppression and ultimately war.

Economists have questioned the validity of Luxemburg's analysis. Whether they are right or wrong is not the question. The point, rather, is that the picture she draws is uncomfortably close to present reality. What is obvious today is that the international system is not operating effectively, either on the economic or on the political level. People felt the same in 1911, though the scale was smaller; hence the prevalent fatalism and what has been called (with, I suspect, a good deal of exaggeration) the 'death wish' of European society. Ten years ago, in

178

the wake of the great surge forward of the 1950s and 1960s, the mood was optimistic. Marxist predictions of the demise of capitalist society, we were told, had been triumphantly disproved. Today, with unemployment rising everywhere to heights unknown since the 1930s, with basic industries such as steel and automobiles in apparently irreversible decline, and with the inflationary spiral, far from being controlled, the triumph seems to have been short-lived. The danger, obviously, is that someone, somewhere, some time, will risk taking a short cut out of the impasse.

There are plenty of people today, modern equivalents of Blunt and Morel, warning us of the danger. Co-operation, we are told, is 'the only sensible path' to follow, the only way to cope with the problems that threaten to engulf us all. Unfortunately, it is easier to understand the need for a global approach to the problems of world poverty, over-population, scarcity, pollution and the depletion of natural resources, than it is to see the way forward in a world of competing national states. Everyone is aware how precarious and unstable the existing situation is, far more unstable than it was in 1911. But, unhappily, it is the world which confronts us.

Is there a way out? Was there a way out in 1911? Looking back, we can all see that the storm in 1911, and the hurricane that followed in 1914, were unnecessary, that the issues were certainly not substantial enough to drive the world into the holocaust. Will that be the verdict on us also? Every age searches for a way out. In 1911 the panacea was the Hague Peace Conferences of 1899 and 1907, full of protestations of good intentions, but bare of practical results. In the 1970s the slogan was 'interdependence', propagated by the Trilateral Commission under Zbigniew Brzezinski before he became President Carter's National Security Adviser in succession to Kissinger. In 1980 it disappeared from the scene, as discredited and out-of-date as the slogan of 'collective security' in the 1930s. Since the onset of the economic depression the world has become less, not more, interdependent, far less so than it was in 1911. What we have instead is a struggle for wealth and power which is rapidly developing into a struggle of all against all, a struggle in which the United States is desperately trying to reassert the pre-eminence it enjoyed between 1945 and 1968, when it was the core of the international *status quo*. That is not far from the position of Great Britain in 1911, and is not, in the long run, likely to be more successful.

In the short run, there are other more immediate dangers. Jean Jaurès, the great French socialist leader who was assassinated by a nationalist fanatic in 1914, looking around the pre-1914 world, foresaw a long period of counter-revolution, a period of 'furious reaction', 'exasperated nationalism', and 'stifling dictatorship'. Or possibly, as an alternative, war as an outlet from the intolerable pressures. The same alternatives face us today, and neither is very palatable. And, almost certainly, the one can lead to the other.

*　　*　　*

The only lesson of history, we are often told, is that history teaches no lessons. That may be true for those who cannot, or do not want to, see beyond the conventional parameters. It is also often said that it is easy to be wise after the event. That may also be true; but, as we have seen, there were plenty of people in 1911 who were wise before the event. It needed no unusual perspicuity in 1911 to foresee, as Bebel did, the great *Kladderadatsch*, the total collapse of the existing system. The trouble was that no one took any notice. If no one takes notice today we can expect our own *Kladderadatsch*, the only difference being that it will be far more complete. In 1914 statesmen and professional diplomats slid into war protesting their innocence and helplessness. 'How on earth do you think this happened?', asked Bethmann-Hollweg, raising his arms to heaven. It could be the same again today. But the millions of dead, the 'gun-fodder' of 1915, 1916 and 1917, were not the victims of a capricious fate, but of their own ruling class. *You* are responsible, said Bebel; *you* are 'pushing things to a head'. Will another generation make the same accusation when it is too late?

To retell the story of 1911 would be pointless if it had no bearing on our present predicament. Readers of the foregoing pages must judge for themselves what its bearing is. Today, we are often told, we are living in a 'shrinking world'. One response – it was the response in 1911 – is to grab as much of the world's resources as one can lay hands on. The deeper the recession bites, the fiercer the struggle for markets and raw materials. That is the conflict Lenin foresaw in 1916. We have, perhaps, a better understanding today than they did then that it is no solution. But do we have any better idea of what to do? In his last address as President of the World Bank in 1980, Robert McNamara warned that the global economic crisis had created 'a climate of apprehension in which the temptation will be strong for both the developed and developing nations to react unwisely'. That was the climate in 1911 and we know where it led. It is still the climate today; the only difference is that the stakes are higher.

180

When we leave Agadir behind us, the only question – or, at least, the most insistent question – is where the next Agadir will be. In 1911, not one person in ten thousand, probably not one person in a hundred thousand, had any idea where it was, nor why it should have mattered. Will the world be held up to ransom once again for something so inconsequential? Will it be sacrificed once again to the false idol of the balance of power? It may be – I make no prediction, but simply register the possibility – that the conflict of imperialism and anti-imperialism will tear the thin veneer of civilization apart. But who, looking around at some of the things civilization has wrought, could complain?

But, finally, the lesson of the whole story is its futility and senselessness. This is not what life is for or about. In 1911, walking in the park with my German Fräulein, neither of us knew that in three years we were going to be deadly enemies, nor would we have believed it if we had been told. Seventy years later, looking out across Boston Common, and watching couples walking peacefully hand in hand and families making the most of the thin, late winter sun, the same sense of unreality is uppermost. Are we in the grip of a senseless demon? Are we simply, like the Moroccans in 1911, pawns in a game in which there are only losers? If Agadir has any lesson to teach – and I think there is more than one – the final lesson must be: no more Agadirs. But, looking round the world today, with all its multiple flash-points, who would dare to predict that? Many things have changed in the world since 1911, but not the capacity of human beings to react irrationally to the changes. That is why the story of Agadir is still worth telling. It is a past that can too easily become a future.

Bibliography

The notes which follow are deliberately short and selective, and no attempt has been made to list all the sources, primary and secondary, which I have consulted. In particular, articles in specialized periodicals, to which few readers probably will have access, are not included. In general, I have referred only to books which deal specifically and in some detail with the events of 1911, and literature on the historical background and origins of the Agadir crisis has been excluded. I have also omitted subjects (for example, Anglo-German naval rivalry, and the Persian question) which, though important in themselves, are only touched upon tangentially in the text. On all these topics the literature is immense, and their inclusion would have inflated the bibliography beyond reason.

1. Most general political histories and histories of particular countries cover a wider span and refer to 1911 only incidentally, if at all. Few contribute anything of substance, but A.J. Ryder, *Twentieth-Century Germany: From Bismarck to Brandt* (1973), deals more fully with 1911 than most, and Golo Mann, *A History of Germany since 1789* (1968), has a particularly perceptive account of the German political scene under Bethmann-Hollweg. For England, E. Halévy, *A History of the English People in the Nineteenth Century*, vol. VI: *The Rule of Democracy, 1905–1914* (1934), is still unsurpassed. There is unfortunately no equivalent work for France. D.W. Brogan had a remarkable insight into French politics under the Third Republic, but his *Development of Modern France* (1940) understandably wastes few words on the uninspiring interlude between the fall of Delcassé in 1905 and the accession to power of Poincaré in 1912. J. Chastenet, *La France de M. Fallières* (1950), is one of

the few books which deals specifically with the French political scene in and around 1911, but is not entirely adequate.

2. The conventional diplomatic history of the Agadir crisis is covered in ample detail. Those who can should go direct to the published documents, particularly the *British Documents* (eds Gooch and Temperley) and the German documents (*Die grosse Politik*, eds Lepsius, Mendelssohn-Bartholdy and Thimme), which, though necessarily selective, are far more lively and informative than secondhand, warmed-up accounts. But the story of Agadir is told, at greater or lesser length, in all the standard histories of international relations (e.g., A.J.P. Taylor, 1954; P. Renouvin, 1955; R. Albrecht-Carrié, 1958) and also in the extensive literature (e.g., E. Brandenburg, 1927; S.B. Fay, 1929; B.E. Schmitt, 1930; R.J. Sontag, 1933) on the origins of the First World War, most of it now superseded by L. Albertini, *The Origins of the War of 1914* (3 vols, 1952-7). There is also a sound and painstaking monograph by Ima C. Barlow, *The Agadir Crisis* (1940). Emily Oncken, *Panthersprung nach Agadir* (1981), reached me only after this book was completed.

3. Emphasis has shifted away today from formal diplomatic history (which G.M. Young once described as the record of what one clerk said to another clerk) to the underlying motivations and the pressures and interests influencing and shaping policy. Jean-Claude Allain, *Agadir 1911* (1976), an elaborate and sophisticated analysis of the crisis and its background, based upon unpublished material in the French archives, is a notable example of the new trend, and an important contribution to the subject. In Germany the change was initiated by Fritz Fischer, *War of Illusions* (1973; original German edn, 1969), an amplification of the opening section of his earlier *Griff nach der Weltmacht* (1961; English trans., 1967), which examines in great detail the domestic pressures affecting the policies of Bethmann-Hollweg and Kiderlen-Wächter. Although Fischer's arguments have been criticized, they have had a lasting impact. It is best seen in V.R. Berghahn, *Germany and the Approach of War in 1914* (1973), which places German foreign policy in and around 1911 firmly in the context of Germany's internal crisis; this book (with a valuable bibliography) is essential reading. So also is Zara S. Steiner, *Britain and the Origins of the First World War* (1977), although Steiner minimizes the influence of domestic policies on Grey and the Foreign Office. F.H. Hinsley (ed.), *British Foreign Policy under Sir Edward Grey* (1976), on the other hand, is

old-fashioned diplomatic history, sometimes informative on particular points, but arid in concept.

4. A broad picture of the political world in 1911, such as I have attempted to draw in chapter 5, has to be pieced together from scraps of information in a variety of sources. Most of the actors on the 1911 stage (Grey, Bethmann, Churchill, Bertie, Schoen, and others) have left us their memoirs, but they are more notable for discretion and reticence than for insight and revelation. W.S. Blunt, *My Diaries* (1919), on the other hand, is deliberately indiscreet, and occasionally contributes a few sidelights. Giolitti's *Memoirs* (1923) are also revealing, though less for his actions than for his psychology. Caillaux poured out apologetics (*Agadir: ma politique extérieure*, 1919; *Devant l'histoire*, 1920; *Mes mémoires*, 1942–7), but the problem is to distinguish truth from falsehood or self-deception, and Lancken's memoirs (*Meine Dreissig Dienstjahre*, 1931), which might have provided a wealth of information about the murky political undercurrents in 1911, are almost totally (and no doubt deliberately) uninformative. E. Jäckh, *Kiderlen-Wächter. Der Staatsmann und Mensch* (1924), at least reproduces some of Kiderlen's correspondence with Mme de Jonina, but is otherwise inadequate. On the other hand, M. Balfour, *The Kaiser and his Times* (1964), gives a lively and rounded view of the charmed circle of the German ruling class; and there are profiles of some of the leading figures in the diplomatic world in Lamar Cecil, *The German Diplomatic Service, 1871–1914* (1976), and Zara S. Steiner, *The Foreign Office and Foreign Policy, 1898–1914* (1969). It is, as usual, less easy to recapture the French scene, but R. Binion, *Defeated Leaders* (1960), provides useful, if rather too indulgent, character sketches of Caillaux, Tardieu and Henry de Jouvenal, with sidelights on many of their contemporaries, great and small.

5. The best approach to the real world of 1911, the world of anxious businessmen and desperate workers, is Arthur Feiler, *Die Konjunkturperiode 1907–1913* (1914), a remarkably perceptive and informed survey of the economic scene in 1911 by the financial editor of the *Frankfurter Zeitung*. It should be supplemented for England by vol. 3 of Sir John Clapham's *Economic History of Modern Britain* (1938), still (surprisingly) the fullest general account of the British economy in the years before 1914. G. Dangerfield, *The Strange Death of Liberal England* (1935), provides a vivid – perhaps too vivid – picture of the revolutionary undercurrents of the time. More recent work, modifying some of

Dangerfield's conclusions, is summarized in J.E. Cronin, *Industrial Conflict in Modern Britain* (1979), and *Social Conflict and the Political Order in Modern Britain* (eds J.E. Cronin and J. Schneer). There has also been much patient investigation of wages, strikes and labour unrest in France, Germany and elsewhere (E. Shorter and C. Tilly, *Strikes in France, 1830–1968*, 1974; W. Kendall, *The Labour Movement in Europe*, 1975; A.V. Desai, *Real Wages in Germany, 1871–1913*, 1968). Much of this literature is technical and specialized, and I am grateful to Professor Cronin for helping me to evaluate it. It supports the conclusion that the situation in England, Wales and Scotland was not exceptional; the economic crisis was a general crisis from which no country was exempt.

6. The imperialism which was the other distinctive feature of the time is described briefly but appositely in vol. 3 of *The History of the Times* (1947). It is discussed in detail by G.W.F. Hallgarten, *Imperialismus vor 1914* (2 vols, 1951), with a truly remarkable command of the contemporary sources. Few historians today will probably go the whole way with Hallgarten, but no one can go even part of the way without him. Otherwise the vast literature on imperialism is wide-ranging and general, and casts little light directly on the situation in 1911. There are some illuminating pages in A.P. Thornton, *Imperialism in the Twentieth Century* (1977); and D.K. Fieldhouse, *Economics and Empire, 1830–1914* (1973), has a useful chapter on Morocco; but the latter, like most literature on the subject, approaches the question from the point of view of the imperialist powers, not from that of the victims. Two more recent books – E. Burke, *Prelude to Protectorate in Morocco: Precolonial Protest and Resistance, 1860–1912* (1976), and R.E. Dunn, *Resistance in the Desert. Moroccan Responses to French Imperialism, 1881–1912* (1977) – present the other side of the medal. They are important correctives.

Index